About the author

Stephen Endicott was born in Shanghai of missionary parents and grew up in China before the Communist revolution. His family has lived in Sichuan province for three generations. He has returned to China for lengthy visits beginning in 1972: his interaction with the people greatly facilitated by his command of the Chinese language. During his year as visiting professor at Sichuan University in 1980-81 he began his interviews and research in the countryside. Most recently, in 1988, he spent six months in China together with his artist wife, Lena Wilson, teaching, doing research and travelling. Dr. Endicott, who is a graduate of the University of Toronto, has received the Killam Senior Fellowship and other academic awards and currently teaches East Asian history at York University. His last book, *Rebel Out of China,* a biography of the Reverend James Endicott, was a Canadian bestseller. The Endicott's four daughters share their recreational interests in camping and white-water canoeing on the rivers of Ontario.

Also by Stephen Endicott

Diplomacy and Enterprise: British China Policy 1933-1937, University of British Columbia and Manchester University Press, 1975.

James G. Endicott: Rebel Out of China, University of Toronto Press, Toronto, 1980.

Wen Yiuzhang Zhuan, (The biography of James Endicott) - a translation with Yin Zhonglai, *et al* of *Rebel Out of China,* Sichuan People's Publishing House, Chengdu, 1983.

RED EARTH

REVOLUTION IN A SICHUAN VILLAGE

Stephen Endicott

To Ann,
A kindred spirit!
Steve + Lena Endicott
Toronto, Sept, 2008

NC PRESS LIMITED

Supported by

University of Toronto-York University
Joint Centre for Asia Pacific Studies

Toronto
1989

Illustrations: Lena Wilson, pages VI, 1, 95, 153
Front cover: Election day at MaGaoqiao village, 1984.
Back cover: Dragon dancers entertain crowds in Junction township at
spring festival time, 1981.

Published by arrangement with I. B. Tauris & Co. Ltd.,
3 Henrietta Street, Covent Garden, London, WC2E 8PW
Copyright © 1988 by Stephen Endicott

Canadian Cataloguing in Publication Data

Red earth: revolution in a Sichuan village

Endicott, Stephen Lyon, 1928 –

Rev. Canadian ed.
Includes bibliographical references and index.
ISBN 1-55021-049-1

1. MaGaoqiao (China) – social conditions.
2. Villages – China – Case studies. 3. Szechwan
Province (China) – Rural Conditions – case studies.
4. China – Politics and government – 1949– .
I. Title.

HN740.M34E54 1989 307.7'62'095138 C89-093501-7

We would like to thank the Ontario Arts Council and the Canada
Council for their assistance in the production of this book.

New Canada Publications, a division of NC Press Limited,
Box 4010, Stn. A, Toronto, Ontario, Canada, M5W 1H8

Printed and bound in Canada

CONTENTS

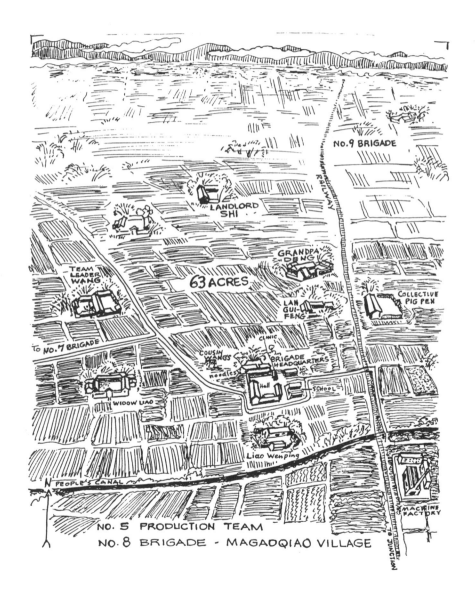

LIST OF MAPS AND TABLES

Maps

List of Tables

Supplementary Tables in the Appendix:

Land Reform and Co-operativization

To the people of MaGaoqiao

ACKNOWLEDGEMENTS

My thanks are due to the peasant families of MaGaoqiao whose friendship and kindness have allowed me to know what it has meant to live on the great western plain of Sichuan province in the first generation after the land revolution of the 1950s.

Over a period of six months in 1980–1, 1983–4, and in the summer of 1986 and the spring of 1988 the villagers took me into their homes, invited me to their celebrations, answered my countless questions about their economy, politics and life-cycle customs. They made me feel part of a collective experience that has intrigued much of the rest of the world for what it may say about the human condition, about new ways of fulfilling life's possibilities in an ancient civilization.

This account of rural revolution begins with the recollections of those who lived the first half of their lives in the warlord and republican eras before 1949. These were years when China was engulfed in warlord rivalries, imperialist invasions, the war against Japan (1937–45) and two major civil wars between the Nationalists and the Communists for the right to rule the country. This was the generation of men and women who were young adults when men on horseback brought the revolution to the village. As they found a new revolutionary identity they joined in, dispossessed the landlords and divided the land among the poor in the years 1950–2.

The story is continued into the 1980s by the middle-aged and younger villagers who inherited the establishment of Red Power. Under the leadership of the Chinese Communist Party they took part in unprecedented efforts aimed at consciously redefining social relations and reshaping the political and economic institutions of the village.

These efforts went in stages, advancing and then retreating like the ebb and flow of the tide, with so many revolutionary mass movements and rectifications that no villager could keep an accurate count. But they were not the kind of experience that could be easily forgotten or ignored either, since by and large there were no mere spectators in this drama.

After the death of Mao Zedong in 1976 and the assumption of leadership by Deng Xiaoping, new directions came to the village, this time through bureaucratic channels, and the search for a socialist identity continues.

The results of my research are mainly arranged chronologically, until the last four chapters, which are thematic dealing with health care, education, women's emancipation and social customs related to the life-cycle of birth, marriage and death.

Like the homing pigeons Sichuanese love to raise in their spare time, I went back to the southwest of China partly because of early training, family associations and childhood memories. Sichuan was the place where my parents, and before them my paternal grandparents, had gone from Canada to strike roots as Christian missionaries. 'There is awful significance in . . . the great millions dying in darkness,' my grandfather, James Endicott, had written to a classmate in the 1890s.[1] Later, after 1925 when my father and mother followed in the same footsteps for twenty-two years, they discovered that China was in the throes of one of the greatest revolutions the world had ever seen. Eventually both of these generations came to accept the novel idea that the best person to lead China was a Communist by the name of Mao Zedong, and they became warm friends of the People's Republic established in 1949.

Many years later when I had the rare opportunity to spend a sabbatical in Sichuan in 1980 (followed by a five-month trip for field research in 1983–4 and several more weeks in 1986 and 1988), I was naturally quite excited by several features of the experience: the chance to make a modest contribution to China's current modernization programme by teaching English at Sichuan University; the time to improve an unused Chinese language ability; the desire to take my artist wife, Lena, to visit the memory-filled houses in Chongqing, Chengdu, Leshan and Mount Emei where I had lived for thirteen childhood years, to discover friends and colleagues of my parents in order to catch up on forty years, to see what remained and what was changed in the towns and villages, how the attitudes of the people and their ways of living had altered after four decades of revolution. Twice I had been to China briefly during the heady years of the Cultural Revolution (1966–76), and after a decade of reflecting on and teaching Chinese history and politics at York University in Toronto, I had a strong professional interest in gaining some new, first-hand knowledge of the course of China's socialist experiment.

Since the focus of my interest was the countryside, where almost 85 per cent of China's people live and work on the land, I requested permission to gather material for the purpose of writing a history of one of the villages in a people's commune.

Without the assistance of the Ministry of Education, the provincial Foreign Affairs Office and Sichuan University in arranging for me to go to the countryside and without the help in translations and statistical analysis of Guan Yaping, Li Guolin, Shi Jian, Zhao Xiaoxue, Zhang Changwen, Zhao Huaisun, Wang Hongjun and Li Xiaoxiong of that university, who at different times joined me as a small research team, this project would have been impossible. While these friends are not responsible for the shortcomings of this book, much of whatever success it has belongs to them.

I owe a special debt to others in the countryside as well, to the leaders of the People's Commune in Junction township for providing a room, meals and briefings, and to the Shifang county government for accommodation and statistics concerning thirty years of the collectivized, socialist experiment in agriculture.

Historical novels by Chen Yuantsung, Chou Lipo and Hao Ran helped to inspire this book as did the reporting of my friends David and Isobel Crook, Jan Myrdal and William Hinton, and others too, whose perspective I may not share but whose search for the realities of modern China I respect and to whom reference is made in the endnotes. I particularly thank Sharon Hare for her assistance in statistical analysis, and Audrey Mills Douglas, Carl Dow, Lena Wilson Endicott, William Hinton, Kate Gill Kemper, Jeanne Keresztesi, Diana Lary, Mark Selden, and Donald Willmott for their helpful comments on earlier drafts.

Finally, my thanks to the Social Sciences and Humanities Research Council of Canada for financial support and to Atkinson College, York University, for the possibility of spending extended periods away from my teaching duties in the department of history.

Stephen Endicott
Sichuan University
Chengdu
July 1988

NAMES OF VILLAGERS
WHO APPEAR MORE THAN ONCE
(Listed Alphabetically)

Chen Guofeng, born 1953, head of the women's group in No. 5 production team at MaGaoqiao after 1983.

Deng Xicheng, (retired secretary Deng), a long-time leader of Junction People's Commune, deputy secretary of the party committee.

Deng Yuanming, (Grandpa Deng), poor peasant, village clerk at time of land reform in 1952, member of No. 5 production team.

Huang Kailan, born 1953, barefoot doctor from 1974 and leader of the MaGaoqiao Women's Association after 1983.

Huang Kaiyao, poor peasant, Korean war veteran, village militia leader, member of No. 5 production team.

Jiang Beixiu, head of Junction township at time of Liberation, executed in 1951.

Jiang Tenglin, husband of widow Liao, deputy team leader, No. 5 production team, committed suicide in 1971.

Jiang Wenguang, middle peasant, No. 8 Brigade accountant 1962–78, then party branch secretary of MaGaoqiao village 1978–85; head of rural enterprises for Junction township after 1985.

Lan Guifeng, enemy of widow Liao, member of No. 5 production team.

Li Shouhui, from Qionglai county, leader of the Four Clean-up Work Team at No. 8 Brigade in 1966.

Liao Lixiu, (Widow Liao), lower-middle peasant, active in forming the Women's Association at the time of the land reform, No. 5 production team.

Liao Moquan, born 1949, middle peasant, a village Red Guard leader during the Cultural Revolution, brother-in-law of cousin Wang, No. 5 production team.

Liao Wenfang, village accountant at MaGaoqiao from 1978 to 1982, village head in 1983 and party branch secretary in 1985, member of No. 4 production team.

Liao Wenping, poor peasant, organizer of a co-operative, expelled from the Communist Party for seventeen years then readmitted, No. 5 production team; a 'ten thousand yuan' household after 1982.

Shi Shufu, born 1919, former landlord, spent five years in prison camp for counter-revolutionaries, member of No. 5 production team.

Shi Zengfa, head teacher at MaGaoqiao primary school.

Tan Qijun, (barefoot doctor Tan), poor peasant, born 1933, member of No. 5 production team.

Wang Daoquan, (team leader Wang), lower-middle peasant, born 1935 leader of No. 5 production team in MaGaoqiao village for twenty-five years.

Wang Dequn, leader of the Women's Federation of Shifang County.

Wang Youming, (cousin Wang), activist during the Four Clean-up campaign in 1966, chairman of the Poor and Lower Middle Peasant's Association at No. 8 Brigade, member of No. 5 production team.

Yang Changyou, (Commune director Yang), long-time leader of Junction People's Commune, became secretary of the township party committee in 1983.

Yang Yongxiu, midwife, women's leader, No. 5 production team.

Yao Shengwan, poor peasant, born 1921, party branch secretary at MaGaoqiao from 1950s until 1978.

Zeng Lingmo, middle peasant, clan elder, treasurer of No. 5 production team.

Zeng Xiancuan, landlord, MaGaoqiao village head 1947–50, committed suicide in 1950.

Zhang Gufu, rich peasant background, head teacher at MaGaoqiao lower-middle school in 1980s.

Zhang Jinghe, (village head Zhang), middle peasant, head of MaGaoqiao village from 1951 to 1978, expelled from the party once, then readmitted.

Zhong Tingyin, school teacher, leader of the Women's Association of MaGaoqiao village from 1976 to 1983.

Zhou Zhizhu, born 1949, female barefoot doctor at No. 8 Brigade.

PART I

SOCIAL AND ECONOMIC CHANGE

1

BACK TO THE BEGINNING

February the first, 1984, in Fangting town. All evening and into the sleepless small hours of the morning barrages of exploding fireworks, some near, others far, some in clusters, some in single volleys like gunshot, crackle through the wintry air as if covering the advance of a phantom, nocturnal army. At dawn just when the last of the firecrackers peter out and drowsy travellers in the county guesthouse gratefully think of dropping off to sleep, the distant beat of drums and clash of cymbals announce the arrival of detachments of peasants, vanguards of twenty thousand or more who will pour into town that day to mark the start of the lunar New Year holiday in Shifang county.

A boisterous scene is unfolding. Village musicians and actors, the dragon lantern performers from the production teams, the colourful *yangge* dancers with their ribbons of silk, and the landboat paddlers push their way up Youth Street. First stop is the courtyard of the army garrison command. Here red lanterns with yellow tassels hang over the doorway, and age-old, almost forgotten salutations are a striking invitation to enter: 'Plain sailing – your wealth is as vast as the waters of the Eastern seas – you'll live as long as the Southern mountains!' These greetings are startling because they express a spirit far removed from the moral philosophy 'serve the people' which until recently has been the motto of the People's Liberation Army.

After a brief performance that attracts throngs of bystanders the actors move on to visit every public building – the court house, public security office, county gaol – and finally to the top of the road where the only remaining gate of the ancient medieval city stands. It guards the inner sanctum of political power, the county governor's offices and the county committee of the Chinese Communist Party. The peasants, apparently uninhibited, push their way through the gate and repeat their noisy salutations.

When these excitements are over, the crowds discover storytellers, tumblers, magicians and other amusements on the broad avenue of the

Town-God Temple. Although the temple is gone, demolished to make way for a cinema several years earlier during the Cultural Revolution, much of the former atmosphere has reappeared, resurrected, it seems, to inaugurate the Year of the Rat. Several teahouses, those characteristic institutions of old China where people, mostly men, gathered to make plans or idle away time, have come back to life.[1] Fortune tellers are setting up shop on the curbsides; people throw dice to win candied figures and play other games of chance; there are itinerant snake charmers from Hunan, monkey performances to help sell aphrodisiacs and other exotic herbal medicines. Such superstitious or questionable activities have not been seen around these parts for decades. Not since the distribution of land to the poor peasant over thirty years before has there been this kind of Spring Festival in socialist China.

The holiday-makers have varied interests: some have come to make money — pedlars cry out their wares, selling sweet noodles, dumplings, cakes and fried beancurd to the festive crowds; others are intent upon seizing the occasion to revive forbidden pleasures from the feudal past; many wish simply to renew acquaintances or visit relatives. But at the core, spurring things on, are newly prosperous peasants, beneficiaries of recent government reforms, who want to express their enthusiasm. As a smiling bystander puts it:

> We have 'turned over' once again. This is Chairman Mao's revolutionary line coming back into the hands of the peasants as in the early 1950s. And some of us say, 'We owe our liberation to Chairman Mao and our prosperity to Deng Xiaoping'.

In contrast to the spartan life-style and egalitarian collective policies of the Mao era, when China felt constantly threatened by foreign aggression, freedom for individuals to become rich before others is the result of new policies introduced by Deng Xiaoping, successor to Mao Zedong on the political stage in Beijing in the more relaxed international situation. Individual peasant households now take responsibility for decisions about production and marketing formerly handled by the collective teams, and increased government procurement prices for farm products have put more money than ever into the hands of rural shoppers.[2]

It doesn't seem to concern the peasants heading for the town this morning that no governor or party secretary, no chief of police, army commander, judge or gaol warden is on hand to greet them. These high officials and their deputies are out, lost in the crowds, strolling with their families, cautiously observing the scene and savouring the festivities in their best, newest attire. What seems to matter is that the doors and symbolic gates of power are open and accessible. Many of these festivities are ritual political expressions dating from time immemorial, frowned upon, even forbidden at times, since the Communists came to power, because they give support to old habits, customs, thoughts and superstitious practices from China's feudal past.

At a deeper level, below the surface appearances, the turn-about in peasant life and fortunes in 1984 imparts a surrealistic, some might say nightmare, quality to this thirty-fifth lunar New Year since the founding of the People's Republic. Locally, at least, it is like a pageant whose many acts unfold without adequate programming. The pageant reveals the warring elements at work in China. The lure of personal enrichment, each family for itself, which was the dominant theme for over 2,000 years of Chinese history, appears to be taking centre stage again this year. It is raising a challenge to the collective ideal of reaching common prosperity through a co-operative re-ordering of social life that has been so prominent in recent decades.

The far-reaching structural changes are not coming easily to this remote inland county far from Beijing. Although Sichuan province has been widely publicized for several years as a pace-setter in reform, in these parts it is just one year since the reforms were started; only the first harvest under the new system has been collected.

Many local people, especially older experienced peasants, have doubts about the reforms. They worry that the collective organizations and the spirit they nourish might be weakened or destroyed by the reforms. The wider implications of Deng's programme are not clear. Is the reversion to household management of farming a capitalist way of doing things, as Mao had warned? Are we going back to the beginning? Or are the reforms just another way of organizing labour within a collectively-owned economy? Will they lead to polarization between rich and poor, to the exploitation of the weak by the strong? Or is it a case of developing 'socialism with Chinese characteristics' as Deng and his supporters are claiming?

For the moment uncertainty about the road ahead is evident and aptly illustrated by the contradictory message that local officials in Shifang have chosen to hang on the gateway at the county centre. 'Persist in Mao Zedong Thought, by self-reliance create a grand future prospect', says the left-hand side in large red characters; 'Study carefully Deng Xiaoping's *Selected Works*, seek truth from facts, create a new road', proclaims the other side; and joining them across the ancient lintel is an enigmatic exhortation: 'For a spiritual civilization!'

Apart from ancient customs that have reappeared in the wake of liberalizing economic reforms, the county leaders and planners feel that they have several reasons to worry about the possible shape of things to come. With individual peasants now making their own business contracts it is evident that inflation and profiteering have appeared in the markets once again. An outbreak of serious crimes has led to a dozen executions in the county. The spectre of a further population explosion looms ominously as peasants seek to increase their family labour power in the more individualistic atmosphere of the times.

The number of people here, as in all China, has almost doubled since 1949, rising in the county to 382,000 from 217,000 and thereby cutting down the available cultivated land per rural inhabitant to a dangerous level. Only a rigorous family planning drive can reverse the trend and prevent a slide into massive food shortages. A campaign with young couples pledged to have only one child is in place; it is reasonable, but unpopular in some quarters. Many peasants have doubts about small families, about a generation that will have no brothers or sisters, no cousins, aunts or uncles.

'How can we have a carefree old age unless we have children?' they ask. 'It is as hard to rear a single child as it is to make a fire from a single stick.' And now, with each family dependent on its own labour power, 'More sons mean more blessings', is a popular local saying.

In response to this backward-looking and sexist kind of thinking and against any tendency to laxness in all the family reunions at the turn of the year, the cadres in Shifang have been mobilized in preparation for the holiday. Working overtime, the sound trucks of the Propaganda Department have fanned out through the countryside hammering home the theme of family planning, while in the county town countless streamers and pennants, blue, red and yellow, are strung high across the streets and lanes with slogans about having one child per couple.

Other exhortations abound urging people to unite around the leadership of the Chinese Communist Party, to support China's drive to modernization.

And warnings. Near the court house on Youth Street silent crowds gather around official posters with large red seals listing those condemned to death the previous September, giving the nature of their crimes – murder, arson, rape. No details are spared. Photographs show twelve prisoners, heads bowed and shaven, arms bound to white staves pointing skyward; Governor Wang Chang-yun presiding at a public rally announcing the sentences; then the bodies lying on the ground, shot through the heart by a firing squad. The first public executions to occur in many years, they reflect an emerging social malaise and carry the clear message that the government is prepared to resort to drastic measures in support of public order.

And finally, the ambiguities. Why had the Propaganda Department decided to play 'The East is Red', a triumphal hymn in praise of Mao Zedong as the saviour of the poor, over the country broadcasting system this morning just when certain peasants are becoming prosperous by following advice that it is 'all right for some to get rich first?' Was it a song of rejoicing or a note of warning? Who could tell?

The exhortations, warnings and ambiguities, the juxtapositioning of Mao and Deng are the subject of teashop conversations this day. The politically seasoned venture their interpretation of the political currents; others, less confident, prefer to keep their own counsel. But the stir of conjecture which fills the air is unmistakable.

2

ANCESTRAL MEMORIES: BEFORE 1950

Prehistoric floods, earthquakes and other subterranean upheavals created a soil in Sichuan that crumbles into reddish loam under the farmers' heavy hoes, making endless quantities of red earth. It is this fertile soil that forms the basis of the 'granary of heaven', a term by which Sichuan is known throughout China.

The village of MaGaoqiao occupies half a square mile of this gently sloping land on the edge of the great western plain. A county railway running north-south alongside the main asphalted highway and the eastward-flowing People's Canal, part of a vast provincial irrigation project of the 1950s, cut the village land into four quarters. To the north are the towering Dragon Gate mountains, usually invisible owing to mist and clouds. They store glacial waters to feed the Shi-ting River, one of several water courses that shape the alluvial plain on which the farmers here have sown and reaped for over two thousand years. To the south, half an hour by foot, is the nearest market town, called Junction.

As one approaches the village from the distance of the railway embankment, it seems to have a steady, ancient rhythm, a unity that can be understood and described. Children cut grass for pig fodder, slow-moving buffaloes graze by the roadside, women wash clothes in a spring-fed stream, a blue-clad peasant with a wide straw hat is repairing an irrigation ditch and the village tractor-driver hauls in a load of coal. Scattered clusters of farmhouses, the village office, school and clinic, all shaded by bamboo groves and stands of eucalyptus, appear to float in the surrounding paddy fields, small islands in a mirage of light brown, turquoise, gold or green, depending on the season. Narrow raised footpaths along the edges of fields act as connecting threads between the farmhouses, supplemented by bumpy, rutted tractor roads leading to the seven larger courtyards of the village. A feeling of physical dispersal pervades; without any main street, tower, tall building or other distinguishing landmarks, it is hard to imagine that this is a community of two thousand souls. It is only when inside one of the bamboo groves

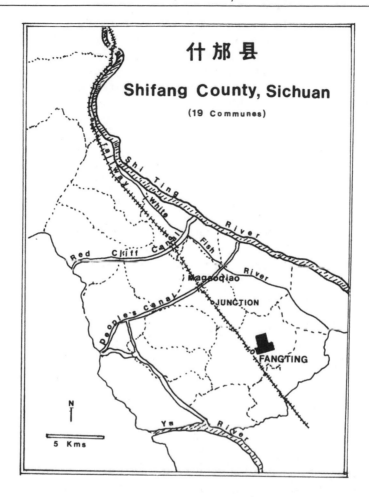

that the closeness, the density, the proximity of human habitation and animal husbandry, the potential for conflict, can be sensed. It is here that the secrets of the village stir.

Within one of these island clusters, at the north end of the village, is the Wang family compound. It nestles tight against its neighbours. Just beyond its confines is a well that is shared with several other families, and each family has a clump of bamboo and a private plot of land for growing vegetables. Inside the Wangs' compound gate the other practical arrangements for work and family life become apparent.

Stretching along the north and west sides of the enclosure are the living-room, kitchen and bedrooms, newly reconstructed of red brick and grey tiles in 1982. The windows of these rooms are gaping spaces each fitted with perpendicular iron bars that give a fortified look. In the eastern wing of the single-storied structure the thatched storage sheds for tools, the toilet, pig pens and a stall for the yellow ox combine to give off a pungent, damp aroma that permeates the air. The south side of the compound is completed by the back of the neighbour's house. In the open central courtyard which is used for sunning grain during fine weather, chickens scratch in the compost heap. Off in a corner beside a pile of coal a watch-dog with no name looks on silently.

Although the residence is new the furnishings of the living-room – a wooden table and several benches on the concrete floor, a single twenty-five watt bulb hanging from the ceiling – give the impression of an austere life-style. This feeling is heightened in the main bedroom which seems quite bare apart from a four-poster bed hung with worn mosquito netting, a small wall mirror, a red lacquer bureau blackened with age and several large rodent-proof jars for storing grain.

The kitchen is the centre of family life. It is dominated by the large brick stove with two built-in cauldrons made of cast iron. Smoke from the straw and coal fire curls up past cured meat dangling from the rafters and finds it way out through the tiles. It is not customary to have a chimney. A panel of family photographs, colourful wall posters and some poetry that team leader Wang Daoquan and his wife, Huang Chengxiu, have pasted on the doorway leading to their bedroom provides a clue to the sense of family feeling that is strong in this household.

Team leader Wang is a seasoned farmer, strong and agile. His alert eyes and lively conversation reveal a sense of humour and quick wit that allow him to hold his own with anyone in the village. Though a natural leader, a curious ambivalence of mind makes him willing to serve but reluctant to lead. Steadfast in his efforts on behalf of his team through changing circumstances and inspired by the prospect of a new and modernized China, he is yet tied to many of the ideas and practices of a feudal past that stand in the way of such a vastly different future.

It was his grandfather who influenced him most in his early years. A smith by trade and at one time a successful farmer who became a landlord with over 100 *mu* of land (a *mu* is one-sixth of an acre), Grandfather Wang took up opium smoking and subsequently lost most of his property. Later through his membership in the Robed Brotherhood, a secret society, he managed to buy a position in a temple and became a monk. His wife and children and eventually their children lived in a small hut not far from the temple and it was here that young Wang spent most of his youth tending a buffalo, listening to the monks tell exciting tales of the Tang and Song dynasties and observing the ways of the world.

In the early 1940s the boy went to private school but did not enjoy the experience. 'In the old school the teacher only explained things once', Wang recalled. 'If we forgot a word the teacher would beat our hands until they were swollen like steamed bread, or he'd strike us on the head. We cried a lot in our schooling time.' Wang soon left school and remained functionally illiterate all his life. He had, however, imbibed various Confucian ethical teachings on obedience, nourishment of a sense of shame, loyalty to one's relatives, respect for elders, veneration of ancestors through appropriate sacrifices and other moral principles which buttressed China's ancient family social system and its culture. When he was fifteen in 1950, Wang's ailing grandfather called him in one evening, entrusted him with the family history book and ancestor tablet and instructed him in his duties as the future head of the clan; it was an assignment that he could accept at this stage without question or worry.

During the years that followed Wang matured quickly. When the revolution came to the village he became active and, in spite of his grandfather's status and dubious connections with the underworld, was eventually recruited into the Communist Party. This favourable political standing in the village did not save him from the common experiences of family sorrows or tragedy: his father died of malnutrition during the difficult years of communization in the late 1950s, and two sisters also met unnatural deaths. The oldest one, married at eighteen to a man who lived in the mountains, was treated cruelly by her in-laws and died mysteriously. 'As that family had money we didn't dare go to the court', said Wang. 'We were afraid of meeting officials.' The younger sister, after a serious quarrel with her husband, threw herself into the canal and drowned in 1964.

In the face of such events, and in spite of his public duties as a party member, Wang faithfully carried on his responsibilities as family head, caring for his mother, helping his three younger brothers get established, and together with his wife raising four children in the private family courtyard that he inherited from his parents.

The negative aspect in the background of the Wang family – addiction to opium, connections with secret societies, illiteracy, patriarchal authority, female suicide, hard times – is not uncommon. The remarkable thing about team leader Wang is that, apart from heading up his own family, he has also become the leader of an emergent socialist collective of eighty-four other families. Hindered by illiteracy and ancient myths and sometimes in spite of his personal inclinations, he has been willing to take a lead in new social experiments. Events would prove that the very duality of his mental outlook – now clan/family centred, now community/collective oriented – made him an ideal cadre type, responsive to the pressures for change, yet sensitive to personal needs at a time of unprecedented upheaval in village life. For two and a half decades he has been at the helm, and is not yet fifty.

As a cold, windless January morning brightens in the unheated brigade headquarters, team leader Wang ushers in several of the elders, men in their fifties and sixties. It is the slack season for farm work and after some gentle coaxing by Wang they have come to talk of village history, of things remembered from childhood. Without their help no outsider could fathom the deep roots of the family-centred culture or guess the course of storms and upheavals, both natural and human, that underlie this tranquil world.

Zeng Lingmo, one of the elders, adjusts a broad fur cap over his ears and rubs his fingers to keep the circulation going. A gentle-mannered man who has acted as treasurer of his production team since 1963, he is the oldest of five brothers still living in the village. Lingmo knows his clan details perfectly, learned from a tombstone in the family graveyard at a place called Goat Crossing near the west gate of Fangting town. 'I went there twice when I was a teenager, but I haven't been there since', he adds carefully. 'Our clan came to Sichuan from Gold Fish mountain in Guangdong province about 300 years ago. It was after the uprising led by "Yellow Tiger" Zhang in Sichuan'.

The escapades of 'Yellow Tiger' Zhang colour the tales of all the clan histories in the village. Lingmo did not know the details, but according to historians it was in the last years of the Ming (1368–1644), before the Manchu Qing dynasty could establish its control, that the peasant rebel, Zhang Xianzhong, attracted a wide following. Within a few years invading Manchu warriors had begun a struggle for power with Zhang. By the time the formidable Zhang was killed in battle by an arrow in his throat, the population of Sichuan was decimated and it had become a land where, according to some chroniclers, famished dogs and fierce tigers attacked the hapless survivors.

Into this depopulated wasteland immigrants like Lingmo's ancestors trekked from other provinces, either land-hungry farmers or unwilling settlers, their hands tied behind their backs, prodded into the far west by a new dynasty in Beijing determined to consolidate its rule.

As the newcomers from Eastern China made their way into Sichuan during the seventeenth century, they brought with them their local dialects and deities, and their traditional foods – a strong sense of their place of origin. They constructed numerous temples and clubs where people from the same native district could gather to preserve their roots. Such establishments nestled everywhere in Sichuan, and grew in wealth and importance, becoming religious and political centres for the surrounding countryside. Thus at the small market town of Junction, with only 500 people, there stood, until the Cultural Revolution of the 1960s, no less than six large temples and social clubs reflecting the diverse origins and affiliations of the population.[1]

Even more than geographic origin however, it was ties of kinship that bound people together most closely. The family ancestral tablets traced the lineage back 300 years, recording the names of thirteen generations. 'Apart from the temples, almost every family clan had its own ancestral hall', Lingmo recalls. He remembers seeing his great-great-grandfather who had the middle name *xian* to mark his generation.

> From him my great-grandfather Qingsheng was born. He had seven sons of which my grandfather Fangao was the youngest. He had two sons, my father Xiangce and my uncle Xiangru. Then comes my generation with the *ling* as the middle name; my grandchildren are named *wei* and the next two generations, as yet unborn, will have the middle names *chen* and *you*.

It was like a recitation from the Book of Genesis – such careful ordering, such earnestness.

The extended family clan included all those in a vicinity who were related by blood and of the same patrilineal name, irrespective of their social class. Male clan leaders acted as custodians of jointly owned land, made loans or handed out charity, and used their prestige to mediate disputes so as to uphold the prevailing morality, prevent the remarriage of widows and otherwise defend what was thought to be good for the reputation and solidarity of the family. The clans thus became such an overpowering influence that to dislodge their hold on village life would require the force of a major social earthquake.

Such an eruption did arrive in MaGaoqiao in the 1950s when another peasant army swept across the province as Zhang Xianzhong and his rebels had done three centuries earlier. This time, using the Marxist techniques of class analysis and class struggle, the threads of a deeply embedded social fabric were pulled apart or broken, starting a process most villagers came to accept and learn to call Liberation.

For some, however, even after thirty years there appeared to be a sense of loss about a tradition that was disappearing without adequate emotional compensation. Lingmo was one who felt this loss. His voice has a tinge of nostalgia as he recalls Spring Festivals past:

> My mother or my father would have us put on new shoes and we walked a long way to visit relatives, going from house to house, from one village to the next. We used to get blisters from the new shoes. After we visited one family they would join us to visit the next; by the end of the morning there would be a great line of happy relatives walking through the fields, as many as two hundred or more. We usually ended up at a relative's in Shuangshen township. He was well-off, with two water buffaloes, and every year he would set up seven or eight tables to entertain his relatives.

The family history book and ancestor tablet, central symbols for developing filial piety in the young, disappeared at the deathbed of Lingmo's grandmother. He laments:

She handed it down, but now I don't know where that book is. The book was handed here and there to this family and that – I guess it is lost. Anyhow I don't know where it is now. During the period of the Cultural Revolution we burned lots of old books; I even burned the ten thousand year calendar. What a pity! It's a very good calendar; from it you can count the years according to the Chinese tradition, and it is helpful for farming, for telling the season. Well, I had it burned.

Team leader Wang Daoquan, intensely interested by this last comment, hurried in a coal briquette firepot to allow the conversation to continue into the chilly afternoon. When Lingmo mentioned that even the local Sichuanese who survived the killings of the 'Yellow Tiger' had their own halls and temples which were called *dizhu gong* – landlord palaces – Wang was unable to contain himself.

Yes, they called it landlord palace! I still remember when we talked about class struggle in the 1960s. As team leader I had to go to talk to the landlord elements once a week. I would shout at them, 'Where have you been?' and they would reply, 'We've been around here working in the fields'. And I would pretend to disagree. 'Oh no, you've been off in the mountains building a landlord palace!' That would frighten them!

Team leader Wang laughs at the recollection. He is clearly less nostalgic for the past than Lingmo.

The elder who condemns the past most eloquently is a poor peasant who scarcely set foot inside the ancestral precincts of his clan before Liberation except as a menial serving person. This is Liao Wenping. Tall, good-looking and exceptionally able, Wenping joined the Communist Party and rose to prominence in the village, only to fall into disgrace and be expelled in the 1960s and then rise again in the post-Mao era to become the first 'ten thousand yuan' family in the hamlet after Deng Xiaoping's reforms in the 1980s.

Although he seemed reticent to converse at first, even a little disdainful, Wenping remembered well the main Liao family courtyard which, in modified form, is now the village headquarters. He described how a protective eight-foot wall made of sun-dried bricks and plastered over wound its way around this complex. The dragon gate or main entrance faced east. A fortified tower higher than the bamboo groves, about thirty feet to the top, occupied one corner. 'It had gun port-holes on all sides and walls several feet thick', he explained. The tower was a place of refuge for the landlord and his family in case the courtyard was broken into and also served as a gaol into which he threw his debtors. Wenping had once spent some time there. The landlord, Liao Shangheng, lived in the manor house with some of his relatives. Their bedrooms were on the second storey of the main building. Around the brick and tile courtyard there were many large, gnarled willow trees, while outside the compound on the west side, in an extensive bamboo grove, the burial ground had magnificent graves with stone facings and carved headstones. All these – graves, walls and tower – symbols of the old order, were levelled to the ground when communization came in 1958; Shangheng and his wife moved into a cow shed.

The Liao family had also come to MaGaoqiao from South China after 'Yellow Tiger' Zhang's uprising. They heard the soil here was good for farming but they were also told that tigers ate people and that wild dogs and bees killed humans, so they were fearful. According to Wenping his ancestors were among those bound and forced to move into Sichuan.

His account of names and numbers were as precise and detailed as Lingmo's had been. There is no forgetting. The annual clan gathering was the most important tradition. On the second day of the Spring Festival every year the Liao clan met in neighbouring Yunxi township to exchange New Year's wishes under a wealthy clansman's roof.

'When we arrived there we would be asked from which generation, from which family ours had descended', said Wenping. Then a lunch was served. After lunch old and young and even the children sat together and listened to the clan history. Each year the senior clansman told them who was the first generation of their family in Sichuan, where they lived, how many sons they had, and from which son their family came, and how many members came from each family. He never mentioned the women separately.

> There were twenty or more tables, almost two hundred people. Those who were officials or who had money were well treated; they were invited into the living-room while the rest of us, the poor members, ate out in the open courtyard.

The purpose of these family gatherings, said Wenping, who glanced over at Lingmo as if seeking confirmation, was to let the generations become acquainted and avoid the error of fighting each other when meeting at a crossroads, or having someone of the younger generation beat a person from the older generation of the same clan. 'As you know,' he said, 'people in the countryside like to call others names, to swear, and if they don't know their relatives they might curse someone from the older generation. That would be unthinkable.'

'When did I become revolutionary?' Wenping paused for a moment.

At the time of the land reform when I joined the Chinese Communist Party, that's when I became a revolutionary. Our wealthy clansman in Yunxi was a big landlord with more than 100 *mu* (sixteen acres) of land. Following the determination of class status, after Liberation, he was classified as a landlord and we burned our family history book. We were in revolution. We were of the same clan but we belonged to different social classes, poor, middle and rich peasants and landlords and we didn't recognize him or the clan anymore.

Wenping grew more animated as he spoke of the effect of the clan ideology. People believed that the location of their ancestor's tomb affected the growth and destiny of a family. His branch of the family was told that, since their ancestor's tomb was not located in the right place, future generations could not become well-off. Only those tombs that were surrounded by large twisting trees with big trunks could make the generations to follow rich. This, according to Wenping, was said to make them accept their lot in life.

Liao Shangheng, a landlord of this village and member of our clan who had large twisted trees around his ancestor's tomb, cursed us saying, 'You poor devils. Members of your branch can never become rich. If people are poor their ghosts will be poor after death.'

'But I don't believe that the reason we were poor was because of the location of our ancestor's tomb', said Wenping with a defiant shake of his head.

It was because the rich and powerful like Shangheng rode roughshod over us. This was man exploiting man and money exploiting man. We were held back by many conditions; their fields were better and nearer to water. Without money you had no power; you had to suffer from his oppression.

Wenping spoke more rapidly.

Relatives exploited relatives. He had money, we had none, so he didn't treat us as a relative. Even if we wanted to borrow money from him he would refuse. If he did lend us money he asked for high interest. Through this kind of accounting he made us poorer and we had no way out. To pay back we would have to go to work for him.

Wenping paused again to light a home-made cigar before going on to explain that at the present time the Liao clan has two big families in the village and a couple of scorned outsiders, one of whom was destined to play a prominent role in the class struggles. Wenping headed one of the big families and the younger brother of the late landlord, Liao Shangheng who died a few years earlier, led the other. In Wenping's branch there were three living generations identified by the *shang, wen,* and *mo* ideographs. As he explained:

> When I joined the Communist Party, Shangheng's position as landlord did not have any effect on my application. No, not at all. To join the party they usually look into your background for three generations. But Shangheng's branch and mine were brothers six generations ago.
>
> Since Liberation we have never carried on with the clan meeting. After our wealthy clansman was classified as a landlord, as an enemy, nobody went there anymore. Now with the leadership of the Communist Party it is not necessary to carry out such meetings and they would not be good for socialism or for the people.

From Wenping's account of the powerful Liao clan, which still has ten households under that name in the hamlet, the memory of familial kindness that so colours the reminiscences of other peasants is almost entirely absent. The clan, by his account, appears instead as a rather crude instrument of social control: fostering the worship of the dead to control the living, a device to perpetuate the rule of the old over the young, the jurisdiction of male over female, the exploitation of the poor by the rich.

Understandings such as Wenping's did not come easily in the village. It was only during the sharp struggles of the land reform in the early 1950s and in the building of new political organizations in the village such as the youth league, the peasants' association and the party itself, where recruitment was by class status rather than by family connection, that different ties of solidarity emerged as an alternative to the views still held by men like Lingmo. As the change in consciousness from clan to class allegiance gained momentum it fuelled a levelling as fundamental and unsettling for the lives of village inhabitants as the geological and political upheavals of the more distant past. This new chain of events, while not completely eliminating ties of kinship, is etched deeply into the memory of every villager over the age of fifty. It began after the fall of the provincial capital to the People's Liberation Army from East China headed by generals He Long and Liu Bocheng, and political commissar Deng Xiaoping, in the last days of 1949.

3

'A CLEAN SNOW SWEEPS THE LAND': LAND REFORM IN 1951

The People's Liberation Army (PLA) captured Chengdu, capital of Sichuan province, in the last days of 1949. By then the civil war between the Communists and the Guomindang was sputtering out and the vanquished Nationalist forces disappeared like the wind-scattered leaves of the sycamore trees that lined the city streets.

Following a short battle to the north of Chengdu in which the 302nd division of the 16th army corps under the Nationalist general Hu Zhongnan suffered defeat, the Guomindang army finally dissolved into roving bands foraging in the villages, stealing food and warm clothing from the peasants and molesting the women.

In the wake of these demoralized troops the fringe elements of rural society up in Shifang county, the opium dealers, bands of thieves, gamblers, petty officials and leaders of secret societies who had reason to fear punishment at the hands of a new regime, took flight. They crossed over county lines hoping to establish new identities. Some fled into the mountains to join the outlaws of Mother Zhao, a tiny old woman from Northeast China who had been decorated by Chiang Kai-shek during the anti-Japanese war and who remained fiercely loyal to him. She became the stuff of local legends in Shifang; it took two years before PLA expeditions into the Dragon Gate mountains, supported by 2,000 peasants to carry grain, could eliminate the armed enemies of the revolution and establish friendly ties with the Qiang minority people who inhabited the highlands. Meanwhile on the plains small groups of PLA officers and men were left behind to help the villages organize their security and build a new political order.

When three PLA men rode into MaGaoqiao on horseback – a political instructor named Wei Saotang and two guards – the peasants hardly dared look up. Soldiers had always meant trouble, beatings and losses. 'We don't beat people', Wei called out. 'We are a different army, we are one family with the poor. We will divide the landlords' fields and give land to everyone.'

At first the peasants didn't believe them. They had no experience with the Communist Party; there had never been a party member in the whole county before 1950. 'How could we get the landlord's fields, we who have no land of our own, not even enough to throw at a crow?' they wondered, for at MaGaoqiao a handful of families owned most of the land.[1] But the Liberation Army said, 'We will help you', and some of the poorer peasants decided to accept the invitation.

Among the most vivid recollections of this time are those that come from the lips of Liao Lixiu, a widow of fifty who thirty years later lives in a low thatched cottage with two unmarried sons. Illiterate, in spite of a year at adult night school, and in poor health with chronic bronchitis aggravated by heavy smoking and the sunless days of a Sichuan winter, she possesses, nevertheless, the rapid speaking manner and rhetorical flourishes of one accustomed to defending her own turf. To hear her speak is to know what it was like to be poor, young and female in this village.

'At that time I was about twenty years old', she began. 'I was in the Village Armed Force and my husband, Jiang Tenglin, was a group leader of the Peasants' Association. I carried a rifle. Both of us were very active.'

There were about two dozen activists and they began by looking for the guns of the landlords and rich peasants. The village head, landlord Zeng Xiancuan, from whom Liao Lixiu and her husband rented twelve *mu* of land, as well as landlord Liao Shangheng and a rich peasant named Zhang, all had weapons. 'When we asked them to hand them over they shook and trembled.' She laughed at the recollection.

Rich peasant Zhang threw his rifle into a well where they found it. Later when his tobacco storehouse caught fire and people came to put it out they discovered another rifle in the loft. Landlord Liao denied having any weapons even after a thrashing with bamboo sticks. It took six months to force him to disclose twelve rifles, left by the KMT soldiers, which he had wrapped in oil cloth and buried. The village head's younger brother told the young activists he knew where the family coins and weapons were buried and he led them here and there digging for silver and guns. He would say, 'They're here', but when they dug there was nothing. Then he would point to another spot and they would dig without result. It was a wild goose chase. They became so angry with him that they dug a trench three feet deep, pressed him into it, placed a small bamboo sheet over his face and buried him alive.

'Of course we only intended to frighten him, we didn't want to kill him', she remarked. 'An hour later we dug him out and he was still alive, but even then he wouldn't tell us the truth.' They escorted him behind the tobacco barn and, ignoring the law forbidding corporal punishment, kicked him to his knees and fired two shots into the air causing him to faint. He still wouldn't talk. 'Now he's still alive', widow Liao chuckled thirty years later. 'He's really had a long life!'

The process of change at MaGaoqiao, as described by her, was not so different from that followed in other parts of China newly under the control of the Communist Party. It was reminiscent of a Chinese proverb that Chairman Mao liked to quote: straw sandals have no pattern; they take shape in the weaving. The army cadres who slipped into the village, almost unnoticed at first, albeit on horseback, had guidelines about main goals, sequence of reforms and work methods, but no exact plans or new leaders to propose. According to party instructions they were to trust the masses by recruiting activists from among the local peasants. The strategy required that the rich be identified and then class struggle promoted in clearly defined stages, leading to a restructuring of the village government in favour of the poor majority. Since the class interests of the poor were usually blurred by other social factors such as clan ties or jealousies, sex roles or generational obligations, not a few false starts were made.

The first attempt to establish a peasants' association at MaGaoqiao was a failure. Instructor Wei had helped set up a core group but the chairman was later discovered to be a leader of the Elder Brothers' Society, a secret organization of the landlords. 'It showed us that the organization was impure and its cadres not reliable', said Liao.

She then described the founding of a solid organization. In the summer of 1950 when the grain was ripening a dozen or more PLA soldiers, headed by battalion leader Zhang, came to the village. This time Liao and her comrades did things on a large scale. After going around to the poorer peasants' households to do some political organization they held several mass meetings to 'speak bitterness'. Here peasants talked openly of their past sufferings. Several hundred peasants went to one of these meetings at the Tang family courtyard by the grist mill. After the PLA troupe performed some skits and dances about things that had happened elsewhere, including songs from the popular opera, *The White Haired Girl*, the meeting began.

'Everyone was in high spirits and a bit nervous', Liao said. 'There was no platform or stage in that yard so we took out a dining-room table and asked the landlords to stand by it with their heads bowed. Bareheaded.'

Liao came forward to struggle face-to-face with village head Zeng, followed by her husband Jiang. They spoke of the evil doings and bullying tactics of Zeng, describing him as a cruel man who liked to throw people around and beat them, who charged high interest on loans and took big rents for his land. According to Liao:

> One evening, we got some water to grow rice in our plot of land
> but Zeng found out about this and sent someone to damage our

dyke so that all the water ran out; he didn't want us to grow rice there. He was so cruel. When people went along the sides of his fields cutting grass for pig fodder he didn't just beat or curse them, he stripped them of their trousers, no matter whether they were men or women and chased after them as they ran shrieking with fear. Then he walked away with the trousers over his shoulder. He was a rough, cruel man!

While she was confronting the landlord, battalion leader Zhang pulled Zeng's ear and said, 'Are you listening to her?' Zeng replied, 'I'm listening, I'm listening.' 'Yes, I struggled with him!' said Liao. 'And my husband, Jiang, as well as Tang Yunwu and Chen Kaishi also "spoke bitterness" at the meeting.' Liao and the others were nervous at first, but after it was over PLA leader Zhang called them together saying not to worry, he would back them up.

To judge by widow Liao's charges against village head Zeng, which were relatively minor crimes, he may not have been the monster she claimed. Nevertheless, he was frightened and a few days later he committed suicide with a knife. Then his daughter hanged herself in her room. Liao said solemnly:

> I was in charge of her. That day when I went to ask her to come out I carried my baby son on my back. As I opened the door I saw her hanging there and I was frightened. I turned back and ran home. I was really afraid. Then we shut all the members of Zeng's family into a tower to prevent other such happenings.

Following these events the peasants established their association and to show their feelings the young revolutionaries changed the name of the village to Build the Country Village. They proudly made themselves a national flag and a seal for the association. From then on peasants wishing to travel from the village had to have a paper with this seal on it so that the village could control the movements of the landlord and rich peasant classes. With the departure of battalion leader Zhang and his work team, the new local leadership faced the task of consolidating its position in the village.

There is still an air of exhilaration in widow Liao's account of the way the young women of the village participated in the class struggle. The process generated a sense of power, a hint of what revolution could bring. But so far it was only a glimmering of light. Male short-sightedness and deeply ingrained Confucian ideas of patriarchy continued to make the village a man's world. Although Liao Lixiu did not refer directly to Confucianism, the reality of its presence and her keen awareness of it were evident as she talked.

> There were some men in the village who opposed the public activity of
> their wives and daughters-in-law. So we formed a women's organization
> and did propaganda work; we danced the *yangge* through the village. For
> a time I was the leader of the Women's Association and we went around
> with the men taking over the properties and fields of the landlords.

Her father-in-law, especially, expressed his displeasure. 'A woman
should not run about outside', he said. 'People think such women are
whores!' If he saw her sitting on the same bench with some man he
cursed at her, saying that it was not proper. Sometimes he even beat
her for being outside, and she broke several of his bamboo pipes while
protecting herself.

> Now Chairman Mao has come, he supports us women, and helped us to
> straighten up our backs. Even if my father-in-law swore at me I'd still go
> out and be active. If he infuriated me, I'd go to the Peasants' Association
> and get him called to a meeting for criticism. The people scolded him
> and talked to him; after that he didn't speak to me about going out,
> he didn't dare.
>   I was angry and I asked him, 'Don't you remember how we poor
> people suffered bitterly in the past? Now that Chairman Mao has come
> isn't it our turn to be pushy? Why shouldn't we run around outside for
> a few days more? How do you think you got your land and pigs?' What
> else could he say? He kept silent.

But she kept it up. 'If it were not for Liberation,' she railed at him,
'would you be able to find a bowl of rice? In the past when you had your
breakfast you never knew whether you would be able to find your lunch
or not. Now you just want to sit in your room and wait for bargains!'
Her husband encouraged her. He said, 'Let my father curse, don't pay
any attention to him. You go ahead and take part.'
    Before long Liao Lixiu had three children. In all she raised five and
bore another three who died. From this time on she was not so active,
but still carried a child on her back to attend meetings when they were
called. She recalled:

> In the old society we country women dared not go out, we didn't go
> to plays or theatres or even to the market. Now that the Liberation had
> come no wonder all of us women were happy! We liked it. We came out.
> How we hated those who held us down! That's why we were so active in
> struggling with the landlords.

Widow Liao's lively version of those early days did not pass unchal-
lenged by some of the villagers. No less a person than the head of the

village armed force in those early years, Zou Jingfu, now aged 68, cast doubts about her militant role.

'Liao Lixiu came over to our house several times to persuade me to allow her husband Jiang Tenglin into the Armed Force,' said Zou, 'but we didn't let him in.' The quiet-spoken Zou, whose eyes almost squeezed shut when he smiled, referred to the fact that Liao's husband was a distant relative of a man named Jiang Beixiu, the township head before 1950 and one of the most hated of the local tyrants.

According to Zou the younger Jiang had participated in some of his distant uncle's shady activities before 1950, even carrying a gun for him during one of his nocturnal raids. And might it not be that Liao and her husband had been able to rent twelve *mu* from village head Zeng because Zeng's wife was Jiang's distant aunt, a sister of Jiang Beixiu's? Zou insinuated a web of clannish ties; the suspicion was that the young couple were merely acting up in a quarrel among relatives. 'Her purpose', Zou continued, 'was to get her husband into the Armed Force so that people would forget the things he had done for Jiang Beixiu before Liberation. As for Liao Lixiu herself, I don't think that she was in our Armed Force either.' All the while Zou's talkative young wife, Lan Guifeng, who appeared to harbour some unstated dislike or jealousy of Liao, egged him on.

This conflicting testimony reflected deep cleavages that had existed among the peasant revolutionaries, cleavages that twenty years later led to tragic results for Jiang Tenglin, by then vice-team-leader. The conflict also suggested a complexity of motives – fear, self-protection, greed, idealism, class or gender solidarity – that lay behind the militancy of villagers such as Liao Lixiu, and also, perhaps, the feelings of disappointment of people like Zou who were not chosen to continue in leading roles beyond the first few years after Liberation.

In spite of the contentions of Zou and his wife, however, there could be little doubt about Liao Lixiu's active record in removing local tyrants from power since it kept appearing in the accounts of other villagers, including their memory of the next great drama when the focus of action shifted to the high street of the nearby market town.

Junction, or Thriving Market as it was known during those early years, is a 'standard market town' of about 500 permanent residents.[2] In addition to its six temples and a primary school, it boasted the usual shops for serving the surrounding countryside: four Chinese medicine shops and two that sold Western medicines; two slaughter houses, two noodle shops, two inns and four restaurants; four wine shops and two distilleries, 'Roly Poly' Li's smoked chicken store next door to 'Chicken Meat' Jiang's establishment; teahouses; a dry goods store, two tailors' shops and a dye workshop. The number suggested a keen element of competition in the marketplace. Two smithies repaired wheelbarrows and carts. Within a short distance stood a clock-watch-bicycle repair store and five shops to make things 'for superstitious activities – joss sticks, firecrackers, paper money and paper houses to burn for the dead. These businesses, strung out along a single, narrow street, much like the main street of any small town, served the masses of peasants and commercial travellers who thronged in on the periodic markets that occurred every three or four days. Junction's setting, where the north-south road meets the thoroughfare coming in from Peng county to the west, and its location in the tobacco-growing district, naturally attracted people from many other parts.

It also attracted the attention of the underworld in the years before 1950.

Chief of the Elder Brothers' Society was a man named Chen Wenlong who controlled 400 guns in Shifang and neighbouring counties. He raked in money by levying taxes on the small dealers and street hawkers, and he ran teahouses where gambling went on day and night. He managed the opium dens on the high street as well as two brothels that, according to the manager of the Official Inn, 'housed prostitutes who came mainly from Chengdu where they could no longer make their mark'. Since Chen's activities were so wide-ranging, when the new government caught him he was tried, sentenced to death and executed in Fangting, the county capital.

The Jiang and Ma families, the biggest local despots in Junction, between them owned most of the shops on the high street. In addition, each operated money-lending businesses and owned large tracts of land. The head of the Ma family, Ma Yusong, committed suicide at the time of Chengdu's liberation and his properties fell forfeit to the state. That left Jiang Beixiu and his four brothers – the 'five tigers' of the Jiang family. The crafty Jiang Beixiu, who, as already mentioned, was township head in Junction at the time of Liberation, managed to hoodwink PLA instructor Wei the first time round, getting himself classified as nothing more than a middle peasant. Unfortunately for him, the authorities sent him to Fangting to attend a re-education class set up for landlords and former village and township heads. There he wrote out his own biography. When this document arrived back in Junction for confirmation it outraged the people by its half-truths and omissions.

Living in MaGaoqiao village with his two wives and sixty *mu* of land won in a card game, Jiang Beixiu was a familiar and notorious figure. Fearing for his safety, he travelled only by sedan chair with a score of armed retainers going before and aft including his special gunmen, two brothers named Xiang. Pistols dangling from their hips, they never left his side. Many people, therefore, came forward with charges and stories of Jiang's misdeeds – his bullying tactics, his corrupt use of public funds, and his gunmen's murderous activities.

After sifting the evidence, the county court decided that by day Jiang had been head of a township, by night the leader of a bandit gang. In the late autumn of 1950, therefore, PLA instructor Wei summoned the leaders of all the Peasants' Associations of Junction township to a meeting. 'We were unanimous', recalled Deng Yuanming, who was then clerk of MaGaoqiao village. 'We said he should be executed.'

A detachment of the township armed force promptly went to Fangting to escort Jiang back for trial in the square of the Upper Fire God Temple on the high street. To mark the importance of this occasion – the most dramatic event to have occurred there in living memory – the county governor, Chen Guang, chief magistrate by Chinese tradition, presided.

Before a throng of thousands a maid servant, Liu Shuzheng, formerly wet-nurse to Jiang's child, spoke first. Shaking her fist at Jiang, who stood on the platform, head shaven and bowed, she told of her bitter life in his house and what she knew of his nefarious activities. The manager of a restaurant on the high street, Huang Dahai, followed her, and then the now intrepid Liao Lixiu.

'My husband and I lived in a house rented from our distant relative, Jiang Beixiu, at a placed called One Tree-trunk Bridge', she began calmly. 'We were relatives going back five or six generations. We cultivated his fields there for a year, but then he poured out a stream of abuse on us and refused to rent us the land again.' Everyone present, steeped in Confucian tradition, would condemn Jiang for lack of 'human feeling' towards relatives, but it was not a crime when directed by an older generation toward juniors. But Liao Lixiu had more serious charges to follow. She continued, her voice rising:

> He was a rough man, and cruel, and so were his running dogs, especially one Xiang Tinmeng. Once when a strong young man was carrying baskets of coal through the village, running-dog Xiang caught him and wanted to sell him as a conscript to the army. The young man refused. Xiang then beat him with his gun and he died on the spot. I saw them drag the body away and no one dared to say a word. Xiang was under the protection of Jiang Beixiu, township head. . . .

Liao finished and a man rushed forward from the crowd eager to recite a verse about the disaster that peasants faced from the former Guomindang government's conscription policy:

> Conscripts, conscripts,
> Swallow our tears . . .
> The township head decides our fate,
> Village chiefs are chicken-footed gods;

The oil of the poor is boiled away,
The king of hell lights the lamps of heaven.

There was not much more to be said. After hearing all the witnesses, Governor Chen asked the meeting rhetorically what should be done about Jiang. 'Kill him!' the crowd roared. 'Cut off his head!'

Revolutionary tribunals executed a dozen people in Junction in that year of retribution. Many others who had committed grievous acts were spared and given a chance to reform themselves. Local peasants still maintain that the bloodshed of that year was minimal compared to the infamies perpetrated by those executed when they rode high. The lines of poetry posted up on either side of their doors when the first lunar New Year after Liberation came round reflected the sense of relief and celebration felt by the peasants:[3]

> The ten directions are liberated
> Hundreds of millions of households celebrate
> A clean snow sweeps the land.

and

> The four seas* wear the light of benevolence
> Several thousand li** are cheering
> Just like a timely rain from heaven.
> (*a poetic expression meaning humanity;
> **a Chinese mile, equal to one-third of an
> English mile)

With the local tyrants deposed and a voice acquired by those so long silent, the time had come to start the land reform and to begin distributing the fruits of Liberation. The peasants impatiently awaited this day.

The Peasants' Association began recruiting activists to prepare for the land revolution in the autumn of 1951 after the grain harvest. From MaGaoqiao the new village head, Zhang Jinghe, and another young man named Yao Shengwan, who became village party secretary, set off for Junction with about seventy other activists from the township for a training session. Between them these two ambitious and outspoken young men proved themselves able to ride out the political storms that lay ahead and held the top positions in the village over the next twenty-five years. But for the moment they were novices.

Upon arrival in Junction they discovered a work team of equal size, seventy people, men and women workers, students, teachers, journalists, writers and professors from all over China, some from as far away as Shanghai and Beijing. It was more than a little awe-inspiring for the young peasants to make contact with such people. This widely divergent group of proletarians, intellectuals and peasants teamed up for two months. To begin they stayed for a week in the Hu-guang temple, eating and living together, learning about each other and about government policy.

For change to take place the peasants had to examine their own role in the feudal economy in the countryside. It was considered crucial that they should understand the land reform as much more than a tactical redistribution of wealth. Here as elsewhere in China, many peasants did not realize the nature of the feudal exploitation, believing instead that they were poor because fate had been unkind to them or their horoscope was unlucky. Now, unless they raised their class awareness by personal struggle against the landlords, their submissiveness would remain and the old élite would eventually return to power.

Nor was the land distribution to come about as a top-down imperial favour. Instructors warned the delegates that if the process was 'peaceful', without the unpleasantness of confronting the landlords in each village, then the peasants might feel that they were taking or stealing the land from the rightful owners rather than redistributing it as a matter of social justice, or alternatively that it had fallen into their laps by sheer good luck. The aim was to overturn an old ruling class at the most basic level of society and replace it by a leadership committed to seeing a social order that gave voice and power to the poor.

The Communist Party's policy was to seize all the property and possessions of any family in the village classified as *landlord* for distribution, leaving the family only an amount equal to that of the poor peasants after distribution. The policy kept *rich peasants* out of power, but left their property intact unless there was a shortage of land for distribution, in which case their surplus was taken. The *middle peasants* kept what they had and became owners of the land they formerly rented. The *poor peasants and hired hands* received the landlords' possessions as the fruits of the revolution. The policy of the party, in short, was to 'rely on the poor peasants, unite with the middle peasants, neutralize the rich peasants and oppose the landlords'.

In all this it was the leniency towards the rich peasants that was most difficult for the delegates to accept; in many cases their living conditions were on par with the landlords. In response to this discontent the leadership explained that consideration for the rich peasant class arose from the fact that their economy and their expertise in farming were vital to revive production from the stagnation induced by years of civil war; if production did not revive and shortages occurred, then hungry people would turn against the government. Internal documents, published years later, also reveal that the Communist Party feared lest ultra-left tendencies among the poor peasants should emerge and make it hard to prevent 'indiscriminate beating and killing' if the party did not draw a clear line separating rich peasants from landlords.[4]

When the training class at Junction ended, a young woman from East China, a male student from Chengdu 'who wore a university badge on his jacket', two house painters from a neighbouring township and one or two others formed a small work team to help the peasants at MaGaoqiao 'turn over' (*fanshen*).

In the north end of the village all family members gathered at the Liao family courtyard, jostling each other good-naturedly as they crowded in to hear the report of the work team. Men, women, and children, everyone came.

The work team began by explaining the main categories, as outlined in the land reform documents issued by the people's government. They told the meeting that *landlords* were those who were able to live without working; *rich peasants* did work but received more than 25 per cent of their income by collecting rents and interest and by exploiting hired labour; *middle peasants* hired helpers on a seasonal basis but gained less than 25 per cent of their income from others; and finally, there were the *poor peasants* and *farm labourers* who owned or rented little, insufficient, or no land and survived by hiring themselves out to others. A family's condition during the three years immediately prior to Liberation determined its class status.

Following these explanations, the meeting to determine everyone's class status lasted several days, sometimes late into the evening, as tension ran high. The excited poor peasants told the landlords and rich peasants to climb up on some upside-down threshing bins, and as a form of humiliation demanded that they announce their own class status. 'The landlords admitted their status,' said village head Zhang, 'but some rich peasants claimed they were only middle peasants. So we calculated their fields, their rental income and other property until they had to admit that they were in the rich or small land lessor category.' At Liao Family Flats (later No. 5 production team), which was fairly typical of the whole village, three families fell into the 'bad' landlord category while fifteen could claim the 'good' poor peasant class; in between were eighteen families of rich and middle peasants.

The land reform work team confiscated the surplus land of the rich peasants, the part they were unable to work themselves, as well as the properties of the landlords – their land, equipment, farm animals, houses, furniture, clothes, everything they owned. Then they classified the land into six grades according to fertility. Each person was to have enough land to produce 500 *jin* of grain per year; (a *jin*, or catty, is equal to 1.1 lb. or half a kilogram.) This meant 1.1 *mu* of class 1-a land, 1.2 *mu* of class 1-b and so on to 1.6 *mu* of class 3-b. The work team described the resulting parcels of land clearly on the land certificates, giving their boundaries north, south, east and west, a description of the neighbouring pieces, notations of any tombs that were on them, how many large stones, trees, what group the soil was in. 'We put a square stamp on the middle of the land certificate', said village head Zhang Jinghe. 'Then we tore the paper down the middle, one part for the village office, the other in the hands of the owner.'

The work team distributed shares to everyone, even new-born babies, on an equal basis. A woman's own name now appeared on the family's land certificate, as distinct from that of her husband, marking an important symbolic break with the past practice of female subjugation. From that time on women kept their own names after marriage. 'Single persons received two shares', said Zhang, 'and a childless couple got three, but for a family of three or more each had one share per person.' The villagers adopted these adjustments and amendments to the main principle of equal shares, following the expression of opinion and voting at village meetings.

For seventy days the land reform movement continued at MaGaoqiao. At its conclusion a higher level cadre came one day to check on the work. 'None of the peasants here complained or appealed against their class status', said village head Zhang with a certain air of pride. Compared to the land reform conducted five years earlier in North China, as described in William Hinton's *Fanshen*, the transition was remarkably smooth, the product of years of practical experience by the Communist Party.

Ironically, when the work team posted up the results of the land reform for the villagers to see, it was the rich and middle peasants who remained at the top (See Appendix Table 1, col. 8). They had about twice the area claimed by the poor peasant class from the landlords. Even the despised landlord families, because they had more children, ended up with title deeds giving them more than the average poor peasant family.

This result should have been enough to turn even the most ardent revolutionary into a cynic. After all the struggle the 'bad classes' came off well, while the poor with their small holdings would have less chance to become prosperous. The villagers were quite matter of fact in their explanations, but it seemed unreasonable even though the pattern was reportedly similar in most parts of China.[5]

The poor peasants were actually not so hard done by. The solution to this puzzle, it turned out, was fairly obvious but was one of those village 'secrets' that fail to appear in any set of statistics and about which no outsider would be directly informed.

The leaders of No. 5 production team had said in passing that they were keeping an area of 93 *mu*, or about 20 per cent of the total land, as a public reserve for future population growth or a winter water reservoir, but they mentioned nothing further about its use. This was the key point.

The reserved area corresponded to the former temple lands and clan holdings which the local gentry controlled before Liberation, land which they often did not register or report to higher levels for tax purposes.[6] After Liberation, with political power wrested from the gentry, the poor peasants took charge of this domain. Possibly they spread the use of these resources among the fifteen poor peasant households, bringing their acreage substantially above the other classes. This seemed reasonable, a matter of natural justice. And perhaps the 'borrowed' part of their economy remained unreported for tax purposes. By way of corroboration in the 1980s, study of satellite data, coupled with ground surveys, convinced members of the Chinese Academy of Social Sciences in Beijing that the cultivated area in China was substantially under-reported by the villages, 'probably by at least 20 per cent'.[7]

When I brought these speculations to the attention of a group of the villagers at an informal gathering one evening in the summer of 1986 the atmosphere seemed to grow still as if before a storm. Those present exchanged glances around the room and it was unclear whether they were trying to suppress frowns or smiles. In the end it was team leader Wang who settled the question. Referring to the challenge and looking across the room he said softly, as if in a stage whisper, 'Only you and I and God know this!' Whereupon everyone broke into laughter and animated conversation.

The 'hidden' asset may help to explain why, when the Communist Party came along with dramatic plans for pooling all the land into co-operative farms in the mid-1950s, the response gathered momentum slowly.

4

TAKING THE CO-OPERATIVE ROAD:
1953–7

After the land reform, farm productivity increased and incomes rose. But many peasants remained at subsistence levels. Even in a place like MaGaoqiao on the fertile Sichuan plain people claimed that the tillers found it difficult to create much surplus. They lacked either the necessary capital or labour power, or sophistication in field planning, crop rotation, water management and animal husbandry.

The former village clerk at MaGaoqiao, Grandpa Deng, said that although output increased the most troublesome fact was a widening gap between the rich and the poor. Those who had more able-bodied people in their families or a buffalo and could grow tobacco as a cash crop became rich in a short time and could 'turn over' in their economic production. These, he said, were mainly the middle and rich peasant classes because 'in the land reform movement we didn't touch their fields'. But families like his own, who were short of labour power and money, or had no pigs to raise, thereby lacking manure for their fields, experienced a steady financial decline.

In the opinion of Grandpa Deng and other old-timers there existed one decisive indicator of unsatisfactory conditions in the village: 'It was still hard for a poor peasant to find a wife; girls didn't wish to marry the sons of poor peasants'.

If things went on this way they believed there would be a return to the miseries of the old society, to the conditions before land reform. One family had already pawned its fields, and six or seven sold their crops to rich peasants in advance at a heavy discount because they were short of food before the harvest and lacked money to buy it.

'The government soon discovered this kind of tendency,' Deng recalled, 'so later in 1953 it started some new policies.' The new policies of the central government, directed by Mao, indeed began flowing to the villages in wave-like progression. Like a storm-swept beach, where each wave piles upon the one before it in overlapping, interweaving, bewildering succession, mass campaigns began to hit MaGaoqiao.

The purposes of these campaigns were varied: to unlock the treasures of nature, to check capitalist practices, to strengthen the hands of the revolutionary activists by building the Communist Party, to strike at counter-revolutionary forces and ultimately to introduce a co-operative, socialist form of agriculture. Inspiration and daring, fright and worry during these mass movements, and the comic relief of seeing an ambitious neighbour fall into a trap of his own making – these were the common experiences of MaGaoqiao villagers from 1953 to 1957 when the Agricultural Producers Co-operative finally included everyone.

The digging of the People's Canal came first. This project made a lasting impression on the villagers. The 150-kilometre waterway cut through the village as it linked six counties to a famous irrigation works on the Min River to the west. It demonstrated the ability of the new government to mobilize the people in transforming the economy.

'In our township we formed a battalion with 500 people', said one of the participants in this project, his eyes lighting up at the recollection. 'Under the battalion', he said, 'we had companies, platoons and squads. Each squad took a certain area to dig.' It was a military-type formation. At first everyone was sceptical.

> We thought such a huge project would fail because of the lack of engineering skills and capital. But the province sent some people to make plans. They drove stakes into the fields and said that water would be brought over from the Min River. Then it turned out that the state didn't have to pay a penny for the land occupied.

In other words, the land was confiscated. This could not have been popular at the time, but in compensation the state announced that the displaced people could settle on public land reserved at the time of land reform.

The speaker was a young revolutionary peasant at that time, Deng Xicheng, now over fifty and retired after almost thirty years of leadership in Junction township. He had a no-nonsense watchfulness and toughness in his character, a hard person to deter once he made up his mind. 'At that time it was easy to mobilize the masses.' Xicheng made a sweeping gesture. 'Ho yo! As soon as you issued a call they would come and follow instructions.'

As Xicheng described building the canal his pride and enthusiasm, his candour and an easy recognition from local people who passed by as he talked, became apparent. This rough-featured peasant, who had carried forward the revolution here longer than any other leader, told of the poverty of his childhood, the quiet desperation of an opium-ridden society, daring exploits at the time of Liberation and then his training to be a leader.

The gist of his story encapsulates something typical of the times. His father died of typhoid fever when he was just one year old, impoverishing the family. After a childhood spent as a hired hand cutting grass for pig fodder, he went with an older brother to help build an airport for the American air force in Guanghan in the 1940s. 'He pushed a wheelbarrow and I gave him a hand by pulling with a rope.'

> My family always lived in a village called Eastern Hills Temple before Liberation. Some of the older people still remember our house – they called it the Deng Family Manure Pit. In the old days we always dug a pit beside the road, so as to collect the shit of the passers-by for our vegetable plot. That's why they called our place the Deng Family Manure Pit.

Xicheng remembered the opium business. Before 1950 opium smoking was common and many people, including his uncles, grew opium poppies as a cash crop.

> During the opium harvest season we went out to the fields with a knife and made diagonal slits on the pods, then on the second day we took a small sliver of bamboo and a red earthen bowl to collect the opium sap. We took the red earthen bowl to the market for sale.
>
> The smokers were mainly load-carriers and rich people; nearly all the carriers smoked to relieve their pain. In the big opium den in Junction, called the Carefree Wineshop, two classes existed. The rich could lie on couches while the poor people lay on the ground to smoke. That place has now been changed over to houses for families.
>
> During the Guomindang period the officials issued orders banning opium and they forbade the growing of poppies. If you didn't obey you could be fined, gaoled or even executed. Sometimes the county governor came down to the countryside by sedan chair to make an impression, to round up the smokers and traders, but they usually hid or ran away. In the last days before Liberation the price of opium soared. Some people turned to using tin foil to sniff morphine; some even broke the former opium containers into pieces, soaked them in water and drank the mixture. Although forbidden you could still buy opium; many families sold their possessions for it and faced ruin.

When the People's Liberation Army arrived Xicheng volunteered to join a grain transport support team. Three times he walked up to the hinterlands close to Tibet. Narrow paths wound through the high mountains and in the evenings the grain carriers slept by the river side. The work was dangerous because of the outlawed Guomindang soldiers, the bandits led by Mother Zhao, whom they nicknamed 'Lady Catkin', and the uncertain attitude of the poverty-stricken national minority people who lived there.

After this experience Xicheng attended a literacy class to train as a cadre. 'I went there with my salary paid', he said enthusiastically. 'The students at that school were peasant cadres, old Red Army soldiers, even young government workers, several hundred of us.' At the opening ceremony the political commissar had said, 'No matter how high your rank, no matter how long you have been working in the party or fighting with the army, you must consider yourself a primary school student here. You must learn to read and write so as to serve the people better.'

Xicheng returned to his earlier story. The five hundred canal diggers from Junction lived and cooked together, each receiving Y5,000 per day, an amount equal to 50 cents after the currency reform of 1955. 'Food and clothing did not cost much in those days', Xicheng remarked. 'We used 20 cents for three meals and saved 30 cents to take back home.' The cash, provided a welcome bonus for the families facing financial difficulty and no doubt helped dissolve the anger many peasants must have felt when the state requisitioned land for the canal. The Junction battalion spent three months without complaint, a whole winter, digging their section of the canal from MaGaoqiao village to the Ma Family Stockade, a distance of about two kilometres; their main satisfaction lay in the prospect of future benefits for the land.

On the day the water started to flow thousands of peasant rose early and marched to witness the spectacle, drums beating, cymbals clashing, volleys of firecrackers, red flags waving and banners reading 'Long live Chairman Mao and the Chinese Communist Party!' 'Long live the irrigation canal!' 'Water is the main thing needed for agricultural production!' It added up to a good beginning.

Hard on the completion of the People's Canal the government began a campaign to change the traditional marketing system. This campaign to restrict capitalist practices sent disturbing shock waves throughout the rural areas.

Until now private traders allied to the more prosperous peasants controlled the marketing of grain, cotton, tobacco, cooking oil and other crops, and prices floated freely up and down as a result of their calculations and speculations. The poor had always complained of price manipulations but most peasants privately hoped that they too would be able to create a surplus and take advantage of the market.

However, under the existing system the government found that it could not secure sufficient products to support the urban industrial revolution at prices that it could afford. Its answer to this problem was to curtail the activities of the private traders by creating a state company with a monopoly for the purchase and sale of grain. In addition, it established Supply and Marketing Co-operatives in every township to compete with the petty capitalist traders in handling the flow of other farm products to the city and the supply of urban industrial goods to the countryside.

Considerable resistance greeted this first attempt to establish a co-operative.

'The private merchants had safe harbours and resources for getting supplies independently', recalled Zhang Shiyuan, leader of the co-op in Junction township. 'They had places for doing business – stores, restaurants, cotton cloth shops, cooking spice outlets; they had the experience and some loyal customers. We had to take wheelbarrows, carts and shoulder poles to deliver our goods to the peasant courtyards.' Using the premises of landlord Ma who had committed suicide at the time of Liberation, the eight co-op workers lived together in one large room and used the rest of the building to carry out their commercial tasks. They sought to win the support of the peasants.

'Gradually the peasants began to help us', Zhang recalled. Quite a few bought shares and the co-operative distributed 10 per cent of the profits to the shareholders; peasant members elected a supervisory committee to watch over the management of the co-op. Sometime after this promising start, according to Zhang, with the private merchants tamed and brought in to a co-operative federation of their own, 'the party adopted a mistaken policy'. The Supply and Marketing Co-operative now expanded greatly, becoming a wholly state-owned organization that lost its democratic style and resulted in all kinds of complaints from the people. 'We collected up some products excessively', said Zhang ruefully, 'and we no longer paid proper attention to the needs of the local people.'

An acute shortage of local leaders plagued the revolutionary regime. The network of trained cadres who actually understood the government's programme was woefully thin in almost all the rural areas. In Junction township an insufficient recruitment of party members delayed the formation of a Communist Party general branch until mid-1953, and another year passed before the party could establish roots in the thirteen villages of the township.

The county party committee tried to remedy the situation with a forty-day training class in Fangting attended by promising activists from each village, but at the end of the session only three of the peasants from Junction proved to be of sufficient calibre to gain admittance as probationary members. Perhaps MaGaoqiao village was lucky, because its applicant, village head Zhang Jinghe, became one of the successful candidates. However, the tragi-comedy of Jinghe's early experience as a party member illustrates the problem of finding suitable people, and offers a glimpse into the crude means that the party sometimes employed to promote its goals.

Jinghe was a middle peasant, a man with deep local roots and a capable farmer who became village head at MaGaoqiao at the time of land reform in 1951. He did well with his political responsibilities, but even after achieving his important new status in the party he could not stop thinking about what was going to happen to his summer harvest of tobacco leaves. It had been a bumper crop for which he expected to reap a handsome reward, and the more he thought about it the more worried he grew, since there were rumours of the government's intention to introduce controlled, planned marketing. One day he quietly prepared two 60-lb. bundles of his best leaves, one bundle for each end of his carrying pole, and without a word to anyone except his wife, without making any arrangements for his duties as village head, he set out for Chongqing, the largest city market in Sichuan about 200 miles away. The 400-mile round trip, which he had to cover by foot and river junk, took about a month. The prices for Shifang county's No. 1 sun-cured tobacco were so favourable compared to what he could get locally that he hurried home and returned to Chongqing a second time.

News of his long-distance trading spread. When Jinghe finally came back the county party secretary summoned him to the county seat and scolded him, telling him that he, a village head and party member, was acting like a capitalist, a speculator! While reassured that his case was only a problem of ideology, not a crime, Jinghe was informed by the party that it was going to make an example of him: 'We want all details about your business in Chongqing and we're going to use them to teach others by negative example.' Jinghe shook his head at the bitter memory.

> I admitted my mistake, I said I was wrong to do that. My error was not as big as it was said to be. They made a great fuss over my case. They built a clay figure in the park in Fangting town and said that it was me, Zhang Jinghe, who was a capitalist. They put on some performances in the park on this theme, with me as the villain who tried to fool innocent people in Chongqing. They made a lotus flower song with bamboo clappers, saying that Jinghe, a middle peasant, takes the lead in promoting capitalism. There were cartoons and all kinds of exaggerations. It didn't prevent me from becoming a full party member, but in the meantime the propaganda was really something!

After that whenever Jinghe went to the high street on market day, in Junction or even in Fangting, people pointed at him from behind saying, 'That's the capitalist Zhang Jinghe'. 'I had to be broad minded', said Jinghe. 'The party used me as a bad example with which to teach the masses. I didn't take it too hard. It was the work of the party.'

Soon the little party branch in Junction township had more troubles. Word came from the centre about a general purification and rectification of party ranks which invited the general public to offer opinions and suggestions. It was called 'a free airing of views and great debates', and was designed to stimulate popular participation in administration. The instructions reflected Mao's belief that the best new members are those who dare to be active in the course of storm and struggle and therefore that recruiting into the party and party rectifications should proceed in an alternating, leap-frog pattern.

The rectification movement provided ambitious peasants with an opportunity to gain public notice, and gave others who risked being labelled as 'rightists' the chance to express complaints. One man, resenting the fact that he could no longer sell his products freely, ridiculed the party openly at the village meeting.

> The party told us we would have electric lights and telephones and we would live in big buildings with upstairs and downstairs. That was just a lie to deceive the masses. The hole in my roof is my electric light; the sound of my children eating porridge in the morning is the telephone; and the party's policy chases people up and down the stairs looking for grain.[1]

The villagers naturally enjoyed this kind of wit and it put the party members on the defensive. People said a member of the old gentry went out that night and wrote a verse on a village wall:

> Chairman Mao's heart is dark black
> He forces us to eat barley.

Hardest of all to take during this rectification was the discovery that the party secretary and vice-head of the township, a man named Wei Zhongqin, had falsified his background when gaining admission to the party. After a spell in Fangting gaol to write out a confession, he was transferred to a job in another township and never returned to Junction.

While Jinghe and the other party members nursed their wounded pride and tried to carry on their political work, the party centre decided to leap-frog in a new direction. Having made clear that the party expected high standards of behaviour from Communists, it was time to curb the party's enemies, especially those deemed to be hidden counter-revolutionaries.

What happened next had a sinister aspect that temporarily, at least, lowered the prestige of the party in the eyes of the masses. Unlike previous campaigns that followed the 'mass line' by involving the people in political dialogue, this one took place entirely within the party and under conditions of great secrecy. Both vice-township head Deng Xicheng and Jinghe vividly recalled this episode.

All the party members from the county gathered in Fangting in 1955 for a training class. Housed in the primary school on South Avenue and not allowed to leave the compound for ten days, they read and discussed documents from the centre. These stressed that counter-revolutionaries were not completely isolated, and that some of the secret society members were still active writing anti-communist slogans and doing damage to some socialist construction. The class stirred to action. As Jinghe put it:

> We exchanged information and gathered materials so as to expose the bad elements. We wrote this down and handed the information to the police station which sent some people out secretly to check if the charges were true or not.

Roused from sleep one morning before daybreak the class was hurriedly formed into small groups of people with two guns. Each group had a different task as they set out before the mists had cleared. They arrested about a dozen people in Junction township that day, according to Xicheng. Wild rumours spread, but eventually the authorities tried and executed only one person, a man from Bell Tower Temple Village, described as a 'former bandit, Robed Brother and big local tyrant who had earlier escaped detection for his crimes'. MaGaoqiao village emerged unscathed, touched only by the lingering memory and talk of early morning raids.

Around this time a small nucleus of members formed the first party group in MaGaoqiao village. All males, it included poor peasants Liao Wenping, Wan Jingfu, Yao Shengwan, and the famous middle peasant Jinghe. A disappointed Jinghe, already village head and a representative to the township People's Congress in Junction, lost his bid to become first party secretary in favour of the relative newcomer, Yao Shengwan. Yao held the top post in the village as party secretary until 1978.

In 1981, the sixty-year-old Yao smoked his habitual cigar while through a small window the soft Sichuan light disclosed a well-built man with strong hands, short-cropped hair, dark penetrating eyes, small moustache and the large ears which among the Chinese foretell longevity. He projected a flinty, slightly overbearing manner, and he spoke with emphasis, speed and rhetorical flourishes, qualities needed to catch the wandering attention of the shuffling, coughing audiences at village meetings. Well-educated by village standards, having attended four years in a Confucian primary school at a time when his parents were prosperous in the 1930s, he became an activist during the land reform struggle in 1951 and later went to a training class for potential cadres. After seventy days at the school in neighbouring Mianyang county where he recalled seeing revolutionary films, studying parts of the *Communist Manifesto* and other documents, he filled out an application to join the party but was rejected.

'I was not steady in my thinking', he mused. Later he filled in another application, but didn't hand it in. 'I heard that those who joined the party would be sent to the fighting in Korea. So I thought to myself, "Better forget it." ' But in 1955 the party in Shifang county came to Yao and others like him whose records they had on file, inviting them to join in preparation for yet another major campaign. This time it was to establish agricultural producers' co-operatives in the villages, one of the most daring, comprehensive and controversial moves the party would ever make.

Yao and his three party comrades, meanwhile, became convinced of the way the wind was blowing: the digging of the People's Canal provided a successful example of collective effort; the planned purchase and supply system took the main farm and vital industrial products out of the hands of the private traders (who might otherwise have been hostile to such a venture); the credit co-operatives, backed by the People's Bank, were able to supply start-up loans for co-operatives at relatively low interest rates; already a number of villagers had visited three model co-operatives in the county to see how they functioned. Since the party seemed determined to move ahead, Yao decided to take the lead.

Any lingering doubts disappeared following the news of Mao's forceful speech in the summer of 1955 criticizing those who 'fear dragons ahead and tigers behind' in forming co-operatives, and who were 'tottering along like a woman with bound feet'.[2] Based on the information that existing model agricultural producers' co-operatives (APCs) were achieving respectably high crop yields, Mao called for the doubling of the number of co-ops in a year so that there would be at least one and possibly half a dozen small semi-socialist collectives of twenty families in each of China's 200,000 townships. Mao's targets were actually quite modest, but when his request became known the local party units translated it into a surging political movement to create APCs in every village.

The four party members at MaGaoqiao decided that they would each try to form a co-operative of twenty families, bringing in eighty of the two hundred-odd families in the village. Several peasants, including an elderly middle peasant by the name of Wu Zhengfu who hesitated to join at first, reconstructed the process of forming the co-op at Liao Family Flats (later No. 5 production team). It was a story of trial and error, dedication, persuasion, hard bargaining, ingenuity, pressure, and in the end the exertion of poor-peasant political power to get everyone to abandon the dream of having a private family farm in favour of another vision:

> At that time Liao Wenping was the only party member in our hamlet and he shouldered a heavy burden. He went from door to door to visit the families explaining the plan. Later with the help of a work team sent from above he arranged a mass meeting to mobilize the people.
>
> From the things said at that meeting we understood co-operation as the way to get all the people rich together. It is a way to avoid two

extremes – the rich and the poor. As for farm production, some peasants are skilled and some are not, so through the co-operative the skilful ones could help the others. They said the way of the collective would be stronger for fighting natural disasters and for improving the farming environment. Also the realization of mechanized farming is difficult with private, small-scale farming.

In our part of the village there were thirty-six families. Of these the fifteen poor-peasant families would probably support a co-operative but that was not enough. So they had to find some middle peasants. There were nine of us in this category around here. At first the middle peasants only said verbally that they wanted to join, but we didn't want to in our hearts and we took no action. Our attitude was that we were already doing all right. But the success of the co-operative depended on us since we had more animals and tools and farming experience.

To solve the problem, Wenping and the party group made a secret re-arrangement of class status – they did this according to the party's central documents – and set up a category of 'lower middle peasants' from among those of us who were not so well-off. They established four families in this new category and approached us. When we came to understand that we would have favourable political status comparable to poor peasants we became interested. Then we went over to visit the model co-operative in Shuangshen township. They proved to us that co-operative output would be equal to or surpass our levels. We talked about it and decided to go in. Two of the lower middle peasants, team leader Wang Daoquan, whose brother is married to my sister, and Jiang Tenglin, were especially important because of their capabilities and enthusiasm and Wang eventually became a party member.

It went like this. If there were twenty households or more who applied, you could set up a co-operative. So far there were only nineteen. We looked around and saw Huang Tianshou, a middle peasant with ten small children. After some bargaining about the things he would have to bring in he was willing to join and then it was enough.

After that we sent our application to the township and then the permission came from the county government. Only in this way could the co-operative be established and gain recognition. Wenping told us things were done this way to stop the old clan associations from coming back under the disguise of forming co-operatives. We heard that in some places such a thing happened.

We counted each *mu* of land as one share, and to join the co-op you had to bring in some other things as well: 8 yuan per share for working capital, 4 yuan per share for fertilizer costs and several bales of straw as fodder for the buffaloes and pigs. If you didn't have enough you could go to the Credit Co-operative on the high street and arrange for a little loan.

Some people did that even if they had enough because they didn't want to take a chance with their own money.

After the co-op was set up we worked together on our fields. We did our production quite well. For the first year we distributed the resulting income according to a principle of seven parts to three parts. Three parts according to our land shares and seven parts according to our labour. Many people felt encouraged by our activity and sooner or later more applied to join.

It was hard to manage things well at the very beginning, especially on how to reward people fairly for their labour since people worked at different speeds. So some people were sent down from higher levels to give us guidance on how to assign work points and how to farm in scientific ways, how to do close planting and deep ploughing. Soon after the establishment of the co-op we bought some new machinery through a loan from the bank. For example, we bought a new two-wheeled plough that took three buffaloes to pull. It was a useless thing. It didn't work well, sank in the mud, and we soon had to leave it aside to rust. The rich peasants laughed at us behind our backs and we felt a little unhappy. Some of them had not given up in their hearts. They were just waiting for a chance to stir up the waters and make waves.

In the early days the village leaders used a hand megaphone to popularize the new policies of the government and the party and the goodness of the socialist road. They called out that 'co-operatives are a golden road to the future', while 'private cultivation is like a single tree-trunk bridge'. Step by step the others began to join us and they put their properties, such as water buffaloes and farm equipment, into the co-op. Of course we all got paid for our things – by instalments.

For those who did not join in and gave us trouble, the co-operative had ways of exerting pressure. Those outside had money and could buy a buffalo, but their money could not buy water. Because the poor and new lower middle peasants held the political power, we in the co-op controlled the water supply. First we irrigated the fields of the co-operative and if water remained they could have it. But if not then they couldn't plant their rice. The same with the fertilizer; when it was available the co-operative had priority in buying it from the Supply and Marketing Co-operative. Their grain was sometimes turned down as still damp or of poor quality by the grain collecting station and then they had to carry it all the way home again and bring it back another day. It was the kind of trick landlords used to play on us poor tenants. So we sometimes exerted that pressure on them.

Middle peasant Wu concluded his account of the way things went at Liao Family Flats by noting that in 1957, after the co-operative moved up to an advanced type in which distribution took place solely according

to labour, the door was opened to the five rich peasants and the three
landlord families. The rich peasants, who had large amounts of land,
were disgruntled when they found that land shares no longer counted
and that together with the former landlord elements they were still
deprived of political rights in the village. Nevertheless they joined; with
80 per cent of the families already in, the pressures became irresistible.
'Now the party doesn't talk about it anymore', Wu said, 'but then, I tell
you, it was all part of a serious class struggle.'

The change brought about by these class struggles in the Chinese
countryside have been described by William Hinton as 'the most massive
transformation of a way of life ever carried through in world history'.
Such a claim is supported on the grounds that hundreds of millions
of peasants, led by the Communist Party, 'abandoned their age-old,
individual mode of production for socialist co-operation'. To Hinton,
who has possibly had unrivalled opportunities to inform himself about
the high tide of collectivization in North China, it looked like a
triumphant achievement done, on the whole, 'without bloodshed,
without any significant destruction of property and without any major
lapses in productivity'.[3] To another able American observer, Professor
Mark Selden, who returned to China for investigations and talks with
prominent Chinese officials after Mao's death, it was the opposite: the
'high tide' had a negative impact on productivity and living standards
and 'despite the genuinely heroic achievement of millions of peasants and
workers, set back the prospects of socialism' by violating the voluntary
principle.[4] The debates in academic circles rage on, and an end is
not yet in sight.

At MaGaoqiao the process, as described by middle peasant Wu and
generally confirmed by others, suggests that, from their own experience
of the way things happened, it included an admissible and supportable
mixture of persuasion and pressure even if the voluntary principle
was sometimes violated. The manipulation of class categories in this
post-land reform period in order to introduce the *lower* middle peasants,
although done secretly, had no apparent sinister or dishonest aspect.
Such a redefinition of class, based roughly upon wealth, allowed the poor
to win more allies. As for statistics on material results, the village archives
reveal nothing; the only figures available are an average preserved by
Junction township that combines results for all thirteen villages.

Twenty-five years later the villagers were positive in insisting that they
had tasted the sweetness after the first two years in the co-operative:
output was increasing steadily and they had felt things would get even
better. What they remembered most was all the pigs they raised and the
abundance of manure.

'We were on the way to socialism', exclaimed team leader Wang
Daoquan. 'We raised our fists high and decided to move to a higher

stage, a fully socialist co-operative.' Others echoed his assessment. As for village leader Jinghe, he claimed that, to judge by the value of a work day worth Y1.30, the co-op that he led was an 'advanced unit'.

The broadly-based township statistics comparing individual and co-operative farm management in these years support claims about the success of the co-operatives (see Appendix, Tables 2 and 3). Oil-bearing cash crops as well as hog production advanced significantly, while grain yields improved at least marginally. Only the output of tobacco declined somewhat under co-operative management.

Since the local statistics did not show dramatic increases across the board, the sense of higher incomes in the peasants' recollections was curious at first. Was it possible that they under-reported their yields in order to minimize sharing with the state? This was an old practice in China and the peasants may have felt justified in doing so because the state collected too much of the 1954 harvest. Faced with angry and hungry people the government returned grain to the villages in 1955 – a small amount, one ton, was sold back to MaGaoqiao and distributed to needy households.[5] Cadres in Junction township denied any practice of under-reporting, but they recalled that the measure of land, the *mu*, was reduced in size in 1955 (one old *mu* became equal to 1.15 new *mu*), with the result that the account-book figures on productivity before and after 1955 are not comparable. When the figures are adjusted (as in Appendix, Table 3) to make them comparable, the results of collective farming are more favourable and more in line with peasant recollections.

The evidence does not suggest that MaGaoqiao was a special case, with extra resources or unusually experienced or talented leaders. The village had its share of difficulty and disappointments, but in spite of them the experience of co-operative farming won many genuine converts to the benefits and possibilities of a collective, socialist way of living.

Although the co-operatives experienced initial success, it was still true that they were fragile organizations. Still not well consolidated, they needed more time to develop. Unfortunately the necessary time did not materialize before China headed into a new, volatile phase of development known as the Great Leap Forward. All the reasons behind the launching of the Great Leap are still not clear, but at least one of the main causes for the change of pace was a worsening of the international situation that seemed to threaten China. Mao and his comrades tried to galvanize the Chinese people into even greater efforts as the US Government, still unreconciled to the existence of the People's Republic, increased its hostile activities on China's doorstep in 1957 and 1958.[6]

5

HOW HIGH THE COST OF FIGHTING 'PAPER TIGERS'?: 1958

The peasants of MaGaoqiao carried their grain, fifty kilos at a time, to the government grain station at Junction. The station is in the spacious compound of the former Upper Fire God Temple, where giant banyan trees shade buildings that once housed prayer mats and clay figures of hundreds of buddhas, and smelt of burning incense. No other facility could accommodate the flow of tax and quota grain that the government bought in these years of bumper harvests. And as they sat resting on their shoulder poles, waiting their turn to weigh in, the peasants, at least the literate among them, contemplated the slogans which the Communist Party had inscribed on the portals of the ancient temple. Their gold and red, slightly weathered characters heralded a world far removed from the narrow, cobbled street: 'Behold the waves of anti-imperialist movements on the five continents', and 'The imperialist powers are declining daily'.

The link between this invisible but vaguely inspiring revolutionary outer world and the peasants' grain could be inferred by the centrepiece: Chairman Mao's portrait. Through the local broadcasting system every-one was familiar with Mao's words. 'In the past others looked down on us,' he told the people in 1958, 'mainly because we produced too little grain, steel and machinery.' 'Wait until we've made thirty million tons of steel . . . and three-and-a-half billion catties of grain . . . When we've achieved this, then we shall be able to negotiate with the Americans with a bit more spirit.'[1] (A catty equals half a kilogram.)

Like the slogans on the temple gate, an unfailing optimism marked Mao's outlook on the world. In the century since the British Navy battered open China's gates during the Opium Wars, and in spite of recent American behaviour in East Asia, the heyday of such imperialist piracy was over. According to Mao, it might take another hundred years for capitalism to disappear completely, but time and the masses were on China's side; imperialism but a 'paper tiger'.[2] This optimism reflected the strategic side of Mao's thought and the peasants relished the imagery.

But progress to a bright future had a tactical aspect in which the balance of power, particularly economic power, would be decisive. China still had to create a position of strength from which to advance and defend itself, and this understanding tempered all optimism for the future.

For a short time in the mid-1950s China's leaders believed that relations with the greatest superpower, the United States, showed some improvement. This was after the settlement of the Korean conflict in 1953, the Indo-China crisis in 1954, and the opening of Sino-American ambassadorial talks in Warsaw in 1955. Under Premier Zhou En-lai's guiding hand in foreign policy, China felt able to cut back on its conventional defence spending and reduced the size of its armed forces. The Chinese expected a relaxation of the American-directed trade embargo, allowing China to restore its traditional markets in South East Asia and to expand its foreign trade elsewhere.

In this improving international environment, Chen Yun, the Minister of Commerce, proposed balanced economic growth for the second five-year plan (1958-62), with more emphasis on agriculture and light industry. Capital for such growth would come from domestic trade and foreign-exchange earnings so that the state could continue investing in defence and heavy industries, while providing the people with modest increases in their standard of living. All this depended upon a friendlier international climate.

In the event, a sudden hardening of US policy towards China in 1957 threw the Chinese leaders into temporary confusion and dealt a fatal blow to their planning. The signal for renewed American hostility was the Pentagon's decision in May 1957 to station Matador guided missiles with a nuclear capability on Taiwan. At the same time US Secretary of State John Foster Dulles bluntly rejected any notion of diplomatic, trade or cultural relations with China. Speaking in San Francisco, he predicted that Communism in China was only a passing phase and said that 'we owe it to ourselves, our allies and the Chinese people to do all we can to contribute to that passing'. Between 1953 and 1958 the United States threatened China with nuclear attack seven times during the crises in Korea, Indo-China and the Offshore Islands in the Taiwan straits.[3]

These American moves, which are analysed in prodigious detail by Professor Franz Schurmann,[4] presaged growing American operational involvement in East Asia, including military deployments of the Seventh Fleet off Taiwan, in the South China Sea and the Gulf of Siam, covert warfare by the CIA, military and economic assistance to buy the support of governments in an arc around China from South Korea and Taiwan down to South East Asia, and eventual involvement in the Vietnam War.

Encouraged by American actions, Chiang Kai-shek never gave up his hopes of reconquering the mainland, and he dispatched reinforcements equipped with the most advanced weapons to the islands of Quemoy and Matsu just off the coast of Fujian province, hoping to provoke an armed clash that would draw even greater US support for his ambitions. How close the Americans were to supporting Chiang in a bombing attack on Fujian airfields may never be known, but according to Schurmann the Quemoy crisis in the summer of 1958 came close to 'plunging America and China into war with each other'.[5]

The Chinese leadership began to feel an exceptional sense of urgency as the probability of another Asian war involving the United States loomed larger. If instead of gradual Sino-American *détente* the environment along the China coast became hostile again, how could they justify cutting defence spending in order to invest in agriculture and light industry? If a blockade interrupted trade, why develop an export industry? And if war was again in the offing, how could they raise people's hopes about a better living standard?

With the foreign policy underpinnings kicked from under Chen Yun's programme of gradual investment in agriculture a new plan had to be devised. In response to the new situation Mao, along with most of China's top leaders, proposed a self-reliant 'great leap forward' to mobilize the vast reserves of peasant labour in revolutionizing agriculture through communes and militias, and they made an appeal for local initiative to conquer China's technological backwardness. 'We can make tables and chairs, teacups and teapots, we can grow grain and grind it into flour, and we can make paper', Mao had observed, 'but we can't make a single motor car, plane, tank or tractor.'[6] This weakness spurred China's desire to catch up quickly, aiming to reach the level of British industry in fifteen years.

If the vision of a great leap forward in steel and grain, and talk in some quarters of moving rapidly from socialism to communism, was driven by a sense of desperate haste to prepare the people for a new international confrontation, it was also based upon the earlier experience in Yenan when soldier-peasants had worked miracles of production against the Japanese invasion in the 1940s through co-operative arrangements and innovative approaches to industry. If this strategy had worked before, why could it not work again?

Added to the worry of a coming confrontation with the United States, China's leaders could not help feeling that an unexpected weakening of their alliance with the Soviet Union further undermined the country's security. Seeking *détente* and peaceful co-existence with the United States, Premier Khrushchev refused support to his Chinese allies in the manner they expected, and denied them help in obtaining the technical ability to build their own nuclear deterrent against

American threats. It was not until 1964 that China successfully tested its own nuclear bomb. In the meantime the Soviet Union, trying to influence China's course of action, demanded repayment of Soviet loans, including the cost of supplies delivered to resist the United States during the Korean War.[7]

In those difficult times, when for more than a decade China faced the hostility of both superpowers, the Chinese leaders searched for new friends. By forging links with the other poor and developing countries of the world, in the 'intermediate zone' which lay between the two powerful giants, they sought to rebuff imperialism and to create a strategy for survival. Therefore in addition to military aid to Korea and Vietnam to resist US intervention, China supported national liberation struggles wherever possible and gave help which it could ill afford to newly emerging nations in Africa and Asia. Billions of dollars were committed as loans for factories, railways and ports to Third World countries from 1956 to the end of 1973.[8]

These waves of foreign policy strategy to cope with the Korean war, the Taiwan crisis, and later the conflict in Vietnam inevitably made ripples on the village ponds throughout China. And MaGaoqiao, in Junction township, was no exception.

Eight teenagers in MaGaoqiao and a hundred other young men from the surrounding villages signed up for the People's Volunteers in June 1951. They acted in response to Mao's call for reinforcements to 'Resist America, Aid Korea'. One of the eight lost his life in battle, another settled elsewhere and the rest came back as local heroes. After a century of humiliation and defeat, the war in Korea was the first victory ever won by a Chinese army over Western forces, and villagers listened eagerly to the stories of the returning veterans.

A village storyteller, Huang Kaiyao, now fifty-one and retired after years as militia commander, was one of these.

> Right on the night of the mid-autumn festival our train passed over a bridge on the Yalu River. Suddenly we heard gunfire. I thought, 'Oh, as soon as we cross the river the fighting begins!' Although we didn't have much training in using arms, I was not afraid. I was young. We got off the train immediately and marched eastwards along the moonlit river. We stayed for a week in a nearby place, learning some basic Korean words and sentences.
>
> With eighty pounds on our backs — a rifle, grenades, a blanket, water bottle, spare foot rags, an enamel bowl and chopsticks, tea, rice and soya flour, in some cases with machine-guns and mortars — we marched south through Renchuan, Beilingchuan and Jiechuan up to the front lines. Many American planes, sometimes a hundred or more at a time, dropped

bombs, cluster bombs and napalm bombs which made everything burst
into sudden flame.

The unit stayed there until July 1953.

> One night the army commander ordered our unit to go up to the
> mountain tops. Heavy fighting occurred before midnight. Then at twelve,
> the fighting suddenly stopped; it went quiet everywhere. The war ended
> and both sides signed the armistice. Our troops climbed into the mountains
> preparing to fight the American armies further in case they had signed a
> false surrender. We stayed there for two more months, until September,
> to exchange prisoners. Then we came back to China.

Clearly it was a rare moment of triumph for an Asian peasant army to
have fought the United States of America to a standstill. But it was also
a time for sober reflection.

Although the peasant soldiers saw the result of the Korean War as a
'surrender' by the enemy, they knew the conflict had taken a heavy toll
among their comrades and the people of Korea. They were unprepared
for the awesome fire-power of the Americans with their endless streams
of aircraft, napalm and heavy bombs and, as the Chinese claimed, the
selective use of bacteriological weapons.[9] The blood-soaked hills of
Korea opened their eyes.

As a result of the sacrifices made in the war in Korea, when matters
became tense again and some tragic events occurred in the village in the
years that lay ahead, the earlier decision of the central government to
recruit peasants for the army from such remote inland areas as Shifang
county proved crucial for popular morale. It meant that a generation
already impoverished by years of war against Japan and faced with
further postponement of their consumer desires would nevertheless
respond to calls for heroic deeds to support the motherland. Peasant
nationalism had been aroused in the hinterlands as perhaps never before
in Chinese history.

This is not to suggest that the people received the demands of high
policy easily. When at tremendous cost[10] the central government began
dispersing the defence industries to safe, remote interior locations in the
mid-1960s, after the United States started intervening in Vietnam, the
peasants often found the consequences difficult to accept.

The experience at MaGaoqiao is instructive of the way in which
contradictions between the centre and the locality, between workers and
peasants, worked out in Mao's China. Some higher level made a decision
around 1965 to construct a medium-sized machine-building factory in
the village. Plans called for an annual capacity to produce 1,200 tons
of strategic and sophisticated electrical and mining equipment, in

addition to the small chemical fertilizer plants that gave the factory its name. Construction of the Chemical Fertilizer Machinery Factory began in 1967.

An immediate difficulty arose from the fact that the factory took up sixteen acres of land between the railway and the highway, some of it good farmland, and, perhaps more disturbing, occupied the village burial ground. In addition, the factory had already recruited its full complement of 1,000 workers from urban places and therefore, apart from some temporary construction work, offered few jobs to the local people. From many peasants' point of view, it was an unwelcome intrusion, cursed by some as upsetting to the ancestral spirits and as a transfer of resources without adequate compensation to the village.

Appealing for recognition of the wider interests of the nation, the local leaders supported the project in spite of objections and it went ahead: five large workshops with an assortment of 300 lathes, drills and presses from Shanghai, Beijing, even some Japanese and Polish models; five-storey red-brick apartment blocks for the families, two schools for the workers' children, a vast complex in the centre of which rose a stack that belched smoke and towered over the green fields, quiet beyond the gates. The ten foot brick and mortar walls surrounding this 'third front construction', as the defence projects were called, gave tangible expression to the gulf separating workers and peasants. Inside the workers ate 'public grain' supplied by the government, had higher incomes[11] and felt secure in fair weather or foul. Outside the peasants fed themselves and could only dream of their children some day entering the gates.

Even though the factory eventually paid 2,500 yuan per *mu* for the fertile land, it took several years to assuage the hard feelings. Graves were moved, if the families requested it, at the state's expense. When some workers turned a blind eye to their children slipping out and stealing vegetables from the fields at night and small quarrels arose, the factory management moved quickly to establish a joint committee with the production teams to solve disputes.

Later, to lessen the resentment, the factory hired seventy temporary workers locally and allowed the nearby production teams to carry off the manure of the factory complex free of charge. It also manufactured some water pumping machines and loaned them out to the peasants during the rice planting season. The factory brought other advantages to its neighbours. It supplied power at cost from the provincial grid for the homes and grist mills of the three nearby production teams five years before the electrification of the rest of the area, and it invited the villagers to weekly film nights at the factory cinema. Not least in importance was the liveliness that 4,000 newcomers injected into the local marketplace for farm products and the attractive marriage prospects. As factory director Ho Yulong recalled:

When we came here we occupied a lot of land and the peasants thought this would reduce their income; it was a sharp contradiction. To reduce the contradiction we tried hard to help the nearby peasants be better-off, to make them realize that the factory would not be a burden to them. As we learned from Chairman Mao's speech on 'The Ten Great Relationships' there are bound to be contradictions between town and country, between industry and agriculture. Following his advice we taught our workers and their families to appreciate the agricultural crops and to strengthen feelings of worker-peasant unity. The peasants, of course, realized that we actually produced machinery to support the modernization of agriculture.

Gradually the 'third front construction' gained acceptance; the transformation of village life and the defence of the motherland took shape hand in hand. This, in spite of the fact that the burden of opposing American intervention in Korea, in the straits of Taiwan, and in Vietnam, of repaying the Soviet Union and building a nuclear deterrent, of relocating strategic industries, and of offering aid to Third World friends all fell heavily on the shoulders of the peasants. The sacrifices and hardships, some of which increased as the result of human errors, were to an incalculable degree the social costs of scaring off 'paper tigers'. Any attempt to understand the years of China's socialist construction that fails to take into account the externally imposed costs must be considered either uninformed or misleading.

6

GREAT LEAP FORWARD: TRIUMPH AND TRAGEDY, 1958–61

Train No. 704 puffs into Junction station daily at 8:37, hoots a few times while people scramble aboard or a freight car is detached and then proceeds slowly southbound. The pace is so leisurely that the entire forty-five mile run from the Dragon Gate mountains down to the mainline at Guanghan takes three hours to complete. Speed, clearly, is not what determines the value of this 'chariot of fire', although an express does run through to the provincial capital on holidays providing a bargain for travellers at three cents a mile. Rather it is the cargoes which make it the pride of its builders; limestone, phosphorus and coal that have done so much to transform the local economy.

The story of the little railway in Shifang county is the story of the nation-wide Great Leap Forward writ small.

The Great Leap was a brief episode, a gathering together of human energy on a scale seldom seen in history short of conditions of all-out war. It mobilized people across the country, especially the 500 million peasants, to convert surplus labour into capital with the aim of producing more iron and steel and of creating greater agricultural and light industrial production. Launched by Mao Zedong with revolutionary fervour under conditions that sometimes bordered on anarchy, it took place from 1958 to 1960. 'Like a sergeant major inducting raw recruits into their new world by bawling his squad into life,' wrote one scholar, 'Mao galvanized his people . . . by the notion that with one supreme effort they might burst the bonds of poverty.'[1]

Allied to the mass mobilization of labour the Great Leap triggered a far-reaching restructuring of social relationships and institutions to make possible that release of human initiative and energy. Whole counties amalgamated, with Shifang disappearing to become part of neighbouring Guanghan. The townships were converted into people's communes combining industry, agriculture, trade, education and military affairs to become the basic units of state power. Villages turned into brigades and agricultural producers co-operatives became production teams within the commune.[2] Organized along military lines in squads, platoons and companies, people worked with revolutionary fervour and led lives of collective equality.

These reorganizations of material and social life, central to Mao's strategy for rapid development, came swiftly in Sichuan during that hot, humid summer of 1958. The communes opened community dining-rooms, nurseries, 'homes of respect for the aged' and other collective welfare measures to emancipate women from the drudgery of the kitchen and presently both men and women began to receive wages for their labour, supplemented by free supply of such items as rice, oil, salt, soya sauce, vinegar and vegetables. 'For the peasants, all this is epoch-making news', declared the party central committee, '. . . (showing) the way to the gradual transition from the socialist principle of "to each according to his work" to the communist principle of "to each according to his needs".'[3]

After forty days of feverish activity, heightened by news of confrontation with Chiang Kai-shek's forces in the Straits of Taiwan, the new structures were in place throughout most of Sichuan[4] and tens of thousands of basic-level cadres suddenly found themselves challenged by unaccustomed responsibilities and new opportunities. The objectives seemed clear. Every production unit would begin by helping to establish small or medium-sized iron and steel furnaces. Using traditional methods, they would produce metal for a technological revolution: wheels with steel ball-bearings to replace the shoulder pole and squeaking wooden wheelbarrow; small hydro-electric stations, gears and taps, diesel and electrical pumps, in place of treadle water wheels powered by human limbs; pesticide sprayers and chemical fertilizers to increase crop yields and improve labour productivity. The tasks were endless and the pressures to succeed intense.

Responding the the party's call for self-reliant participation in the Great Leap, the county government asked each village in Shifang to recruit about seventy of its best, most capable young men and women for the new production front. Thus Junction People's Commune organized 900 peasants into 'iron-and-steel brigades' and sent them off from mass meetings in the high street. To the beating of gongs and fireworks 11 per cent of the commune's work-force marched out, banners waving, with their bed-rolls and cooking utensils, to discover ore bodies and to establish a blast furnace high in the Dragon Gate mountains. It was the same in other communes and soon the county mobilized 12,000 people for the task. Participants still recall the times with a sense of excitement and a feeling that 'those were the days!'

As they found relatively small quantities of ore the immediate results of the iron and steel campaign were disappointing. And the crude blast furnaces produced pig iron of inferior quality. Nevertheless, for two years they persisted in this work, gaining technical knowledge and new skills in social organization. In the meantime while digging in the mountains they came across large seams of coal, limestone formations and high-grade phosphorus deposits.[5] When local leaders realized the implications of these discoveries – their value for creating electrical energy, for home cooking, for construction materials and for chemical fertilizer – the way opened for a new advance. After summing up their experience and estimating the possibilities, they considered how to haul out the treasures of the mountains. The Shifang railway project began to take shape.

The county dispatched squads to other areas to see how to build railways.[6] They learned that for a narrow-gauge railway the rails could be cast directly from the pig iron they had already created. Soon thousands of peasants started working on the project, moving houses, grading the roadbed, building bridges and smelting crude iron into rails.

'I was transferred down from the mountains where I had been building roads and smelters and assigned to the command office of the railway construction department in charge of materials, housing and labour supply', recalled retired commune cadre Deng Xicheng. 'The railway project began in the winter of 1959 and work went on until the spring of 1960. It was a narrow-gauge track at first. We tried to use our home-made pig-iron rails but they could not bear the weight of the trains.' He shrugged. 'It was a real mess, so we had to cast them again.'

According to Deng the peasant builders worked without wages, except for money which he called 'a subsidy of several yuan a month' for daily necessities. 'But they had their work points recorded at home', he noted, 'and they still got their share of grain and cash distribution from their unit at the end of the year.'

'This was not unpaid or slave labour!' he said hotly in rejecting the suggestion. 'The entire collective supported the builders so they received the same treatment as everyone else.'

'We also set up public canteens with free meals along the railway and served different kinds of food – grain, sweet potatoes, and then when supplies became tight even pig fodder (turnips).' Deng grimaced.

'At that time', he said, 'the whole country took part in big projects so the movement carried us along in spite of the hardships. The state didn't have to pay anything for the land occupied by the construction; labour was free and land was free. That's how we built the railway. It has no debts.'

Deng's account alternated between matter-of-fact understatement and evident enchantment. In less than a year locomotives began hauling freight out from the foothills; each engine could pull a load that would have taken a thousand peasants to carry on their shoulders. In a place where the carrying pole and wheelbarrow continued to be the main means of transport and motorized transport was virtually unknown, the railway was something bordering on the miraculous.

In the midst of the excitement surrounding the building of workshops, opening mines and constructing the railway an unforseen tragedy took shape on the home front. With the best leadership and core of the workforce off in the mountains, agricultural production fell. There was a shortage of labour to plant and harvest the crops. Morale dropped and those who resented the levelling that had taken place (when people in poorer villages received the same rewards as those in wealthier villages) dragged their feet. An exhausted workforce labouring long hours could not keep up. To compound matters further, those in charge of agricultural work admitted any shortcomings only reluctantly. While trying to maintain the flow of grain to the state, in spite of falling output they resorted to exaggerations and boasting in reporting crop yields.

This resulted in the food shortage that turned into a man-made famine. The party secretary in charge of agriculture in Shifang recalled the time:[7]

> In the beginning of the Great Leap in 1958, development was smooth. But presently there was a tendency to boasting and exaggeration and a communist wind of levelling and transferring of wealth came. This wind cooled down the enthusiasm of the masses and in the end, by transferring out, they drained the commune members' family resources. Eventually in agricultural production there came a great regression . . . It was really a nightmare; hunger, serious illness, unnatural deaths . . . tens of thousands of people had no grain to eat.

Even after the leadership of Beijing recognized the imbalances in the Great Leap, they failed to change the direction quickly enough and in the winter of 1960 conditions of starvation became widespread in many parts of China. The battle for progress in Shifang county turned into a struggle for survival.

The collective memory of the 'three hard years' at MaGaoqiao stirs uneasily. Sensitive to possible shifts in the political wind, the things villagers remember and talk about vary. While some do not seem to bend with the latest gusts, they all appear to have a sixth sense of what to avoid mentioning, especially when speaking to outsiders.

Initially, when I talked with them in 1981, they made proud references to 'remaking the rivers and mountains'. And there was an enthusiasm among the women over the new relationships of equality between men and women that appeared as a result of the community dining-halls and nurseries. As midwife Yang Yongxiu recalled:

Our slogan was 'Long live the public canteen'. In the past all households (women) cooked, and looked after their own children while at the same time we women had to work in the fields. But with the opening of canteens cooks prepared meals for all the people. Special people raised pigs collectively and the children had kindergartens and nurseries and all the people who worked in these areas were elected by the commune members. My husband and I were both committee members of the team. We women began to receive wages for our work. I was the happiest I'd ever been.

This midwife's happiness and the favourable conditions for women's emancipation were short-lived.

Gradually references to agonies and sometimes stories of unspeakable sadness and tragedy filtered into the conversation. Villagers avoided using the words 'death from starvation' at first, employing instead such phrases as 'illness caused by the swelling disease'. But two years later, in 1983, after a resolution on the party's history characterized the Great Leap as a leftist error by Mao and the central leadership causing serious losses to the country and the people,[8] retired village cadres admitted bluntly and without qualification that 300 villagers died of starvation in the Great Leap.

Three hundred starved to death in a single village! The mind is numbed at the thought. Could it be true? Or was this more exaggeration to support the latest pressure from higher levels to denigrate everything about the Great Leap? If true, it meant that one in five of the population perished of hunger in the winters of 1959 and 1960. Even the most sensational reports of an unfriendly international press in the past seldom put forward such casualty figures.

Demographers in China have so far not attempted to give an overall figure for the losses, perhaps because accurate detailed birth and death statistics for 1958-61 are lacking or perhaps because they are too embarrassing. Western demographers, on the other hand, using statistics published in China since 1981 estimate that thirty million people died prematurely in what may have been the largest famine in human history.[9]

Population statistics preserved in the village archives begin only after the Great Leap, in 1964. At that time they record 1,336 residents in MaGaoqiao. Figures at the commune headquarters are more useful. From a series that combines information for all thirteen of the villages in the township beginning from 1949 certain inferences may be made.

Table 4 cols. a and b (see Appendix) shows that the registered population of the whole commune fell by 3,059 to 15,447 from 18,506 between 1957 and the winter of 1960, a reduction of 16.5 per cent. Part of this decline is accounted for by the transfer of 900 able-bodied peasants for projects in the mountains (cols. e and f) leaving a loss of

2,159 or 11.7 per cent. Some of this remaining decline may have been the result of transfers or migration out of the area, because it is reckoned that there was an influx of about twenty million peasants into the cities of China in late 1958 and early 1959,[10] but the influence of this factor cannot be determined from the available statistics.

Since MaGaoqiao has about 8.3 per cent of the commune's population, its proportional loss of the 2,159 would have been 179, which is considerably less than the 300 reported to me, and it suggests that one in ten perished.

In normal times, based on current average birth rates of 35/1,000 and mortality rates of 10/1,000,[11] an estimated village population of 1,535 in 1957 (i.e. 8.3 per cent of the commune's 18,506) would have grown to 1,820 by 1964, which would have been an increase of 484 instead of an actual decrease of 199 to 1,336. This is an even wider gap. Times were not normal, however, and birth rates dropped to half in the absence of conditions for settled family life:[12] about seventy young men and women of marriageable age at MaGaoqiao, for example, postponed their marriages and were away from home for two or three of these years opening mines and building the railway. It was the same in the other twelve villages of the township. Villagers confirmed this, leading one to suspect that the number of deaths was somewhat less than the cadres stated. But whether one in five or one in ten died, it was a tragedy of major proportions, entirely unexpected in the New China. How did it happen?

The first explanation given by everyone concerned the influence of natural disasters. This reason was part of the official government explanation at the time. It is well documented that the worst typhoons and flooding in fifty years affected almost half the cultivated land in China in 1960-1, and in some areas insect pest and plant diseases followed severe droughts which greatly reduced yields.[13] But did such conditions hold true for Shifang county?

Some cadres said that drought occurred, especially around the planting season; others thought that it rained too much at harvest time. Figures obtained from the provincial weather bureau (see Appendix, Table 5) confirm some suggestion of abnormality in the weather: except for a dry rice-transplanting season in May, 1961, The Great Leap years had more rain than the ten-year average and more than in the two good crop years that followed. But in a rice-growing area such abundance of water, while possibly having some influence on the yield, does not spell disaster unless there is actual flooding by the rivers which no one suggested had happened.[14]

Others mentioned the sudden decision of the Soviet Union to cancel its scientific and engineering aid to China in the summer of 1960 as a disrupting factor in the economy. While peasants in Shifang knew and spoke of this bad faith, no Soviet-aided projects in fact existed in the immediate area. The main burden in this respect was the heavy shipments of grain out of the district, needed, as one peasant said, because 'the Soviet revisionists were forcing us to clear up our debt to them'.[15]

There remained the factors of human error and miscalculation. In 1983, team leader Wang indicated that he could be more candid about the past. 'The upper levels', he said, 'told me that in talking about our situation we should be neither haughty nor humble, neither overbearing nor servile, neither supercilious nor obsequious; we should seek truth from facts.' Feeling free to be natural he then related the story of the Great Leap as it affected himself and his neighbours. It was a time of hope and pain, of expectations dashed, of thievery and self-deception, of the tragic absence of democracy and the right to express doubt, of passions, ambitions, fears and animosities aroused during the social upheavals that accompanied the Great Leap.

> When communization came we thought it was much better. The collective was bigger . . . the commune was the size of the township. All expenses were covered – food, clothing, medicine, child-delivery, even your haircut – and you still had your wages. It was very good. There were no private plots to care for; all land went to the commune. What's the use of a land certificate when you have all this! We got paid every month instead of having to wait for the distribution of shares in June and December. My mother rated three yuan. I was in the seventh rank – seven yuan. The party branch secretary's wage was nine yuan.
>
> We started public canteens and all ate from 'the one big pot'. At first we had three communal dining-halls in this team; later we merged them into one hall. This was from the autumn of 1958 until 1961 when the broad bean season began. People didn't have to eat sweet potatoes – even if they were cooked they didn't eat them because we had plenty of rice. That was in 1958. The canteen was open to everyone; even the passers-by could come in for a meal. When food was free and the commune members had pork and there was a holiday, then the members liked it. In the busy season we had no holiday – when planting or threshing – but otherwise we had one day off in every seven.
>
> We did our production work in large military formations – battalions, companies, platoons and squads. We did many good things. When the leaders at the higher levels said we should have some auditoriums and meeting places in the countryside we thought it a good idea and we built a large auditorium at the Ren Family Mill. We even invited a Sichuan Opera group to come and give performances there. Zhou Jinghong, the commune party secretary, was very happy to see our initiative and gave us warm support. He once said to our village head, Zhang Jinghe, 'You've raised collective pigs well; if you can raise even more, then we will send you to

Beijing as our representative and you will be received by Chairman Mao.' We were excited by this prospect and bought even more piglets.

Our team did not have a steel blast furnace but the commune organized some people to go to the mountains to mine iron ore and we sent about thirty able-bodied people to join that work. We had three groups. For pocket money people got paid according to seven grades, from two yuan at the bottom to nine yuan at the top and everyone got a free supply of food. Clothes, bedding, food, medical care were also free; the commune supplied everything. When our iron-and-steel-brigade came back they all returned wearing new clothes.

But by the end of 1958 the tendency of the 'four highs' and 'five winds' came into our area.[16] Every production team and village was boasting, they were boasting about their production, about their high output of grain. In this atmosphere production team members didn't do the farm work seriously, and we wasted grain. The people in charge of feeding pigs and chickens all asked the team to provide grain; they wanted to do their own work well and they argued and quarrelled with the leaders of the team, so we had to give them grain. We fed one hundred fat pigs by using grain. Everyone came clamouring for grain to do their work.

After a few months we began to run out of rice and we could not satisfy our hunger so we started eating sweet potatoes. People began to complain and they didn't want to work in the fields any more.

Because of the boasting the higher levels thought we had more grain than we had and they gave us big quotas. The higher levels pressured the lower levels to make more sales to the state.

One day Deng Yuanming, our team accountant, went to the commune to report on our output of grain. He told them it was 500 *jin* per *mu*. They turned him away saying, 'No, that's not the number. You can't pass the gate.' We talked it over and sent him back a second time to say it was 700 *jin* per *mu*. Again they said no. They told him that if the number wasn't up to 1,000 *jin* per *mu* then he could not get his figures accepted. So he said, 'Yes, yes, it is 1,000 *jin*.' Then he passed.

Actually output of 1,000 *jin* per *mu* is not impossible, we are now over that level. But today it is a real figure. Before it wasn't so. We peasants working in the fields could not be deceived. Once we saw the crops in the fields we could figure out how many *jin* of grain a field could produce . . · So we were unhappy in those years. I wanted to act according to facts. I thought we could cross the river by finding the stepping stones. Some people said we were using these inflated figures to scare the Soviet Union.

In Zhao Guo Commune they transplanted the ripening crops from several fields into one field and claimed an output of 2,000 *jin* per *mu* . . . (elsewhere) they put down a bundle of straw in a warehouse and then covered it with grain to make it look like a big pile. Everybody was brought from all round to look at it. This happened because those who could show best results had a better chance to become a model or to become an official. It was another kind of competition.[17]

Many false accounts were sent to the higher levels. We had two sets of accounts, one with the inflated figures and the other with the real figures. On the falsified book every peasant was required to put his thumb print as he carried in his grain to the grain station. The cadres explained to them why we should have this inflated account book, and the peasants said, 'If the cadres aren't afraid of it, neither are we'. We also had two books for the expenditures, one with the false and one with the real figures. Everywhere such accounting practices were carried on.[18]

Because of our boasting and the high quotas, lots and lots of grain was transported from our area. The government sent representatives right down to the production teams; one of them came to our village and as soon as the grain was harvested from the fields it was collected and carried away. It went to Guangyuan and there it was loaded on to the train and shipped away. At that time the cadres took a lead in handing in grain. We did this in the daytime and sometimes even until midnight; even the strongest able-bodied got worn out doing this strenuous work. At that time it was said the grain should be handed in to support the iron and steel production and to guarantee our foreign trade.

In the spring of 1959 Chairman Mao became worried about the results of boasting and urged us not to accept unreasonable demands,[19] but in 1960 things became still more difficult for us; we were short of food. Even in that tough situation, however, nobody raised doubts openly about the commune. We said 'Long live the general line for the building of socialism!', 'Long live the great leap forward!', 'Long live the People's Commune!'. Several 'long lives'. These were the three red banners. If people had some inner doubts, they didn't dare speak them out because they noticed that cadres were dismissed for raising questions about the way things were going.

Formerly when the co-operative was being created the party called for people to speak out freely what was on their minds. That was in 1957. So after we read the newspapers we too said whatever we wished. Meetings were held and we could say such things as the present policy is wrong, or should be changed, or even 'Down with the Communist Party!'. Soon we learned that the movement changed to an anti-rightist direction and then we began to hear exaggerations in the newspapers. For example, we heard that one production team in Henan produced 7,000 *jin* of grain per *mu* that year. Impossible! But how could you dare say anything? If you spoke people would say you were against the three red banners.

In 1959 there was a measles epidemic and some children around or below ten years of age died of complications. There were so many to be buried. When someone died in the measles clinic we gave whoever buried the dead child one or two bowls of food from the canteen. Take that turtle's egg, Liao Shangmo, he buried quite a few of them as he wanted the extra food. One day as he was carrying away a big bowl of rice after burying a child I saw him and criticized him. 'How did you bury the child? You only covered it with a few bamboo leaves and some pieces of stone.' He looked embarrassed and said, 'I didn't have the strength to dig a grave.'

At the end of 1959, beginning of 1960, some of the older people started to die. In some families people could not find anyone to carry the dead body out, so I went to help do this; I always carried the head, the heavy end. My own father also died, he was fifty-six and already in poor health.

At that difficult time I was called away to Guanghan town to attend a training class. It was after my application to join the party had been accepted. I was there for forty days. We were able to eat, but the food was unpalatable – rice husks, pig fodder and some thin porridge.

Yes, in our platoon some people did die, but the numbers were less than in No. 2 platoon down there at the southern end where Liao Wenping was in charge. There almost all the male persons, young and old, died. The widows around the age of thirty all remarried and left here. Many of the teenagers went out to the fields and stole vegetables to survive.

The situation in my canteen was not so critical. We had corn in our storage, lots of it. We had it hung up around the walls drying. We had grown it on every available space – along the embankments, on the edges of the fields – and we were able to keep it in the village. Nobody came to steal our corn at night as we had posted guards and militia members to keep watch over our storehouse. So although we couldn't provide the members with rice, at least we could supply them with something to eat.

After a while the county government sent a work team to squat at our village to see how the public canteens were functioning. The second platoon had no grain left, and no salt even. They didn't run their canteen strictly and they had some thieves. Many people died of hunger there. At the neighbourhood clinic in No. 2 platoon I saw three corpses. As soon as they were moved out, another body came. It was terrible. I thought they had turned the clinic into a morgue. Because of their critical situation we divided their group up, we in No. 4 platoon got one part, and No. 5 and No. 7 platoon each got a part. The platoon I led was by now the biggest, with 530 people in it. People pointed over at us and said, 'Look, the food tubs in Wang's canteen are filled to over-flowing', but actually we didn't have much.

When the work team discovered the bad situation in our village the county grain storehouse was opened to us to save us. They found that because of the boasting, after we had fulfilled the state quota not much was left to us. Our party branch secretary Yao was transferred somewhere else but Liao Wenping could not give a clear account of the grain used in his platoon. Since he didn't exaggerate the output, the upper level cadres could not understand why the output was so low. They suspected that his platoon had kept back grain for their own use. So when people from No. 2 platoon went to the commune for help the cadres said, 'Go and ask Liao Wenping what he has done with the grain'. They accused him of under-reporting output and as a result he couldn't get help for his platoon. They were short of grain, more so than the rest of us.

Liao was taken before a mass meeting of over 1,000 people and had to stand there with his head bowed for hours, sweat running down his face – beads of sweat as large as yellow beans. He didn't even get any lunch. When we went back to the high street in the afternoon after lunch, he was still standing there with his head bowed. Beat him? No, he was not beaten. He was criticized for a whole day and then expelled from the party.

The reason for his treatment was that he didn't give false numbers for output, he was honest, he didn't exaggerate the production figures, and also so many members of his production team died of hunger. It was for these two reasons. He couldn't get them any grain to eat; he was considered responsible for that. Liao got back into the party when Hua Guofeng was chairman and Deng Xiaoping came back. It was almost twenty years later, in 1978. We took out Liao's file and decided that it had been a mistake to kick him out. I went to talk to him and asked him to write another application. he said, 'Forget it, forget it, I'll just go and be a carpenter', but later he was persuaded to re-enter the party.

The class struggle sharpened during the Great Leap and we made the former landlords work hard. They did field work by day and at night we sent them to cut firewood since we lacked coal for the canteen. Any still alive? Yes, in our team there is Shi Shufu . . .

Former landlord Shi took up the story from team leader Wang. He differed from Wang in his perspective on the Great Leap and this was natural because he spent the whole time in prison.

A short, unprepossessing man of sixty-eight, Shi has an accepting, forgiving, almost stoic nature. This bearing makes it nearly impossible to imagine that for twenty-six years he has been a village counter-revolutionary. His round face is likeable but its easy-going expression, one thinks, must surely be a mask since his status suggests that he has done bad deeds. Or perhaps it is the face of a person who is emotionally drained, because for five of those bitter twenty-six years he lived far away in a prison camp designed for class enemies and when he returned to the village he discovered that his whole immediate family had perished in the Great Leap. As he talks Shi reveals a remarkable tenacity for survival – from depths of despair to a sudden return of full citizenship rights – and like all survivors it is apparent that he learned how to keep his calm, to cling to hope, to adapt and inch forward when some change of circumstance offered the slightest chance to improve his lot.

'I was born and grew up here', he says quietly, 'and I went to a private school where I learned the works of the master. Even now I can recite some things from *The Great Learning* and I can still read, but I can't write properly any longer because of my eyes.'

The young Shi was at home during the land reform movement and witnessed his family's buildings and land divided into the hands of the poor. 'I now think this was good', he says. 'It's no use to save up money and gather up land for yourself. In the old days if you had money in your pocket you would be afraid of robbers and bandits every day. You could not live peacefully.'

To illustrate and perhaps reinforce the sincerity of these remarks he recalls an incident when, at the age of sixteen or seventeen, a group of bandits robbed his family one night. The hired hands and other family members heard the noise and ran away but Shi was still in bed when the bandits broke in. They took the chickens and the ducks and pigs away and tied him up and took him too. They held him for ransom in a place about a mile away. After six months his family got him back by paying twenty-eight yuan.

'After Liberation, as a landlord element,' said Shi, 'I was the target of many movements. I didn't take it too hard; I've survived. Since I had so much land I was not able to farm it myself; since I had so many rooms my family could not use them all. So it was right to divide it up for others.'

When the village co-operative admitted Shi's family into membership he worked as a tradesman responsible for repairing farm equipment. He thinks this was in 1957 and it was in this role that misfortune befell him. One night, as he tells it, a piece of wall collapsed on a wooden paddle wheel for raising water and damaged it.

> The paddle wheel was now the collective property of the co-operative, where before it had been mine. Since it was badly damaged and would cost one hundred yuan to fix I said that I couldn't do it. The leadership claimed that I was making trouble for the collective. Some even said that I was the one who damaged the paddle wheel out of spite. In those days Wu Zhengcai was the leader of the co-operative and he attacked me with a black heart. The village militia came and seized me.

By now Shi's hands were trembling a little and he turned away to wipe his eyes. 'The militia sent me to the public security office of the county', he continued after a moment, ' and shortly after that the court sentenced me to eight years reform through labour.'

How could a relatively minor matter lead to such a severe sentence? Was there something else? Or were the authorities making an example of him, 'killing a chicken in order to scare the monkey', in the words of a Chinese proverb? It is impossible to know with certainty now because Shi's accuser is long since dead.

'What was it like to do reform through labour?' Shi repeats the question and then continues without hesitation.

> I was sent to a state farm in Xichang district of southwestern Sichuan. It was a huge place. I was told there were more than seventy brigades working there. In each brigade there were 140 people. There were nine state cadres in charge of us in each brigade. There were also soldiers and policemen around. They had circled the area for about thirty or forty square *li*. There were also women there, about twenty brigades of women who were prisoners as well.

Shi appeared to have no hesitation in revealing the details of his incarceration.

In the first two years of his stay Shi worked with other prisoners in the fields. They planted rape seed, wheat, rice and vegetables for their own consumption. The farm was in a national minority area, a mountainous area of the Yi nationality, but 'we didn't see the people around as the soldiers had the area encircled'. When Shi arrived there were only about 1,200 *mu* of rice fields, but they terraced the hillsides in the winter slack season and by the time he left they had 10,000 *mu* in production.

In Shi's account of prison life there seemed to be no suggestion of harsh or unusual treatment. Was he hiding something? He reinforced the impression of normality further when he described the daily routine. It sounded remarkably like ordinary village life, except for the fact that the prisoners were separated from their families:

> Every day we got up at 6 a.m. After breakfast we went to work in the fields and we had study in the evening. We had political study, farm technique and agricultural knowledge study. We read newspapers and some books. Every evening each one of us was assigned to specific farm work for the next day – such as ploughing, harrowing, seeding and so on. Every month we saw two or three movies. The projection team came to the brigade and we gathered with our stools to see the films.
>
> After the first two years I became a cook. I was asked to cook for the state cadres who were in charge of our brigade. I cooked their three meals and for their families. So in the third year I was allowed to go out to a small town nearby. I went out every morning to get cooking supplies – salt, spices, meat and vegetables. Other people did the cooking for the prisoners in our brigade. When on the high street I saw some of the

national minority people, but I didn't talk to them. I just went directly to the store and came back.

After political study, I sometimes spent my time watching or listening to Sichuan opera performances. All these performances were put on by the prisoners. Some prisoners were good at singing and acting; we had all kinds of professional people in the brigade.

During the first two years of his stay Shi wrote letters home and received letters from his family. 'But later I didn't feel like writing to them so in one letter I said not to write to me any more, then I won't have to reply to you. So they didn't write me any more.' After five years Shi was suddenly paroled.

I came home in the early 1960s, I can't remember when exactly, but it was after the public canteens were closed down in the village. During the period of the public canteen all the members of my family died, but nobody informed me of this. One son died of schistosomiasis, another of leptospirosis and the third of diphtheria. My wife and daughter also passed away. When my nephew wrote he just said that all members of the family were well but that nobody could work in the fields. If he hadn't written to me of their difficulties I would have stayed in Xichang. I would have still been there now. That would have been better than coming back. I'd rather have stayed there. Even the cadres in charge of my brigade didn't want me to leave. And some of their wives said, 'Why don't you stay, you're such a good cook!'

But one of the cadres in charge of the camp said, 'There is a letter from his home saying that none of his family members can work in the fields. We'd better let him go home to look after them.' For that reason Shi returned home before completing his sentence, to discover the disaster that had befallen his family in the Great Leap and from which he had been spared by being in prison.

After I arrived at the commune here, the first person I ran into was production team leader Wang Daoquan. I met him on the high street before reaching home. He said, 'Oh, so you've come back!' I said, 'Yes'. He didn't say too much to me and didn't mention anything about my family.

When I reached the village I learned that all my children and my wife had died during the period of the public canteens. I cursed my nephew. 'Why didn't you tell me that my family all died when you wrote me? Why did you write to say that the nine people in our family were all well? If you'd told me the truth I'd have stayed where I was.'

Shi's vehement preference to stay in the prison camp was surprising but understandable. There he was treated the same as everyone else, even respected as a cook, while back in the village he remained a class enemy.

> Once again I went to the workshop for repairing farm tools and ploughs. I also wove bamboo baskets. If there weren't any such jobs to do then I worked with the others in the fields. I could get eight work points per day. But I was under control and the public security office appointed two of my neighbours, Wu Zhengfu and Lo Jitai, to supervise my actions. I had to ask their permission before going down to the high street or to visit some relatives. They usually allowed me to go if I was visiting my relatives, but sometimes they didn't agree to my going to the market. They would say, 'You'd better not go if you don't have much to do there. You'd better stay at home.'

It was humiliating for Shi and it seemed unreasonable to keep the class labels of the land reform for so many years after those social realities had changed. This idea was also in the minds of the Communist Party leadership.

One day in 1981 Shi received an unexpected call to go to the commune headquarters on the high street. All the former landlords and rich peasants were there for a meeting where a commune cadre announced that the government had decided to abolish the old class categories. 'The government took off our landlord and rich peasant "hats" ', said Shi, 'and freed us from any kind of supervision. The cadre told us that from this day on we could vote and have all the rights of a Chinese citizen. He said that he expected us to work hard and behave well.'

Shi reached into his pocket then thrust forward a special certificate that announced his new status. 'Now life is good', he breathed a sigh. Together with his nephew he had learned how to plant crops in a scientific way, raising output by using chemical fertilizer and by adopting the complicated techniques for tobacco planting and hybrid rice seedlings. Together they were raising five pigs and would slaughter one during the Spring Festival. 'This Spring Festival I plan to go to Linjie township to visit my relatives there', he said.

Meanwhile Shi's reputation as a cook for high officials spread widely and with the help of his nephew he cashed in on this skill. 'Many peasants in our co-operative and nearby areas know about me, they know I am a good cook', he said. 'Some of them hire me to cook for them when they have special parties for engagements, weddings or funerals. I can look after myself.' As a lonely afterthought he added, 'I have no desire to remarry; as a single person I am at leisure.'

Although some consequences of the Great Leap will remain with former landlord Shi for the rest of his life, the Leap itself ended in 1961. A movement which began with such a fanfare of high hopes in 1958, aiming to have China overtake the British economy in fifteen years, petered out in three, leaving in its wake economic disorders, social chaos and a badly divided leadership in the Communist Party.

With a budget deficit of two billion yuan the national economy, according to President Liu Shaoqi, was 'on the verge of collapse'. In some rural areas a decline in popular morale and local disturbances arising from the food crisis reportedly led to seizures of power by elements variously described as landlords, rich peasants, counter-revolutionaries, rascals, hoodlums and corrupt militia units, who used their official positions to seek class revenge or to pursue personal profit by engaging in unlawful activity – beatings, seizing grain, arresting innocent people, corruption, open robbery, rape and manslaughter.[20]

While continuing to insist on the correctness of the Great Leap development strategy, and publicly denying that there would be any reversals, Mao made self-criticisms, 'we bungled a lot', '. . . in socialist construction we continue to grope our way without clear vision', and he agreed to retrenchments of the collective organizations. This led to the closing or scaling down of many economic and social projects. Peasants were allowed to extend their private economic activities through the three 'small freedoms' – private plots, free markets and side-line enterprises.

During the time of panic in 1961, when Liu Shaoqi remarked that deaths in the Great Leap were more than 'those caused by the building of the Great Wall', the government made even more concessions to small-scale farming, and the system of assigning production quotas to individual households became unofficial general policy. In some areas peasants reportedly divided up as much as 30, even 50 per cent of the land and individuals left the commune to engage in private farming. Upon hearing this Deng Xiaoping, who was then general secretary of the party, offered his famous observation that 'white or black, so long as cats catch mice they are good cats', reflecting a philosophy that accepted any method which increased output regardless of ideological perspectives.

To Mao Zedong, on the other hand, whether to allow independent farming or not was a question of taking the socialist or the capitalist road; and he described some of the economic plans of senior colleagues as capitulation to the bourgeoisie. He demanded that the party never forget the class struggle. As Roderick MacFarquhar has said, for Mao 'the cardinal sin was a loss of nerve in the face of difficulty and danger'.[21]

Debates within the leadership in Beijing led to some abrupt changes. As a result confusion and demoralization spread among many basic-level cadres who saw the smaller scale of the collective and a trend to privatization as reversals of previous policies. The retreat from commune-level ownership and accounting to brigade or team ownership, payment according to labour without any free supply, and other changes diminished what some considered to be the superiority of the commune. Many cadres worried that the restoration of private plots, free markets and other material incentives would revive capitalism and bring back speculation, profiteering and price rises, and that families without much labour power would fall behind, leading to a renewed polarization of rural society into rich and poor.

Eventually, in the late summer of 1962, with a better crop assured and imports of grain from Canada available to ease the crisis, the party reached a new consensus on rural development. It affirmed the 'small freedoms' for private economic activities but kept them within limits that prohibited division of the land or assigning quotas to households; and it recommended the production team (an average of thirty to forty households with acreage comparable to a small family farm in less populated countries) as the basic unit of ownership, management and accounting.

The leadership turned its attention to the modernization of agriculture through the progressive development of machinery, chemical fertilizers, irrigation, electric power, fuel, transport, new seeds and construction materials. It declared that the great mission, the major order of the day for the entire party and the whole people, was the technological reform of agriculture, to be accomplished over four five-year plans.[22] In order to raise the morale of the peasant producers the government raised grain procurement prices by almost a third, and reduced the direct agricultural tax by a similar percentage. These measures and a substantial increase in agriculture's share of state investment contributed to immediate improvements in peasant incomes and welfare and led to a revival of the economy.[23]

In this more sober, cautious mood a new phase in China's history began, the time of the People's Communes, an era of unusual social and economic development that continued for the next two decades.

7

THE PEOPLE'S COMMUNE: 1962–72

The nucleus of Junction People's Commune is located in one of the old temples on the high street. Atop the imposing temple gate with its massive wooden doors is a large red star and the words 'Serve the people' in Mao Zedong's calligraphy. On either side in balanced eight-character couplets are further mandates: 'Take grain as the key link, promote all-round development', and 'Bringing into full play the spirit of the Foolish Old Man Who Removed the Mountains, transform China'. Lower down at eye-level two small white signboards announce that this is the Revolutionary Committee of Junction People's Commune and headquarters of the local Communist Party.

Inside the gateway a series of low, single-storied wooden buildings are arranged in three courtyards, one leading through to the next in traditional Chinese fashion. There is a large meeting hall, smaller reception rooms, offices, a kitchen and mess hall, and finally the mosquito-netted bedrooms of the commune cadres and their assistants. There are five main, full-time salaried cadres. These are the party secretary, the commune director in charge of agriculture, the vice-director in charge of civil affairs and security, the leader of the Women's Association, and the secretary responsible for rural enterprises. All local people, they are appointed and paid for by the state.

Tacked on the wall in one of the reception rooms is a faded, poster-sized commune map of the mid-1970s. From this one can see that the commune is shaped something like a pine cone, eight kilometres long and five at the widest point.

The map's legend contains basic information about the commune. It has thirteen brigades consisting of 118 production teams. In these teams are 5,188 peasant households with 21,926 members of which 11,098, or about half, are able-bodied labourers. Of the able-bodied labourers 741 work in commune and brigade-run industries and the rest in farming. With 548 people per square kilometre it is a rural population density seldom matched anywhere in the world. There are 23,791 *mu* of arable

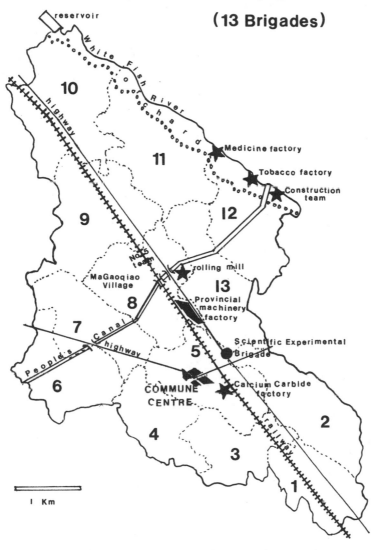

JUNCTION PEOPLE'S COMMUNE
(13 Brigades)

reservoir

White Fish River

hard

highway

10

11

Medicine factory

Tobacco factory

9

Construction team

12

North team

rolling mill

MaGaoqiao Village

13

8

Provincial machinery factory

Canal

7

highway

People's

Scientific Experimental Brigade

5

6

COMMUNE CENTRE

Calcium Carbide factory

2

railway

4

3

1

I Km

land, (3,965 acres) amounting to 1.15 *mu per capita* – about half the national average. Draft animals number 499 and there are an astonishing number of pigs – 21,678, an average of about one pig per person. Mechanized equipment includes 102 generators, pumps, threshers and about 50 medium and small-sized tractors.

Supported by Y900,000 in grants from the state the peasants had invested more than 3 million labour days in basic farmland capital construction. According to information on the map and other commune records, they dug twelve branch canals totalling 48 kilometres and straightened and paved another 300 irrigation channels and field ditches. This immense investment of time and labour basically guarantees stable yields regardless of the weather and systematically eliminates the habitat of the snails that breed the dreaded schistosomiasis fluke. Tractor roads were built into every brigade and production team; a small hydro-power station on the People's Canal, several agricultural machinery stations, some rural processing enterprises and an orchard had been established. Across the bottom of this impressive documentation of collective co-operation was written the slogan: '*Boldly strive to build our commune into a Dazhai-type commune*'.

The commune director, Yang Changyou, soon to be promoted to party secretary, has been a successful farmer in Junction township all his life. He is a stalwart man, now in his fifties, straight in the shoulders, his amber-brown eyes always alert, and he smiles quietly in response to a question. 'That slogan is out of date', he says, referring to recent reports in the news media. 'Dazhai is no longer a model; it was a Leftist deviation with "everyone eating out of one big pot"; and it is said that some things were falsified.' (Dazhai is the name of a small brigade in Shansi province that Mao selected in 1964 as a model for developing agriculture, and he urged all Chinese peasants to emulate it. It is a small community of eighty families in the semi-barren Taihang mountains whose economy and houses were devastated by a flood. Based upon the collective experience learned since the days of resisting the Japanese occupation they fought back with perseverance and, in the spirit of 'putting public interest first, self second', they reclaimed land in the river bed, terraced the sides of Tiger Head mountain, built irrigation viaducts, and within a short period succeeded in gathering-in rich harvests. Using a distribution system they considered equitable, they built a village school, a small hospital and new housing for all the families, leaving none out. Mao reasoned that if a poor village like Dazhai could succeed then so could others more favourably placed and he promoted Dazhai's leader, Chen Yonggui, to the national leadership of the Communist Party. Premier Zhou En-lai in supporting Mao's idea stated that to learn from Dazhai meant to put politics in command and ideology first, to have the spirit of self-reliance and hard struggle, and the Communist style of loving the country and loving the collective. After Mao and Zhou died in 1976 policy changed, public works yielded to privatization, collectives dissolved into family contracts; Dazhai was dropped as a model and the reformers attempted to destroy its reputation and denigrate its achievements as a socialist collective.)

It is difficult to know exactly how much Yang believes of this recent repudiation of the famous Dazhai model. As he talked about the commune's history in 1981 he was already aware that the day of the People's Commune was almost over. It would be disbanded within a year and he was preparing for a revival of an earlier township form of government. Two years later he and the others were willing to explain what they thought was wrong in the way they learned from Dazhai and some failures in the commune experience, but for the moment the accent is on the positive results.

Yang told how he and several others from Junction People's Commune made the trip to Dazhai in 1967 to learn the secret of its success and that they were impressed by what they saw and heard. After that visit they tried for a number of years to do things 'the Dazhai way' in Junction.[1] By mobilizing the surplus labour during the winter slack season with labour-intensive, land-saving technology, as Dazhai had done, Junction commune accelerated agricultural output, and from the collective accumulation funds that this generated they invested in modern scientific and technological inputs.

Since it was not easy to motivate people for such strenuous work the commune had to do two things, according to Yang. It had to discourage people from avoiding the community efforts. To achieve this end it cut down the number of rural market days, thus limiting the time peasants spent on their own pursuing private money-making activity.[2] Then, on the positive side, it offered people encouragement. Apart from some kind of symbolic material rewards – a towel, enamel cup, straw hat or cash award – whenever a group or individual achieved excellence in a task or demonstrated some advanced social or political consciousness for the collective interest or in the study of Marxism-Leninism and Mao Zedong Thought, the commune revolutionary committee presented them with a certificate of honour in the movement to learn from Dazhai. This custom explained the thousands of colourful documents bedecked with red flags and handsome calligraphy that decorated brigade and production team halls and the living rooms of many commune members. The movement to learn from Dazhai, as explained by commune director Yang, was basically an appeal to the production teams to increase their support for voluntary social labour (by crediting participants with work points) as a means of increasing productive capacity in a self-reliant manner, without causing a burden to the state.

Below the commune is the brigade, which is the middle level of a three-tier structure — commune, brigade, and production team. At the brigade level the most important and knowledgeable person is the party branch secretary, someone who is able to supply basic information.

No. 8 Brigade, which is MaGaoqiao village, is located near the heart of Junction People's Commune. It has a population of 1,920 people in 461 households that live on 340 acres of land (2,041 *mu*, or 136 hectares); of this land 32 acres (191 *mu*) are in the form of private family plots. Brigade members were raising 1,832 pigs in 1980. Able-bodied labourers number 1,017, of whom 66 work in commune-run industries, and 48 in brigade industries. The rest are organized by seven production teams into twenty-seven groups to do field work.

The production teams, the bottom tier in the commune, are the basic accounting units. That is to say, they control the land, organize the labour force and arrange the distribution of grain and cash to commune members after the harvest and at the year-end accounting.

Among the assets shared by the brigade and the production teams are fifty water buffaloes and a collection of machinery that shows considerable progress in mechanization: two medium tractors — the 27 hp *Harvest* model and a 40 hp *East is Red* — and seven small hand tractors owned by the production teams, a seventy-five kilowatt transformer, seventeen electric motors and five diesel engines for water pumping, threshing and driving seven grist mills. With the help of these assets and other resources of modern science the grain output in the brigades rose to record heights. The figures in Table A show that within fifteen years yields of grain doubled.

The brigade party secretary who conveyed this remarkable fund of knowledge all from memory was in his late thirties, a broad-faced, handsome male member of the Jiang family who seemed reserved in manner, almost shy, though not unfriendly. His middle peasant origin

TABLE A

Grain output under the People's Commune and after 1963–85
No. 8 Brigade, Junction People's Commune

Year	1963	1965	1970	1975	1980	1985
Total grain production (tons)	550	543	808	826	929	967
Grain yield (tons/hectare)	3.3	3.8	5.7	6.4	7.5	7.3

Source: No. 8 Brigade, *Statistics 1949–1985*, Junction People's Commune.

had allowed him a better than average education before 1950 and, from 1958 until he accepted his present post in 1978, he had been brigade accountant. He knew the workings of the brigade economy inside out. Shy or not, in conversation he spoke with a liveliness accompanied by the occasional gesture of his large hands.

From the flood of new impressions conveyed by Jiang, the most important basic fact seemed to be that a breakthrough had occurred in production since the early years of the People's Commune. In the 1960s the brigade had seventy-two wheelbarrows and twelve waterwheels but no tractors, no pumps or electricity and their annual grain output was only 550 tons. By 1980, on the same area of land, 70 per cent more grain and 50 per cent more cash crops were being harvested, and some of the hardest, back-breaking labour was done by mechanized equipment. The income of the brigade, as illustrated in Table B, doubled in the first decade of the commune and then doubled again in the next ten years even allowing for inflation.

How this impressive, escalating advance occurred was described at a gathering of four people, each of whom occupied a position at different levels in the rural structure: production team leader Wang, brigade party secretary Jiang, retired commune secretary Deng, and Wei Xiongru, a young woman cadre from the county's Family Planning Department.

Water was the first topic. There could be no high and stable yields without adequate and guaranteed supplies of water. This was a truth known to the farmers here since the beginning of irrigation works on the Sichuan plains two thousand years earlier.

The People's Canal, built in 1953, ran through the southern portion of No. 8 Brigade and provided gravity irrigation for three of its teams. But since the alluvial plain slopes southward water had to be raised from the canal for the other four teams on the northern side. This was more expensive and put them at a disadvantage. Three of the other brigades in the commune were totally disadvantaged, being on the higher ground.

TABLE B
Increase in total income 1962–82
No. 8 Brigade, Junction People's Commune (MaGaoqiao Village)
Unit: yuan

Year	1962	1972	1982
Brigade income	146,248	284,033	687,373
Per capita input	122	160	356

Source: Ibid., pp. 29–30.

And beyond them were several other people's communes on the northern slope, even further out of touch with guaranteed water supplies.

With the water problem too large for a single brigade or even a commune to solve on its own, a solution was sought elsewhere. Taking the Dazhai text 'love the country, love the collective', the prefecture (an administrative level below the province encompassing half a dozen or more counties) produced a unified plan that required the co-operation of three counties. Using this plan they built a new major waterway paralleling the People's Canal fifteen kilometres to the north giving gravity-fed water to all the land in between the two canals.

For projects that rely on large bodies of peasant labour, the most difficult task is to distribute the burden of construction fairly. Seeking to avoid the errors of the Great Leap Forward when indiscriminate transfer of labour and resources took place, the government adopted new regulations on the people's communes in 1962. These regulations recommended signed contracts defining the rights and obligations of the units concerned.[3] Labour power contributed by units which derived no or few benefits from such projects was to be offered reasonable compensation. In spite of these precautions it turned out that the peasants in Junction People's Commune got less than they expected from the new canal project, a circumstance that still slightly irks team leader Wang.

Planned in 1965 and constructed during the winter slack seasons of the next three years, the canal was named by its builders, wishing to honour heroic deeds, the Red Cliff canal after Premier Zhou En-lai's famous operations centre in Chongqing during the War of Resistance against Japan.

The story of this enterprise, seen through the eyes of some critic, could possibly be pilloried as a saga of forced labour, while in the hands of the author of *Ivanhoe* it would become a tale of high adventure and romance. Team leader Wang's homespun recollection recreates the scene more simply and directly and in the telling suggests his sense of its underlying morality:

> When we first arrived at the construction site of the Red Cliff canal with the commune battalion, 400-strong, we held a meeting to encourage the participants.
>
> In the afternoon we went to look over our work site; others arranged the camp site, some made the beds, others began to prepare the evening meal.
>
> On the second day the work started. We worked in squads. We engaged in competition to see who could do the job best. In those years of 'politics in command', Chairman Mao's portrait, quotation boards and red flags were everywhere on the construction site.
>
> In the evenings we had recreational activity. The younger men and women did some performances and we all joined in doing the loyalty dance

to show our support for Chairman Mao. In the morning while standing in front of Chairman Mao's portraits we spoke of what we were going to do that day; in the evening we summed up what we had done. Near the construction site some young people's propaganda teams did some things to encourage and praise those who had worked hard. At that time the water was cold, but we rolled up our pants and waded into work.

The living conditions were rough. There were 'five brings': bring your own food (grain, vegetables), utensils (bowls and chopsticks), shelter (bedding, fuel), tools (hoes and iron bars), and transport (wheelbarrows and carts). When we were arriving with all our equipment, our banners flying, we could see thousands of others coming from all directions; it was like a great army moving across the plain. Our excitement was high. We didn't get any payment but we received our work points and distribution (cash and kind) from our production teams at home.

At first, owing to a shortage of cement, we built our dykes of clay, and sometimes they were washed away. Later when the county heard about it they helped us to buy cement and we were able to use cement and stone to build firm walls.

This canal serves five communes in our county, so there were five battalions converging. We finished our part at Ding Family Hill. The people in Mianzhu county built their share of the canal towards us and we linked the two. Then the water flowed past and we got less than we expected. Later, during the dry season, thousands of peasants from our communes stood along the side of the canal with their poles, wanting to get more water. The people from Mianzhu came with iron bars and pikes and there was some fighting over the water. Since we forgot about Chairman Mao's teachings the county had to send some people to stop this fighting. The provincial authority decided that two-thirds of the water should be for Mianzhu and only one-third for Shitang county.

We had to accept this. An irrigation plan was drawn up by agreement between the communes for 'Red May', the busy season when everyone needs water for transplanting the rice shoots. The plan allows water to flow during certain hours to certain ditches for various teams. Leaders of brigades and teams go to the streams and canals armed with this timetable to control the flow of water and to prevent fighting or stealing of water. Because of the organization of the county the distribution of water is done well; anyone who tries to steal water will have their water reduced and fines will be levied. Before, the more people you had on hand, the more water you could take. Things are more settled and reasonable now.

In some respects the events described so candidly by team leader Wang are neither new nor revolutionary. Large-scale hydraulic works built by muscle and iron are part of a Chinese tradition that stretches as far back as the time of the first emperor in 200 BC. Nevertheless, it is a 'drama whose wonder never grows old' because it has been only at rare moments in history that the imagination, determination, leadership, organization and support among the people have emerged to make possible the expenditure of so much energy in favour of community betterment. In this case, even by Chinese standards, the Red Cliff canal and other concurrent projects on the western Sichuan plains were quite phenomenal: by extending the canal system to the marginal areas and peripheral counties where the terrain was more difficult, in a matter of two decades an irrigation system that had existed for two millennia was expanded by 40 per cent.[4]

The other topic of the four-level tête-à-tête was farmland reconstruction. It proved to be a more controversial subject.

For several years, especially after 1970, farmland improvement became the major preoccupation in the rural areas and as with the irrigation works there was a constant underlying question: how much unpaid, social labour could a production team be expected to support?

No. 8 Brigade in Junction People's Commune carried out capital construction on about one-third of its arable land. They changed small fields into big ones suitable for tractor ploughing, levelling and squaring them to make it easier to calculate fertilizer needs and production costs and results. They straightened and narrowed irrigation channels to save precious crop land, planted mulberry trees along the paths as well as fast-growing poplar for firewood, and built seven kilometres of roads so that tractors, large carts with pneumatic tyres, and machine-drawn ploughs and harrows could reach the land of all seven production teams.

Party secretary Jiang shook his head back and forth slowly. 'We were a little tired by all the labour,' he said, 'even exhausted at times.' Some of the peasants complained about all the mobilizations and cursed because the top soil was disturbed, adversely influencing output. They raised the slogan 'beat the drum lightly, move the soil slightly'. But after several seasons output recovered, 'and now the peasants think its a good thing to square the field,' Jiang mused, 'it's more convenient for working.' As Jiang ran through the achievement his face brightened, and the others expressed agreement with his concluding statement that 'we did the farmland reconstruction well, we have gathered in the fruits of this big effort and we did it without taking on any loans or debts'.

But the brigade's own projects were only part of the farmland reconstruction scheme. In the movement to learn from Dazhai both the commune and the county levels were also expected to have their farmland capital construction plans. And these plans, although they might have other sources of capital, had to rely on the same voluntary social labour of the commune members in the production teams.

The higher level projects induced controversy because they would usually be a few miles distant from the village and the benefits were less obvious or immediate than those of reconstruction work nearer home. It took an imaginative commune leadership, strongly rooted among the people, to devise strategies that would meet the requirements of the movement for reclaiming wasteland, protect the commune members from insupportable burdens and yet still create something of lasting value to the community.

Junction People's Commune was an example of a commune that had such leadership. They proposed to reclaim 100 acres of land in a dried-up riverbed, turning it into an orchard, and to dig a 150,000 cubic metre water reservoir the size of three football pitches that could also be used to breed fish. By linking the farmland reconstruction movement with another preoccupation of the county government – how to develop forestry and fisheries as part of an all-round diversified economy – they were able to have their proposal adopted as part of the county plan as well.

'We liked to work on our own projects,' said retired secretary Deng, 'so we wrote a report to the county government which they approved. The county gave money for materials too.' Deng, who was in overall charge of the White Fish River project, as it was called, explained how the idea came about and how the commune organized the work and the method by which they distributed the final benefits to commune members.

There had been a great flood in 1935 in which the waters of the Shi-ting River spread over the fields, creating a spill-way that became known as the White Fish River. Later the waters retreated leaving 250 acres of bare, rocky riverbed.

When the movement to learn from Dazhai reached Junction people in every unit discussed its implications and some suggested that if the Dazhai people could change their hills and gullies into terraced fields, then 'why couldn't we transform the dry riverbed into fertile land?' After further discussion in all the brigades and after approval from the county, the commune made its decision to go ahead. This extensive consultation, it was explained, was the 'mass line' in practice, the Chinese form of participatory democracy.

At this moment Wei Xiongru, of the county government, interjected that the pressure had been too great. 'We accomplished something but we hurt the enthusiasm of the masses', she said. 'It was a form of egalitarianism and transfer of resources from one unit to another, a "leftist" mistake.' She was expressing the judgement of the post-Mao leadership in China. Retired commune secretary Deng, however, did his best to ignore the remark politely and continued with the story:

In the spring of 1970 we set up the White Fish River construction command office in the Ma Family Ancestral Temple near the site, and to show our positive attitude all the cadres from the commune centre moved over there, so if anyone needed to do some business, needed the seal of the commune on some document, they had to come over to the White Fish River. Only during the busy season for agriculture did we move the offices back to the high street.

The soil to cover the riverbed had to be carried some distance and it took 180,000 labour days spread over three winter slack seasons. The reservoir required another 100,000 days spread over seven months. Recalling the size of the undertaking only made Deng wax more enthusiastic:

> People on the site were full of vigour. All the party members from every brigade were there headed by their party branch secretary. The county gave us encouragement, popularized our construction throughout the district and people from other communes came to visit and learn from us; we took the lead in the whole county to 'transform the rivers and mountains'.[5] On the construction site there were red flags, and billboards with Chairman Mao's quotations everywhere. Some model peasants and construction workers were selected on the spot. Everyone was in high spirits. Once during the high tide of construction we had more than 7,000 people there; ordinarily there were 2-3,000.

The work was organized by assigning each brigade a certain section to transform, a task that would take it 15-20,000 works days to accomplish. 'The commune members were quite willing to work on the construction', said Deng, 'because they all got work points from their production team for doing this labour. The burden was carried by the collective, not by the individual.'

For the production teams, of course, the immediate result of giving out work points at the White Fish River was to lower the value of the working day for everyone back home (i.e. 'brigade income *divided* by work points *equals* the individual's share', becomes 'brigade income *divided* by [work points plus "x" number of work points given out for White Fish River project] *equals* individual's (smaller) share'). In that sense it may seem like a transfer of resources from one unit to another, as Wei claimed.

But Deng maintained that the arrangements were fair, there were mutual benefits all-round. He supported this view by pointing out that when the landfill was completed each brigade had it section for growing produce. They planted cash crops such as peanuts, sugar cane and vegetables while waiting for the fruit trees to mature. In addition, each brigade was able to reduce its crowded conditions by moving a dozen or so families over to the new land. It was a rational and fair distribution of the benefits in a project that, to Deng's mind at any rate, was crowned by success: by 1980 there was a harvest of twenty-five tons of peaches, pears and oranges and the water reservoir section was producing two tons of fish each year.

The success of the White Fish River construction had ultimately rested on the labour power and co-operation of 118 production teams. In spite of Wei's negative opinion, team leader Wang, reflecting a view from the bottom, unreservedly confirmed Deng's estimation, and he casually added another piece of information that could leave little doubt as to how the production team members felt.

Wang's No. 5 production team was responsible for creating 5.7 *mu* (just under an acre) of the orchard, and it sent thirty able-bodied people to work forty days, for a total of 1,200 labour days spread over three seasons. It also sent seventeen people, mainly members of their militia platoon, for the reservoir for another 1,000 workdays spread from August until March. 'We arranged things to suit our conditions,' said Wang, 'when the cold weather came we stopped for a while because the cement would not set.'

As for the burden on the team, Wang seemed quite unconcerned. The value of their labour at the then level of 66 cents per day in No. 5 production team was Y1,452. In return for their contribution of labour the production team received some goods – a ton of peanuts and 300 kilograms of brown sugar, together worth Y650 and the right to transfer six people permanently to the orchard. In the first year alone this transfer would save them Y630 in grain and cash payments, so at most the team's contribution to the commune's 'learn from Dazhai' project would be Y200. But then Wang added the decisive point: 'Actually our labour did not cost us anything because no wages are ever paid by the state for yearly county projects anyway.'

From time immemorial in China there was a system of corvee labour by which the state required every able-bodied male in the countryside to donate some labour for road work or improvement of the irrigation system. After Liberation and the establishment of collective ownership of the land, the same practice was continued by the county government. It was called voluntary social labour, applied to all able-bodied persons, male and female, and amounted to four or five days a year per person.

The voluntary social labour for the 165 able-bodied members of Wang's team at the rate of four days a year over four years would have amounted to 2,640 labour days. But since the White Fish River construction had been declared a county project it had included their voluntary social labour for those years and furthermore since it had only taken 2,200 days they had actually saved 440 labour days! This was certainly a deal for which even the most mercenary team member could hardly criticize the commune leadership.

There were other continuing benefits too. At first when the fruit trees were under the care of people sent by each brigade, the results were unsatisfactory as the people were unskilled, did not spray properly or allowed some trees to die. In order to strengthen the management the commune took it over, established a party branch among the people there and set up a commune fruit farm. From then on the profits went into the commune accumulation fund. 'With this fund,' said Wang, 'the production teams have received help for training our scientific experimental group and some subsidies for buying modern farm supplies and equipment.'

The mass mobilizations to change the water ways and transform the land were an important part of China's development strategy during the period of Mao Zedong's leadership. And the progress documented on the faded commune map clearly represented success for the methods of organization and motivation devised by Mao. Without profiteering contractors or any public or private debts to burden future generations, the people, through their own labour, had moved forward together and had made tangible material improvements in the rural communities.

But the object of Mao's design was not the endless repetition of a cycle of hard toil. Rather it involved the creation of a society based on modernized technology in which peasants, while still living in the countryside, would lead culturally enriched lives more akin to those of the urban working people. The formation of a worker-peasant alliance, therefore, was another aim of the commune system. It was an objective that required the introduction of urban-based science and technology, and local industry, into the rural areas.

8

WALKING ON TWO LEGS: 1972–82

There is a saying in China about 'walking on two legs'. It means taking a balanced approach. It means being open to the new and the modern while not overlooking the tried and trusted, being willing to adopt Western methods while not forgetting traditional ways.

The expression on first hearing seems too obvious to bear repeating. Is there any other way to walk? But just asking the question opens the mind. Without realizing it, one may be dragging one's feet or hobbling along on one leg. The saying is an equivalent of the ancient Chinese way of thinking in terms of the complementarity of pairs of opposites, like heaven and earth, male and female, rough and smooth, the *yin* and the *yang* aspects of all phenomena. It is a philosophical concept favourable to looking at issues from all sides.

In contrast to the mass movement to 'learn from Dazhai' in irrigation and land-saving, the technological transformation of agriculture began cautiously with tiny steps. For many years the advantages of walking on the other leg – modern science and technology – were less apparent to the villagers, especially as they watched costs rise steeply.

An instruction in 1963 to appoint one team member as a sparetime experimental worker was the first inkling the production teams in Junction People's Commune had that something new was starting. This person was the lowest level in a co-ordinated science network that gradually spread from the county Agricultural Science Research Institute down through a commune agro-technical station and a brigade scientific experimental group and finally to the production team.

The next year word came that production teams should hand in cash deposits if they wished to be included in the first large allotments of hybrid rice seeds, chemical fertilizer and electric motors expected to arrive in the county by the end of 1964. Excited by this prospect team leader Wang persuaded his production team to put down Y1,000 – about twice as much as any of the other teams in No. 8 Brigade. He was eager to try 'walking on two legs'. But when it came time to use the new short-stalk rice seeds the team committee was afraid of failure and they voted to limit them to one *mu* out of 347. Wang had to accept this restriction but to the surprise of everyone Wang and the scientific experimental worker were able to produce 725 *jin* on that field. This compared to an average yield of 448 *jin* in the fields using the old seeds.

Success converted almost everyone in the team to trying the new seeds. Almost. The exceptions were a few older, experienced peasants who remained sceptical. They concentrated on the fact that the hybrid rice took more fertilizer applications, required more skill and labour to care for it and would be more costly to produce. If the team switched over they wondered if the chemical fertilizer would always be available in sufficient quantities to avoid a disastrous crop failure, and would the price of grain rise enough to cover the new costs? In addition they pointed out that after the harvest of the short hybrid rice there would be no stalks left for thatch or fuel. They argued for limiting the new and continuing the familiar, natural economy. They were criticized for not being willing to 'walk on two legs'. But when the government announced a rise in the procurement price of grain by 17.9 per cent for 1966, coming on top of an 8.3 per cent increase in 1965,[1] even the sceptics were won over and the team ordered as many of the new seeds as the commune's agro-technical station could supply.

Over the next half decade results were unsteady. In 1966 and 1967 the team harvested a record 133 tons of grain each year, but the following year in transplanting early to 'grasp the season' low temperature damaged the seedlings. The harvest fell to 111 tons. Feeling a little panicky they returned to more familiar seeds the next year, reserving some fields for a new improved hybrid variety with a shorter growing time. The latter did so well that in 1970 the team again turned to hybrid seeds and for the first time 'crossed the Yangtze River', meaning they reaped over 150 tons of grain. This was the figure set for a production team of this size in this geographical area by the National Programme for the Development of Agriculture. Having mastered the new techniques and bolstered by guaranteed supplies of water, from that time forward they were always a place of high and stable yields. For a farming community this is something near to heaven.

Urged on by the party committee to 'take grain as the key link in achieving an all-round development', the commune members pushed grain output up year after year, reducing the amount of land used for other crops by 20 per cent, until in 1978 with multiple cropping they reaped 187 tons on 620 *mu* (4.5 tons per sown hectare, or 11 tons per actual hectare) which was about twice the output at the time of land reform.

While the villagers could be justly proud of this achievement there was a strange paradox: the more grain they produced the poorer they became. Their shortage of cash was related to two things.

The first was that after 1966 the government did not increase the procurement price of grain again until 1979. It was a point the sceptics had raised, that income failed to keep pace with rising costs.

The reasons for this astonishing twelve-year lapse, variously attributed by the peasants to right-wing swindlers of the Liu Shaoqi type or else to ultra-Leftist plotters like Lin Piao, was and remains a mystery to the commune members. It has never been convincingly explained. Some members of the post-Mao central leadership place the main responsibility on Mao, saying that he was arrogant and insensitive to reality. Many commune members understood it at the time as belt-tightening for defence purposes after American troops landed in Vietnam in 1966 and as conditions along the Sino-Soviet border deteriorated, but this has never been stated in so many words by the central authorities.[2]

Whatever the actual reason, in the face of escalating costs for the modern inputs needed to produce such high levels of commodity grain – the chemicals, plastic sheeting, hybrid plants, electricity, and tractors – the government's failure to adjust the price of grain upwards during this long period of time was a policy disaster, a blow to the solar plexus of the people's communes. By 1975, ten years after the introduction of modern science to farming, expenses rose sharply from 15 to 26 per cent,[3] while the annual *per capita* income from the collective collapsed from Y51 to a reported Y17. As shown in Table C, the value of the working day at No. 8 Brigade fell from almost Y1.00 in 1965 to Y0.47 in 1975. With their incomes undermined, the peasants' faith in the superiority of both modern science and the socialist road reached a low point. It did not

TABLE C
Value of the work day 1963–82
No. 8 Brigade, Junction People's Commune
Unit: yuan

Year	1963	1965	1970	1975	1978	1980	1982
Value of a day's labour	0.71	0.95	0.66	0.47	0.57	0.89	1.37

Source: No. 8 Brigade, Junction People's Commune, *Statistics 1949–1985*, pp. 35–6.

begin to recover until the government made a new policy decision in December 1978 to raise the procurement price of grain for the 1979 crop by a whopping 40 per cent.

The other reason for the peasants' shortage of money had to do with the pattern of cash cropping. The reduction in the amount of land used for cash crops in favour of food production has already been mentioned.[4] Apart from this, there were the uncertainties of trying to make money by growing tobacco which is the principle source of cash income for the farmers in this area.

Shifang county has long been famous for sun-cured tobacco; its 'cord tobacco' and Lion brand cigars are available across the country and sold abroad. The British consul, Alexander Hosie, who was making a trip through Sichuan to investigate the cultivation of the opium poppy in 1903, noted the excellence of the tobacco leaf in Shifang and predicted that the industry would have a great future, especially in foreign markets.[5]

But it is a difficult crop to cultivate, requiring great amounts of labour, and over the years it had become prey to a cycle of various kinds of insect and bacterial diseases. The result was that the farmers could never be sure from one tobacco season to the next whether they would do well or suffer a crop failure. In the old days this anxiety was calmed by an Earth God Temple in the fields behind the village headquarters run by the landlords. They collected money from the peasants to hire priests and musicians who came to beat the drums on ceremonial occasions. According to team leader Wang Daoquan, the peasants 'feared that if they did not participate and bow down before the clay statues, pests would eat their tobacco seedlings'. Lacking pesticides, this was the way to deal with insects.

In addition to its natural enemies, tobacco has a long growing season, stretching from October to late June or early July, that overlaps with the vital time and land needed for rice cropping by several weeks. When the country's priority was to increase food crops, especially grain, the long growing season for tobacco was a major drawback. These two problems – plant disease and the need for a shorter growing season – could only be solved, and in fact were solved, by 'walking on two legs'.

But first, since so much time and labour are expended on tobacco growing in this community each year, it is instructive to follow the cropping cycle. The scene of peasant labour bending to the task, from seedling to sprout to large verdant leaves drying under the eaves, as painted by Consul Hosie when he travelled on foot through Shifang county almost a century ago, remains the same except for one vital new scientific discovery in 1977. This is Alexander Hosie's description:

The seed is sown in a seed-bed in October and the bed is then watered with liquid manure and covered with rice straw. When the seedlings have attained the height of half an inch the straw is removed and screens made of rape stalks are set up to protect them from frost, snow, and cold, to which they are exceedingly sensitive. If the weather is dry during the winter months the seedlings are watered several times. In March they are sufficiently advanced to be transplanted into rows 18 inches apart, and a like distance between the plants. A considerable interval is left between each set of two rows forming a bed of fine black loam about 2½ feet wide, with plants near the edges, while the intervals between the beds are converted into trenches 2 feet deep by 2½ feet wide at the top, and narrowing to about 1 foot at the bottom. These trenches are the irrigation channels . . . After banking up has taken place the trenches are filled with water every morning to within a inch or two of the surfaces of the beds and as the plants are close to the edges their roots are easily irrigated. Every four or five days, however, liquid manure is applied to the plants instead of water. By the middle of May the plants have grown to the height of a foot or more, and the tops are then snipped off by hand to prevent flowering and to divert the sap to the leaves which have already attained large dimensions. Irrigation now practically ceases unless the weather is exceptionally dry and the crop is harvested from the middle to the end of June . . .

The leaves are harvested by knife, and each stalk is cut close to the stem of the plant. Two inches of the end of each stalk are bent over to form a hook, and by this means the leaves are hung on cord or rope stretched under cover in sheds or under the eaves of houses . . . The leaves are in this way exposed to the air for twenty days. At the end of that period they have changed from green to brown and have shrivelled up laterally. On the twenty-first day they are hung outside the sheds for one night and exposed to the dews of heaven. Next morning they are taken in and rolled up tightly with the cord in bundles of about 20 catties [jin] in weight. After two days the bundles are opened, suspended under cover for two days and again exposed for one night in the open. This takes place a third time when the leaves are removed from the cord and assorted according to size. They are now ready for market . . .[5]

It is a realistic account of patient, intensive labour by the peasants. For all its detail, however, the English traveller's diary does not include the fluctuations of output. The farmers had always been baffled by the capricious influence of the Earth God Temple, and decades later were still frustrated at not being able to count on their main source of cash income. The fluctuations are recorded in the village account books of the 1970s. In one sequence, for example, the yield of tobacco was 158 *jin* per *mu* one year, the next year it was down to 86 *jin*, to be followed by a better harvest at 142 *jin* and then down to 77 *jin* the fourth year.

The vice-director of the county Science and Technology Committee, an impressive man by the name of Chen, explained this puzzling pattern and how it was eventually solved. Formerly a peasant who became an expert in agricultural science, Chen wears a black worsted jacket popular as dress among rural cadres and Western-style leather shoes. Stocky and broad-faced, he is a confident talker with the rhetorical questions of a public speaker, repetitive for emphasis not for lack of words, a man plainly accustomed to having the listener's attention and to winning converts.

The gist of his explanation was that eighteen different plant diseases attack the tobacco plant, of which the most serious is the mosaic disease. By experiment the county research institute discovered that without the presence of the tobacco plant this disease could not remain in the soil longer than 250 days. If they could keep the soil clear of tobacco for that length of time they could break the cycle of the disease. A constraint on doing this, Chen said, is that to get high output 'you have to get first and second growth leaves from the same field which takes about 120 days'. The challenge then is to create faster growing seeds and new planting techniques to reduce the required time from seeding to harvest by two or three weeks. In addition, if this could be done then the land would be ready in better time to plant the late rice crop and thereby solve another constraint on the tobacco industry, namely the government's call to 'take grain as the key link . . .'

Researchers found a solution by adapting the experiences of Japan and other countries to local conditions. The method required an additional transplant from the seedbed at an early stage, using a method called 'nutritious cups' and plastic sheeting to form temporary greenhouses. The plants were then at an advanced stage of growth when re-transplanted into the fields.[6]

'At first the peasants didn't accept it', said Chen. 'They said the new planting method took too much trouble, too much labour and was too complicated in the fields.' But step by step as they saw the results in experimental fields they were won over and became excited by the benefits of scientific farming. In 1977 the per *mu* yield of tobacco in Junction People's Commune was an average of 179 *jin* and with the new methods output rose steadily for nine years to reach 350 *jin* in 1985; the peasants' cash income increased in corresponding fashion. No. 8 Brigade, as shown in Table D, did even better than average.

'Now you can't stop the peasants', Chen laughed. 'Even at Spring Festival time you see them out in the field working carefully on their seeding beds and at the market they are buying plastic sheeting. The new technique alone has created a product value of eight million yuan in the county.'

TABLE D
Yields of cash crops 1963–85
No. 8 Brigade, Junction People's Commune (MaGaoqiao)
(7 production teams)
Unit: *jin* per *mu*

Year	1963	1965	1970	1975	1980	1985
Tobacco	91	187	144	77	266	374
Rape Seed	78	239	311	312	333	422

Source: No. 8 Brigade, account books for relevant years and brigade *Statistics, 1949–1985*.

Success in technological transformation of the tobacco and rice cultures, which started with such small steps in 1962, began to produce large economic gains twenty years later. Commune members were beginning to understand and really appreciate the philosophy of 'walking on two legs'.

Although the new tobacco planting techniques required more labour it was not enough to absorb the surplus farm labour in the villages. By the mid-1970s, after the completion of the large-scale irrigation and field reconstruction projects and the beginnings of farm mechanization, Junction People's Commune reckoned that if everyone worked to capacity it had about 3,000 more people than necessary to do the agricultural work, almost 30 per cent of the workforce. Fifty of these were in team leader Wang's No. 5 Production Team. As long as this superfluous labour remained tied to the village it lowered productivity and was a long-term source of discontent, especially among the younger people.

In the past in other industrializing countries the classic response to the problem of displaced labour power, apart from city slums, has been to send the surplus population abroad as colonists to some new land. The possibility for China to do this in the mid-twentieth century is limited.

Nor is large-scale internal migration feasible since the old settled areas are already over-populated and the mountains and deserts of China's hinterlands do not provide a ready environment for new settlers. Some movements of population from the crowded cities of the eastern seaboard to the interior of China occurred after 1949 but with few exceptions the state decided that the rural areas would have to retain and look after their own rapidly growing populations in a self-reliant manner. The government's plan to help solve this problem, apart from a birth control campaign, was to propose the development of small-scale rural enterprises in the people's communes so that, in Mao's words, 'the peasants can become workers right where they are'.[7]

This idea became a central focus for the people's communes and it has many implications for the way China is trying to industrialize. In the first place, the choice of industries directly related to the needs of agriculture results in fairly quick yields in terms of consumer goods and higher incomes. Later, as these small workshops become more sophisticated, they supply spare parts and accessories to the more technologically advanced industrial sector and thereby make a substantial contribution to China's modernization.

Apart from these considerations, there are social benefits. The dispersion of industry gradually turns peasants into rural workers and brings the standard and styles of living of the peasants closer to those of the more favoured urban workers. It lessens the contradictions between the cities and the countryside and encourages a willingness by commune members to stay in the rural communities to work hard and save for further local improvements. Furthermore, the significant degree of control by the commune provides an education in socialist co-operative organization and minimizes the need for new layers of bureaucracy. And at one time Mao argued that as the income from rural industry overtook income from agriculture, the members of the production team would freely accept raising the level of ownership from team to brigade to commune as part of the transition to a higher form of socialist public ownership.

The first attempts, made during the Great Leap Forward (1958-60), to establish the 'five small industries' as they were called (agricultural machinery, coal-mining, hydro power, chemical fertilizer, and building materials) had only limited success and Mao's plan was set back. After the collapse of the Great Leap the 'Regulations on Work of Rural People's Communes', adopted by the government in 1962 when Liu Shaoqi was in charge, stated that the communes should not build new enterprises 'for years to come' until existing ones were able to function well.[8]

In spite of this restriction Junction People's Commune made a new start in 1966 adding an agricultural machinery workshop and a building construction team to the five small enterprises that had survived the Great Leap. But, according to commune director Yang, state policy was not yet favourable to the promotion of rural industries.

> It was either not allowed at all, or if allowed then no help was given to get it going. Once an official from Chengdu, at the provincial level, helped us start a brick kiln, but then got into trouble for it. We could not get loans and our construction unit, with about thirty people, was not given permission to operate in the towns.

Sometimes the failure to support the growth of rural industry is blamed on the leftist 'gang of four' who held a large share of the national leadership for a few years, but explanations offered by the head of the agricultural section in the Financial Department of Shifang County suggest that it was simply a question of allotting scarce resources according to a plan.[9]

> We carry out our work according to the party's policies. First we supported water conservation and land reclamation to get more grain. Then from 1974 to 1976 the slogan in our country was to realize mechanization in three years, so we mainly supported this work – helped the communes to buy tractors and set up farm machinery stations. And from 1976 the emphasis shifted to rural enterprises so we switched to that.

The record of government loans to rural enterprises shown in Table E supports this interpretation of the facts.

The mushrooming growth of the rural enterprises in Junction People's Commune began in 1976 (when the 'gang of four' were still in power) with a decision of the party to strengthen them by transferring some existing small industries that were under the No. 2 Bureau of Light Industry, and, most important, with the arrival of a new commune party secretary. He was Zhao Biao, a novelist and playwright, who until then had worked in the county cultural centre. A young man of thirty, in the prime of life, Zhao decided that he could not 'be like a monk striking a bell all day', whiling away the time when there was so much to be done. Together with a young assistant, Zhu Molin, who was a technical school graduate and worker in the county's farm machinery factory, he made a survey of the commune's resources – industrial crops (rape seed, tobacco), available raw materials (sand and stone in the riverbed, coal and limestone within the county), convenient rail and highway transportation, electricity from the provincial grid, labour power (two or three thousand more people than were needed for agriculture) – and then prepared a plan of action.

TABLE E
Government loans to rural enterprises 1965–82
Shifang County
Unit: yuan

Year	1965	1971	1974	1978	1982
Loans	41,000	81,000	150,000	1,728,000	18,200,000

Source: Yu Yunli and Tang Zhiqin, managers, Agricultural Bank of Shifang, interviewed in December 1983.

According to a report in *Sichuan Daily* of 10 January 1980, industrial production 'advanced by leaps and bounds' in Junction People's Commune after Zhao Biao 'formed his cabinet'. From the original seven enterprises, the commune soon had twenty-three, ranging from a tailor's shop and film projection group to a tobacco factory, a Chinese medicine pharmaceutical plant, a rapeseed oil processing workshop, a honeycomb coal briquette factory and an electrometallurgy factory producing calcium carbide and ferrosilicon. The output value after Zhao Biao's first year was Y750,000, an increase of 100 per cent over the previous year. Six years later, in 1982, the commune's rural enterprises employed 1,500 workers and turned out products worth Y10,000,000. This remarkable advance, as shown in Table F, was aided by a three-year tax holiday, grants and loans from the state, and technical advice from the provincial-level Chemical Fertilizer Machinery Factory that was located on the commune's territory.

The trend continued to gain momentum. Success at Junction, which according to county officials stood out as one of the better efforts in the county, allowed the gross value of industrial output in the commune to surpass its agricultural product by 1980, five years ahead of the national objective.

The two young men, newcomers to the commune and acting like visiting firemen, were a strong combination for the difficult task of getting things started. They acted on the assumption that it is people not things that are decisive in making progress. Zhu, with his technical knowledge, was in a position to select and train capable workers for a

TABLE F
Growth of commune rural enterprises 1965–85
Junction People's Commune

Year	1965	1975	1980	1982	1985
Number of Enterprises	5	9	20	23	22
Number of Workers	103	301	1,056	1,504	2,300
Gross value of output	Y32,000	Y391,000	Y6,200,000	Y10,400,000	Y18,900,000
Net profits	Y4,800	Y41,000	Y347,000	Y317,000	Y960,000

Sources: A document, 'Industries and Services Run by Junction People's Commune 1965–80', given to the author, and interviews with Yang Wenju, Director of Shifang County Office of Rural Enterprises and Jiang Wenguang, Manager and Party Secretary of the Industrial Corporation of Junction Township, June 1986.

modern industry. 'The peasants have knowledge about agriculture', he said, 'because they have been working in the fields from generation to generation, but they don't know how to work in industry.'

At first when some people, ignorant of the different sizes of nuts and bolts, were sent to buy them in Chengdu, they failed to get the right ones so that time and money were wasted. Others didn't know what an electrical circuit was and knew nothing about voltage. Zhu explained:

> When we want new workers we divide the quotas out to the brigades and tell them about the qualifications. This is the system of democratic recommendation, selection by the masses, and it is different from the vulgar organizational afflictions of the past – getting somewhere by exchanging flattery and favours. Candidates have to be between seventeen and thirty years of age, in good health, have at least lower-middle school education, be politically sound, enthusiastic, have revolutionary drive, and they must face an examination on their cultural level when they come to the factory. What we run are modern factories. Without education we cannot do a good job.

As part of an effort to broaden their horizons, Zhu sent a group of workers to East China on a study tour of the highly publicized rural industries in Wuxi and Suzhou districts.

Zhao, on the other hand, concentrated on getting financial support from the county government and on recruiting people to manage the factories, perhaps turning his experience in creating fictional personalities to the task of judging character.

> A snake cannot crawl without a head, and a business cannot be run with 'scientific illiterates' who have no knowledge of science and technology or have no head for economics. In the past it was the custom here to use the record of service in appointing people, applying the theory of the unique importance of class origin or whether or not someone is a party member in selecting leaders for commune and brigade enterprises. These enterprises were the gateway to privilege in the villages, many people wanted to use personal connections to squeeze in by the back door.

When Zhao 'formed his cabinet' he told factory directors from the start that it was not a life-time appointment and that to receive reappointment after a year they would have to be chosen in a secret ballot by the workers in their factory. If they failed to fulfil the task or quota without objective reasons, they would be replaced and could return to their production team to do farm work.

Commune members responded to this leadership with an enthusiasm that led to some unexpected difficulties. The tobacco factory became so successful that it began influencing the output of the County Tobacco Factory, so much so that the county decided to incorporate the commune factory as part of its operations. The commune had to be content with a smaller share of the profits. In another case the commune's honeycomb briquette coal factory began taking customers away from the County Coal Co. which until then had had a monopoly in supplying briquettes for domestic cooking. The commune factory delivered higher-quality briquettes to the customers' doorsteps, even carrying them upstairs in apartment buildings for the same price as the state factory which operated on a cash-and-carry basis. Presently the commune discovered that it was having difficulty getting supplies of coal from the county mines; its trucks were being sent back half empty on some bureaucratic pretence.

A frustrated Zhao Biao finally got in touch with a reporter in Chengdu who filed a story in the *People's Daily* of 15 August 1979 entitled 'A striking contrast between two honeycomb briquette factories in Shifang county', which brought the embarrassed state company to heel. Apparently the reporter had also sent in a general account of what he had learned of the development of rural enterprises in the commune and this document came to the attention of the central committee of the party. Subsequently the general secretary, Hu Yaobang, sent a letter of support that greatly encouraged the commune members to strive even harder. The coal briquette story illustrates the importance of informal channels and the role of the Chinese press in helping to make the system function.

But perhaps the aspect of the rural enterprises that enthused the peasants most was what they called its socialist orientation, its mandate to serve the people's livelihood.

Sharing out the new jobs to all the production teams in a democratic manner was much appreciated as was the fairness of the system of payment for labour. The factory credited each worker supplied by the production team with work points and sent the cash (except for bonus money) to the production team for the general year-end distribution in which the workers also took part. Since factory work paid more than farm work, these work points boosted the value of the whole team's work day rather than just benefiting a few individuals, and at the same time no widening gap appeared between the incomes of the workers and the peasants. In 1980, for example, this system boosted the average value of the work day on the commune from 78 cents to 90 cents, with the result that the average annual *per capita* income in the whole commune rose by 21 yuan – from Y152 to Y173.[10] The local party members took pride in speaking about the fairness of this system.

Apart from the system of labour payment, the way the rural enterprises distributed their profits also affected the people's livelihood. After the contribution to the state through taxes (from 3 per cent to 40 per cent depending upon the industry), plus the reserve for expanded production and administrative costs, the profits were distributed using two methods.

The first was in the form of grants in support of schools, medical care, farmland reconstruction, purchase of farm machinery, or as bonuses to families that agreed to have only one child, according to the wishes of the various brigades. The other involved a direct distribution to the commune members known as 'money of real benefit'. Team leader Wang still blushes when he recalls the first time this occurred in 1980. All the production team leaders assembled at the commune centre for a solemn ceremony. The cash, 88,000 yuan wrapped in bundles of red paper, lay on the head table as the party secretary reviewed the history of the commune and praised the achievements of socialist industrialization. 'We have brought into full play the spirit of the Foolish Old Man Who Removed the Mountains', he said. 'We are transforming China.'

Then one by one each leader went forward to receive his team's share. Wang was called last as his was Y1,560, the largest amount, and to him fell the difficult honour of saying a few words. 'Right,' he stammered as everyone grinned, 'small-scale industry is good. And next year, if a new industry is started our teams will assure it of a labour force.'[11]

Even if he was not much of a public speaker, Wang took his responsibility as a party member seriously. He had always been prepared to take a lead in working for the material changes brought about under the signboard of the people's commune – impressive changes by any standard of measurement. From irrigation works and farmland reconstruction that guaranteed high and stable crop yields, from basic mechanization of the hardest physical tasks – pumping, milling, carrying – to the beginnings of scientific experimentation and industrial development, Wang had led his team forward to meet each new challenge.

But the greatest challenges lay elsewhere. They were in the demand of the party to refashion old habits, old customs, old ways of thinking and acting considered unsuitable for entering a new socialist society. As the Chinese media repeatedly state, a genuine socialist revolution takes place both externally in the physical environment and internally in the minds and hearts of individuals. It is a 'revolutionary movement of our people for developing socialist construction and transforming the objective world. It is also a revolutionary movement for transforming our subjective world and raising our ideological consciousness.'[12] This demand found expression in various mass movements and especially in a socialist education movement, popularly known as the 'four clean-ups', that ran parallel to and overlapped the mass movements for material progress during the 1960s. It is the awakenings, excitements and traumas of this movement that remain uppermost in the memory of Wang and his fellow villagers when thinking of the past.

PART II

IDEOLOGICAL AND POLITICAL CHANGE

PASSING THE GATE: 1966

After consolidating the communes in 1962, following the difficulties of the Great Leap, the central leadership of the Communist Party became increasingly concerned over the direction of agricultural policy. There were reports of widespread misbehaviour by basic-level cadres who used their positions to take more than their share from the collective.

The national leaders were not of one mind on how this trend should be handled and the centre issued several conflicting guidelines. A drift to individual farming, known as 'three freedoms and one contract', troubled Mao, whereas deputy chairman Liu Shaoqi and the general secretary of the party, Deng Xiaoping, favoured allowing that trend to continue. The 'three freedoms' were the extension of plots for private use, increased frequency of peasant markets and more small enterprises with sole responsibility for their own profits and losses; the contract involved the fixing of output quotas to individual households. These policies all tended to undermine commitment to the collective. Eventually Mao issued a twenty-three-point directive emphasizing the continuing nature of the class struggle and warning about people *within the party* who were taking the capitalist road. He called for a Socialist Education Movement to re-educate those who had made mistakes and to raise everyone's consciousness about the meaning and benefits of socialist collective farming.

The conflicting approaches to the problem blunted the progress of the movement to some extent, but in spite of the differences the party was able to launch a 'four clean-up' campaign. This involved a demand that the production teams clean up their procedures for handling the accounts, the warehouse stores, the use of other assets and the practice of favouritism in handing out work points to team members. To ensure that this campaign progressed effectively the leadership agreed to send work teams from outside, as had been done during the land reform movement. The local cadres would have to 'pass the gate' of mass criticism or else lose their positions. The 'four clean-up' campaign developed from one county to the next in turns, and did not reach Shifang county until the middle of 1966.

One hot July afternoon in 1966, team leader Wang and several others were working in a field of tobacco. The crop was blighted by disease again and commune members were unhappy about the worst harvest in memory. It was so bad that they were cutting down the stalks, not bothering to wait for the second leaves, and they planned to plough the field quickly in time to plant a late crop of rice.

As Wang straightened up a moment to mop perspiration from his neck he saw figures appear at the horizon on the railway embankment. He counted six men and two women striding along in straw hats, each with a bedroll, enamel cup and bag of rice strapped to their backs. He did not recognize any of them but it seemed that they were coming on some business and intended staying for a while. 'Which way to the brigade headquarters?' one of them shouted. 'Over there', Wang pointed as they moved on with hardly a pause.

As the group disappeared down the path leading to the village the peasants stopped working and gathered around Wang. Rumours had been circulating for some time about a work team that would be coming to boost socialist education and carry on with the 'four clean-ups' begun two years earlier. Nothing particular had happened at that time; the county sent some people to inspect the account books and to issue warnings about embezzlement or other corrupt behaviour. The wind had died down quickly without disturbing much. Now with outsiders coming again it looked as if things might be more serious. As they chatted Wang tried to reassure his production team members, but an uneasiness stirred within him as well.

Their premonitions were well-founded. The work team was to stay for six months and turn things inside out, creating a turmoil in the village such as had not been experienced since the sharp class struggles of the land reform fifteen years earlier.

Arriving at the brigade headquarters Li Shouhui, a man in his late thirties, produced a document with the seal of the provincial committee of the Communist Party and introduced himself to the village head, Zhang Jinghe, and to party branch secretary Yao as leader of the 'four clean-up' work team. During polite conversation over cups of tea the younger man revealed that his group had come from Qionglai county, some 150 miles distant, but he gave no further indication of plans to the brigade leaders except to say that he wished a public forum of all villagers over the age of sixteen to be called for the next morning. After taking possession of the brigade account books and household registers and a stroll around the brigade, Li and his team retired to their rooms leaving the village leaders to their own speculations. The power that Li held in his hands was great, much like that of the school inspector when a general inspection takes place and the principal is temporarily removed from office.

Li is a serious, confident man. When his interest is greatly aroused by some topic his neck veins stand out and he punctuates his conversation with head shaking and the exaggerated gestures of a traditional Chinese storyteller, but normally he is relaxed, almost retiring. In a sub-district of Qionglai county he had been in charge of financial and commercial work, supervising the buying and selling of pigs, grain, vegetables, the credit co-operatives and branch banks.

He was well acquainted with the purposes of the 'four clean-ups' because he had already been through three experiences of the campaign – once in his own village and as a work team member in two other counties. And he was well briefed now because preparations for the movement in Shifang had been thorough, with a small advance group coming in March. Three months later he joined the main work team of 1,000 members, almost a third of Qionglai county's government cadres and some others from Dayi county as well. They arrived in a convoy of thirty trucks, enough personnel to assign one person to each production team in Shifang county. They had studied the central committee's documents for a week in the county town and received their assignments. Then they dispersed to the commune centres. At Junction Li made a list of all the cadres in No. 8 Brigade. There were forty of them. He learned as much as he could about which ones would be likely to have problems and who the possible local activists in the movement might be, and then led his small group to MaGaoqiao.

As he sat at a table working by candlelight on the first evening Li mulled over in his mind the movement he was about to launch in this strange, yet very familiar, place. His own village was also on the Western Sichuan plain, with similar crops, except for the tobacco, and irrigated by the same hydraulic system; but by the look of it, MaGaoqiao was more prosperous. Although the peasants also still lived in thatched, pounded-earth houses situated in bamboo groves, at home work points were worth only 40 cents per day, while here the value was 90 cents, and the grain output was higher.

And he wondered about the cadres. He knew from his enquiries at the commune that the brigade leader, Zhang Jinghe, had a reputation for speculating on the market and other capitalist tendencies, but that was long ago and perhaps Zhang had reformed. Of course, there would be complaints and real problems. But he would not make the mistake of expelling cadres to meet a quota. If there were no cadres with serious crimes, then that was that. 'I am a party member', he told himself. 'What we do will be judged by history; we don't just work for the moment.'

He recalled the 'four clean-ups' in his own village almost two years ago. The attitude of that work team was, 'How can there be no reactionaries! If you say that, then you are the reactionary! If you can't find a problem, then you are the problem.' At that time no less than eighty-three outside cadres had come to the village, a human wave. The commune members were cowed and people had said, 'It's like General Tsao Tsao of old, leading 830,000 troops across the Yangtze river!'

This time, guided by the twenty-three-point document from the central committee, Li mused, things would be different, more reasonable.[1]

The main point was to educate the masses to love the country and to build up the collective. Misdeeds of cadres weaken trust in the collective. Therefore the first job was to mobilize the poor and lower middle peasants to tell the work team of any problems and any corrupt practices on the part of their brigade leaders and of the five big cadres in each production team – the team leader, vice-leader, accountant, grainkeeper and treasurer. Guided by the results of this investigation the work team would move to the second stage of public criticism and denunciation of those who had done wrong, always bearing in mind Chairman Mao's advice to 'learn from past mistakes to avoid future ones', and to 'cure the sickness to save the patient'. Success at this stage depended upon recruiting activists and backbone elements willing to speak out in a way that could generate psychological pressure. Otherwise, how could the cadres be encouraged to confess publicly and repudiate their mistakes?

As for the cadres, they would be 'sent upstairs to wash their hands and take a bath', i.e. to write out self-criticisms. If they did not reveal what the work team learned from the commune members, then they could not come downstairs and would have to make a further self-criticism. Only when their confession was in a form acceptable to a meeting of commune members could they 'pass the gate' and take up their work again. Those cadres guilty of serious wrongdoing would have to make reparations or suffer some demotion or penalty.

After Li had finished making an outline of the various stages and points to be remembered, he closed his notebook, locked it in the desk and prepared for bed. As he washed his feet in the hot water solicitously provided by brigade leader Zhang Jinghe, he felt relaxed, ready for next day's launching; the vice-leader of the work team would be making the main speech at the public forum leaving Li free to gauge the mood of the crowd.

Next morning production team leader Wang hurried over to the brigade auditorium well before nine to be sure of getting a good seat, and found several hundred nervously excited people already there. By the time vice-leader of the work team, Zhang Guolin, rose at the front to speak, more than 700 commune members filled the hall, waiting expectantly. They were not disappointed as Zhang was a fiery speaker.

After some preliminary remarks about the generally good situation in the countryside, he turned to the existence of class struggles and enemies who were against socialism trying to restore capitalism through peaceful evolution. Quoting from the Twenty-three Points, he quickly came to the crux of the matter. The aim of the current movement, he said, was 'to purge the capitalist roaders in authority within the party [and] thus further consolidate and develop the position of socialism in the urban and rural areas'.

There was an audible stir in the auditorium at these words, everyone listened even more intently, while team leader Wang and the other twenty-three party members shifted uncomfortably in their seats. The speaker continued:

> Some [cadres] do not draw a clear line between the enemy and ourselves, lose their proletarian stand, and shield their own relatives, friends or old colleagues who are engaged in capitalist activities. An overwhelming majority of our cadres want to travel the road of socialism but some of them do not have a clear understanding of socialist revolution, trust those who are unworthy, make no serious examination of work, and commit the error of bureaucracy.

Zhang explained that there might be four kinds of cadres: the good ones, the comparatively good ones (these categories would probably include 95 per cent), those with many problems who should be criticized and removed from office, and those with serious problems who should be struggled against and labelled as class enemies.

To all the listeners this was a remarkable, astonishing turnabout. For ten years the party branch had been a tight little group. It had accepted no new applications for membership since the drive to form co-operatives. The branch had shaped the destiny of the village, held the power to reward or punish in its hands. Now its members were to be put on trial as it were, called to confess their misdeeds and account for their behaviour in detail to the very people over whom they had held undisputed sway. If it was not a fake, then this was something without precedent in local memory; earlier rectifications of the party paled by comparison.

As for methods, the speaker went on, the masses should be mobilized freely to classify the cadres according to the four categories. However, 'make no blast but produce facts, reason, and prevent simplistic and harsh methods. Beating up or other forms of corporal punishment are strictly prohibited, and confession under duress . . . must be avoided.'

Zhang concluded by outlining the criteria for a successful conduct of the campaign. It would depend on whether the poor and lower middle peasants truly mobilized or not; whether the 'four clean-ups' problem among the cadres was solved or not; whether the cadres took part in labour or not; whether a competent leadership core emerged or not; whether the commune members themselves exercised supervision

over any bad characters to help them become new people or handed
contradictions on to the upper level for solution; and whether production
increased or decreased.

As the meeting broke up in a babble of conversation, Zhang appealed
to the commune members to come forward to exercise their judgement in
distinguishing good from bad, and urged those eligible to become active
in the Poor and Lower Middle Peasants' Association.

From this time on the activities of the movement took place after
working hours and unfolded on several different levels as the work team
sought to dispel passivity, coolness or a misty atmosphere. The village
did not produce any major scandal leading to heavy penalties and prison
sentences. Nevertheless, there was sufficient evidence of embezzlement
and bullying by the cadres to create considerable interest in the clean-up
movement. It was a more telling and thoroughgoing process of popular
participation than any of the general elections could provide. For ten
days the work team members proceeded to visit the homes of the poor
and lower middle peasants, not including those of the party members.
They took along their grain and ate a meal with each family as they
sought out the peasants' complaints. At first most commune members
were reluctant to say anything. One women told her guest, 'The work
team is like water, it comes and then flows away. If the cadre we criticize
cannot be overthrown then later he will make us wear smaller shoes.'
Her husband added:

> Yes, he will make us wear smaller shoes made of glass that can't be seen
> but you feel them. If the brigade leader hears us he will make mental notes
> and our son will lose his chance to join the army, our daughter will miss
> a turn to work in the factory.

The work team countered by forming groups of the Poor and Lower
Middle Peasants' Association in each team. It would be a permanent
organization remaining after the work team left with power to supervise
the work of the team leaders. Since the poor and lower middle peasants
were over 50 per cent of the population they would have some
effective power.

With such assurances they started to get results. People began to say
that their work points were worth too little. The work team encouraged
them saying,

> 'See, this is what the cadres have been doing to you. They control
> you and don't give you what you have made. They have put money
> into their own pockets but they've ignored the 10 per cent for the
> accumulation fund, they've ignored the part for enterprise and production
> funds.

Soon other complaints and charges began to roll out.

One of the targets of the work team, brigade militia leader Huang Kaiyao, the one who had been to the Korean War, described how the work team mobilized the masses:

> They gave loans of grain, or money for the time off to encourage people to go to meetings. But to the cadres or party members they were very serious and even rude, and pressured them heavily.

Those villagers who did most to expose the cadres and party members 'were thought of as leftists and they were "good".'

> If you didn't take part in exposing the cadres you might be accused of having some kind of unsuitable relation with them. In this way many purely fictitious claims were made against the leaders. Team leader Wang Daoquan got lots of false charges raised against him. The leaders could not defend themselves; if they did they would be accused of trying to suppress the masses.

Huang claimed that he was not afraid of anything.

> I hadn't done anything wrong. I wasn't afraid of what people would say. Fortunately at that time I was the leader of the village militia company; I had nothing to do with money or grain. But some of the militia claimed that I treated them badly and rudely. Some people whispered that I had some illicit sexual relations. That was not true, they were not able to come up with any facts to support their statements.

As it turned out Huang was right and the masses accepted his self-criticism at an early stage. He 'passed the gate' and joined the Poor and Lower Middle Peasants' Association, becoming chairman of the brigade group in the last stages of the movement.

With one important exception, the problems of the other brigade-level cadres were also solved early. Party secretary Yao emerged virtually unscathed, being criticized only for extravagance in his use of the brigade's hospitality fund; in the busy season when county tractor-drivers delivering chemical fertilizer had to be bribed he provided dinners with wine and chicken, where, according to the commune members, 'it is common that the guests are few and the hosts are many'. Yao apologized, handed over Y20 – a fairly stiff fine, the equivalent of half a year's cash income from his collective distribution – and was forgiven.

Some commune members also had doubts about the brigade account-ant, Jiang Wenguang. They could find nothing wrong with his books, but they suspected that he was really a rich peasant who had escaped proper classification at the time of the land reform; it was rumoured that he had some land elsewhere which he failed to report. After grilling Jiang for a few weeks, two young activists went elsewhere to investigate but found no substantiation for the stories, so Jiang kept his classification as a middle peasant and emerged with a clear record.

The exception was veteran brigade leader, Zhang Jinghe, the one who had been pilloried for his speculative tobacco trading in the 1950s. The work team classified Jinghe into the third category and he was unable to 'pass the gate'.

People had complaints about him stemming from the bitter memories of the three hard years 1959-61; they said he had a big stomach and when he could not satisfy his hunger in one canteen he went around to other canteens to get more food. They complained that his work method was too simple, his voice too loud as he shouted at them.

From his own perspective Jinghe became a scapegoat in the movement and to this day he is unable to accept the verdict:

It was claimed that I had eaten more, occupied more and taken more than my share. I was forced to return Y370 to the collective and 750 *jin* of unhusked rice. And that was not all. Some people claimed that I had problems in my personal political background. Before Liberation I once joined the Robed Brothers secret society but I didn't take part in any of their activities, except that I had a photograph taken with them. I was standing at the end of the back row in that photograph, that shows how unimportant I was.

Jinghe shrugged his shoulders.

Everyone knows me as a local person. How can that incident be blown up so big! The only thing was that I didn't mention it when I joined the Communist Party. So in the four clean-up movement the charge came that I was two-faced. In the end at a mass meeting the work team stripped me of my posts both inside and outside the party. I had to stand there with my head bowed as they kicked me out of the party.

I was told privately that all these matters would be checked over again at the end of the movement and that the collective would return some of the rice and money to me. But unfortunately this problem was not solved before the movement ended. Another movement started up and the four clean-up work team ran away, leaving my problem dangling there, unsolved.

I went to the commune and to the county many times asking to have my problem solved and for them to give me a final answer. They just comforted me saying they would look into things, but they did nothing. Party secretaries kept changing in those years, one after another, so my problem about the money and the grain was never cleared up and nobody mentions it any more. The commune told me that the decision was from a mass movement, it came from the people.

Later the party branch had special meetings to discuss my membership and they handed in a report to the county. The county sent someone for a heart-to-heart talk with me, speaking of my long service since Liberation and asking what I thought. I said I had no opinion. No matter whether I was in or out of the party I was working for the party with one heart. I had no other heart. I said that, although I had been kicked out, I was still a farmer of China. I had no other allegiance, I was not of two minds. The discussion went round and round for half a year. Finally they decided to restore my membership in the party, but I was no longer a cadre, just an ordinary commune member in No. 6 production team.

Since I was getting old the brigade assigned me to light work in the agricultural science station, to look after the public buildings and I fed some pigs.

That's my experience of all those years. I worked as a cadre for over twenty years; only in 1959 and 1960 did people have complaints about me which they brought up in the four clean-up movement. Of course, peasants suffered a lot when we had the public canteens. But I also suffered in that period. I was so worried about conditions of the people that I fell ill because of worry. I got tuberculosis and was sent to hospital for a month. That was a very difficult time. My health is not that good even now, but they've found me something to do so that I can make a living.

If proceedings went relatively calmly at the brigade level, with the exception of Jinghe, the same was not true in the production teams. Five out of the seven production team leaders could not 'pass the gate'. Two of them, found guilty of taking more than their share, had to return some cash but since they were non-party members they received no further attention from the work team. Another, the head of No. 7 team, was expelled from the party along with Jinghe. His problem was that he failed to distinguish between classes. As work team leader Li explained:

Sometimes he went to the restaurants and met landlords, and they arranged mutual guarantees, especially in 1962 when Chiang Kai-shek boasted that he would return. The landlord element said, 'When Chiang Kai-shek comes we will protect you.' In return the production team leader divided the land in his team back to the individual peasants.

The case of team leader Wang Daoquan of No. 5 production team aroused great interest. The work team knew that Wang was in a fairly strong position because the production in his unit was good and the value of the work day at 96 cents, while not the best, was 2 cents above the brigade average. Nevertheless, as they went around they began hearing enough to make them feel that he was weak politically and a dubious influence on the party. Their call to form a Poor and Lower Middle Peasants' Association in his team brought a strong turnout from the twenty-five families in those categories (excluding the families of the five party members). This was encouraging, but among these only about half a dozen were willing to try to pull Wang down. They became known as the leftist group, a term of approval in those times.

From the statements and investigations of this small group the work team drew up its private bill of indictment: Wang, they charged, had embezzled Y276 and 140 *jin* of grain over the past few years, he unfairly disciplined people he didn't like by deducting their work points or by assigning them less farm work so that they could earn fewer points, he spread superstitious beliefs, he reviled the party by inference and attacked Chairman Mao by inuendo.

Wang, who was still trying to write a suitable self-criticism, had no idea about these points until an anonymous big character poster addressed to him appeared on a wall one day. It asked three questions: Why do you point at the mulberry tree while abusing the locust? Can a Communist Party member believe in superstitions? How clean are your hands?

As Wang read this poster he felt the tension rise inside his chest. How much did they know, he wondered, and what exactly did these questions refer to? What would he have to put into his self-criticism in order to pass the gate? While still puzzling over the work team's socratic lesson, he was secretly helped out of his dilemma by cousin Wang Youming, an illiterate but highly articulate twenty-eight-year-old peasant, who managed to have himself elected chairman of the team's Poor and Lower Middle Peasants' Association. As chairman Wang recounts:

> I still remember having several heart-to-heart talks with Wang [Daoquan] during the movement. He had been production team leader for quite a few years by then. People naturally have some complaints about this or that, there was no doubt about that. But some of the criticism of him was not exactly based upon the truth. Some people could make something the size of your fingertip into a huge matter and distort the facts. It was hard to avoid such things in the movement. Of course, those meetings were held by our association, so we have to take the responsibility for some of the mistakes. As chairman of the association and as a close relative of Wang's — his grandfather was my father's brother — I had to listen to the opinions of the masses, otherwise they would go to the brigade and charge me with protecting Wang because we were related.

According to chairman Wang, his cousin got into trouble for two reasons. The first was that several of the activists had ambitions to replace him. They were team members who had weak clan connections in the village and wanted the protection that comes from holding power. They went around spreading rumours and claiming that they had been mistreated, and one of them nick-named Wang as 'dog officer Wang'. Team members thought the image of Wang as a dog-catcher a great joke and schoolchildren spread the expression widely, creating quite an impression on the work team.

The other reason was that Wang liked to talk a lot, was fond of using metaphors and embellishing ancient tales he learned from watching the Sichuan opera. He was once heard to say 'If you stand in front of a full manure pit you can see the Tian An Men' (Gate of Heavenly Peace in Beijing which appears on the national emblem). He intended this as a way of encouraging team members to contribute their manure for production, but after the work team came looking for class enemies some villagers recalled this saying with less respectful inferences. Similarly during one of the difficult periods he had entertained some team member with an ancient story about a willow tree; in the 'four clean-ups' this was taken as an attack on Mao, whose first wife was named *Yang*, meaning willow.

On another occasion he told some team members of a dream he had had. It was after his sister drowned in the People's Canal and his mother insisted that he go looking for her body. He followed the stream for five days but was unsuccessful. When he came back, with this matter wandering in his mind he dreamt about his sister. In his dream she walked along the riverbank and called to say that she was playing there and would be back soon. The very next day her body was found at a place called Five Trees in Mianzhu county and was returned to them. He thought it quite a coincidence, but now his attackers said he spread superstition about the power of dreams. In the same vein they also pointed out that he still followed the Confucian tradition by having a family clan tablet in his living-room.

Hearing all these things from his cousin, Wang Daoquan became depressed. For days he reviewed the past, wrestling with his conscience. He talked things over with his family, his wife and mother who gave him encouragement. Finally he decided to stand firm and not give in to the pressure. He would not confess to being superstitious or to reviling the party, because it was not factually true. Practically everyone in the village had an altar to their ancestors, it was a matter of respect not superstition. If some of his stories could be interpreted in different ways there still ought to be room for a sense of humour. Nor would he admit to taking Y276 from the collective or any grain. He figured perhaps he had taken Y100 over the years for which he would apologize and offer repayment. And of course he would express regret for those occasions when he had been harsh or unkind and would pledge to do better.

When called before a mass meeting of the fifty-nine families in his team in an effort to force him to return the money, Wang could hardly control a nervous shaking of his hands and clasped them tightly behind his back as he stood before the crowd. The leftist group, encouraged by the work team, were on their feet shouting examples of his misdeeds but Wang, head slightly bowed to show humility, kept silent or shook his head in rejection of their taunts. Asked to make a self-confession he stepped forward slightly to show confidence, glanced at his wife and made a brief statement:

> Commune members have been encouraged to say what they know, what they've heard and what they've guessed. I have used a little more than Y100 belonging to the collective. This is illegal. I am sorry and will repay it. The comrades of the work team are asking for more but it is not according to the facts.

It was an impressive display of character for which many team members secretly admired him, but no one spoke in his support. It was the time for confrontation.

The work team was not satisfied and determined to bring him before a mass meeting of the whole brigade. There political and ideological questions were added to the charges, but Wang stuck to his confession. He was unable to 'pass the gate'. The brigade supported the work team; they voted Wang into the third category, stripped him of his post as team leader and forced him to repay the larger amount. Then the work team, fearing that production might drop without Wang's leadership and wanting to make clear that he had not become 'an enemy of the people', announced that it would propose to the commune committee that he be eligible as a deputy-leader of the team.

As if this were not enough humiliation for Wang the work team had more ideas for the future of No. 5 production team. It wanted to leaven the party group which he led with new blood by encouraging a number of leftists to apply for party membership. This was according to party policy which held that no collective could stand still and remain healthy. Eventually the work team sponsored four young men to join the party and together with the existing five members they were to form the leadership core of the team. These included, as well as cousin Wang, two brothers, Zeng Fanjing, aged thirty, and Zeng Fanbao, aged twenty-one, and Huang Kaiquan, aged nineteen, all three of whom were 'outsiders', not belonging to any of the clans in the village.

This selection passed over two women leftists who were engaged to be married outside the village as well as two other male activists who might have had a claim except for personal shortcomings. They were not considered up to the standard for a party member.

One, Song Faxi, vice-chairman of the Poor and Lower Middle Peasants' Association, was a soft, willing, uncontentious, sheepish sort of person. As chairman Wang explained:

> He does just as you say. If you say this is a circle, he will agree that it's a circle; if you say it is a square, he will say it's a square; if you say one, he will not say two. Song is a good friend of mine but in our party we don't bring up the kind of person who has no ideas or thoughts of his own, who could not support his own opinions.

The other person was the one who invented the 'dog-officer' nickname for team leader Wang, but cousin Wang warned the work team that if he made application it would not even pass at the brigade level because he was too self-centred, had a tendency to factionalism and 'his hands and feet were not clean', meaning that he too stole things from the collective and had pick-pocketed people on the high street in Junction. Moreover, his father had been a landlord in another village. How could he be admitted into the party?

Before the work team finished its task it had enlarged the Communist Party branch from twenty-four to forty members in the whole brigade and established Poor and Lower Middle Peasants' Associations in each of the teams. The latter had power to play a continuing supervisory role over the team cadres.

In this fumbling, sometimes errant, fashion the village followed along Mao's path to keep the revolution going, to check the emergence of a socialist bureaucratic class prone to function as a law unto itself. While the process illustrated the continued presence of personal ambition, residual clan loyalties, and economic self-interest, it also showed how more selfless political and ideological commitments could be encouraged and strengthened as the village struggled to renew itself.

Fifteen years later brigade party secretary, Jiang Wenguang, who was the accountant at the time, looked back with an appreciative eye at the 'four clean-ups' and its results for the Communist Party.

> Some criticisms of the masses might not be true to the facts. In one's past work one must have offended someone and as a result a few people gave unfounded criticisms. But the achievements of the movement were great. It was a good thing.

Jiang believed the movement touched the innermost soul of those who had made mistakes.

Through this movement, it was clear what is right and what is wrong in ideology, politics, economics and organization, and the embezzlers, grafters, inveterate speculators and profiteers now set their mind to working in the fields.

Jiang stressed the therapeutic effect of integrating criticism with self-confession:

The cadres were asked to believe in themselves, to educate themselves, liberate themselves and after this those of us who were good or comparatively good could join the struggle without any burdens; we could march with light packs as we continued our work as cadres. Those who were proved to be bad were overthrown. The leadership at all levels was put on a sound footing and that made the masses and cadres more closely linked.

Jiang said that in elections held shortly afterwards most of the cadres were re-elected, including team leader Wang Daoquan, but that without the cleansing effect of the 'four clean-up' movement 'there would have been many more twists and turns during the Cultural Revolution because it was brought about in a rush'.

The Cultural Revolution to which he referred began in Beijing in the summer of 1966, overlapping the 'four clean-up' movement. It was launched by Mao as an escalation of the Socialist Education Movement by employing new methods. During the autumn it made little impression on the Sichuan countryside which was already preoccupied with the 'four clean-ups'. Then one day in early December student Red Guards from Chengdu arrived in Shifang county to spread news of the new movement. The 'four clean-up' cadres from Qionglai, realizing some important change was coming, came to a quick decision that this was no time to be so far from home.

'The work team left the village suddenly one night', recalled cousin Wang. 'We were not sure what happened.' It was past midnight when the chairman of the Poor and Lower Middle Peasants' Association was awakened to be informed that the work team would depart before dawn.

The haste created a temporary sense of alarm. The new supervisory organ of village politics had hardly got itself established and here were its patrons proposing to disappear in the middle of the night. The whole village, Wang feared, would be convulsed with laughter next morning.

Determined to put a good face on the matter cousin Wang roused his executive colleagues to send the work team off as if it had all been planned. 'We saw them to the edge of the village', he said. 'It was cold that morning; it was in the winter, freezing cold and our teeth were chattering.' Cousin Wang, now a party member as well as chairman of the Poor and Lower Middle Peasants' Association, felt just a little unnerved by the thought of his new responsibilities as he watched the eight members of the work team, bedrolls tied to their backs, disappear down the railway embankment and fade into the early morning mists.

10

THE CULTURAL REVOLUTION: 1966–76

After Mao died many Chinese described the Cultural Revolution as 'the so-called cultural revolution'. It has also been pictured as 'a power struggle at the top' to determine who would succeed Mao, as 'ten years of chaos', as 'the folly of an ageing leader, a throwback to feudal despotism', or more positively as an effort 'to create revolutionary successors'. Perhaps in the end, when it got out of control, it became a mixture of all these things.

But in the beginning it was different. The manifesto of August 1966 that launched the Cultural Revolution set the goal of starting a new and deeper stage of the socialist revolution emphasizing proletarian culture.[1] For Mao felt that, although the former ruling class had been overthrown, its members continued to use the 'old ideas, old culture, old customs and old habits' of the exploiting classes to corrupt the masses, capture their minds and to try to stage a comeback. As for how to go about creating proletarian culture, Mao believed that in the main the masses had to discover it for themselves. It could not be done for them by others, there were no short cuts.

However, to encourage the movement he chose to activate students in the high schools and universities. In response to Mao's manifesto, the students quickly formed themselves into detachments of Red Guards and began spreading the news about his ideas as they understood them.

Before long China's great cities were in turmoil. In Chongqing, just 200 miles from Shifang county, rival factions of Red Guards engaged in bitter argument, all claiming to be the best followers of Mao. Eventually they went so far as to raid the military arsenals and take up arms in order to seize power from the Communist Party headquarters. Artillery shells volleyed across the Yangtze River, Red Guard snipers and bloody street fighting killed thousands of people. Although the provincial capital, Chengdu, remained relatively calm, the mayhem in Chongqing and other provincial cities in 1967 assumed the dimensions of a civil war and was only quelled by the army in 1968.

The school gate at MaGaoqiao (Ma Gao bridge) village in 1981 with the leaders of No. 5 Production Team. Wang Daoquan, team leader for 25 stormy years, is third from left. Note: All photographs are from Author's private collection unless otherwise designated.

*Liao Lixiu, militant young woman's
leader at the time of land reform, as
a widow in 1984. (page 19).*

*Alongside their thatched home Widow Liao's family tend to their private
plots. This private sector provided about 40% of the peasants annual income
during the collective period.*

The famous People's Canal as it flows through MaGaoqiao village providing vital irrigation water for cropland. (pages 32-34).

Old photograph showing the tedious man-powered paddle wheel method of irrigation used at MaGaoqiao as late as the 1960's.

Leaders of the Poor and Lower Middle Peasant's Association at MaGaoqiao in 1981. From left, Zhou Yuquan, Liao Wenping and Deng Yuanming.

Zhang Jinghe, middle peasant and village head 1951 to 1978, dressed for winter.

Former village landlord, Shi Shufu, who returned in 1961 to tell his story after five years in a prison camp for counter- revolutionaries. (page 61).

Twice a week on market day the sound of bargaining voices surges along Junction high street as crowds of peasants sell their wares and provide services to each other. (page 23).

Stephen and Lena Endicott by the imposing main gate to Junction People's Commune which carries the slogan "Serve the people," in Mao Zedong's calligraphy. (page 68).

Banners raised to encourage the collective spirit, commune members are digging the Red Cliff Canal in the winter of 1967. (page 74.) – Shifang County Archives.

Li Shouhui of Qionglai County led a work team into MaGaoqiao village in 1966 to organize the socialist education movement.

Train No. 704 puffs out of Junction Station on the railway built during the Great Leap Forward in 1959-1960. (pages 51,53).

Reclaiming land from the White Fish riverbed in the 1970 slack season to create the commune orchard. (pages 77-79). – Shifang County Archives.

"Grasp revolution . . ." at the White Fish River construction site in Junction People's Commune in 1971. A youth leader speaks, waving the little red book, Quotations of Chairman Mao. *–Shifang County Archives.*

Liao Wenfang, a farmer and later village accountant as secretary of the party branch at MaGaoqiao in 1985, relaxing with his cup of tea.

Driving pigs to market when Shifang became a successful "Dazhai-type" county for pig-raising in 1971. (pages 121-3.) – Shifang County Archives.

Accompanied by a portrait of Chairman Mao (centre) and the slogan, "We must grasp grain production tightly," peasants transplant rice seedlings, Spring 1969. (page 127). – Shifang County Archives.

City-educated youth take part in a literacy campaign in 1974. Wall poster says: "Down with capitalism, boldly build socialism." – Shifang County Archives.

Members of the Communist youth league in No. 5 Production Team at MaGaoqiao in 1981, led by team leader Wang's daughter, Zhouzhi, centre front.

Formerly of the rich peasant class, Zhang Guofu became head teacher at MaGaoqiao school.

Brother and sister help with farm work during two-hour school lunch break, 1984. The girl is wearing a Mao badge on her coat.

The full-day nursery school at MaGaoqiao with teacher Liao Mozhi, aged seventeen.

Hanging noodles out to dry.

The grist mill and noodle factory of No. 5 Team is an eight-member co-operative. (pages 213-14).

This gaunt-looking structure belongs to one of Junction People's Commune's thriving rural enterprises. The electro-metallurgy plant, begun in 1979, employed 205 people by 1986. (page 90).

*Daoist layman, Li Dangdang,
right, burns "spirit money" before
interment of the ashes of deceased
in the township burying ground in
1984. (page 209).*

A village funeral procession. The bolts of cloth are gifts of neighbours.

Practising the village dragon for competition with other villages.

The dragons meet on the high street in Junction, 1981.

Home-made poster pasted on a door during Spring Festival celebrations in 1984. (pages 3-4).

The six female members of the Communist party at MaGaoqiao in 1984.
Front (left to right) comrades Zhang, Yo and Shi. Back row: Li, Zhang and
Zhong Tingyin. (page 185).

The new brick and tile house of team leader Wang in 1983.

Team leader Wang Daoquan operates one of seven hand tractors in the village. Owned collectively until 1982, the tractors were sold off to the highest bidders during a wave of privatization sponsored by the Communist Party. (page 137).

Open air village meeting to prepare for county and township elections in 1984. (page 148).

But at Junction People's Commune things did not go that far. Violence was minimal, anti-climactic compared to what happened in the cities. For a year after the youthful Red Guards stormed into the commune headquarters, in January 1967, to seize power from the Communist Party (which was paralysed from then on, unable to conduct its business or to hold any meetings for five years), there was rivalry among the contending groups and uncertainty about their role. Finally, in 1968, the rebels, revolutionary cadres, and representatives of the commune members formed a coalition with an army man acting as moderator.

This revolutionary committee took the initiative and led the commune until 1982. Its strong, self-reliant and co-operative efforts in basic farmland reconstruction and other capital projects, which clearly gained their impetus from the Cultural Revolution, are the subject of previous chapters. Nor did the revolutionary committee neglect current production. During the years of greatest turmoil, from 1967 to 1971, the value of production, as shown in Table G, rose by almost 30 per cent. In view of later doubts and negative images surrounding the Cultural Revolution as a time of chaos and 'naked power struggle', it is worth noting that Junction People's Commune was able to provide for its members' on-going needs and that production levels there were not unique.

The claims of Mao's successors that China's economy would have made even greater strides had it not been for the political movement can neither be proved nor disproved. But the State Statistical Bureau affirms that during the years 1967 to 1971 there were 'significant increases' in economic development.[2] What is more, the production figures referred to in its report do not take into account much of the communal work of this time. No estimates or published statistics exist for the billions of labour days invested by the peasants in basic farmland capital construction from one end of the country to the other during the Cultural Revolution. If such calculations are ever made it is safe to say that they will dwarf the

TABLE G
Production during the Cultural Revolution
Junction People's Commune
Unit: '000 yuan

Year	1965	1966	1967	1968	1969	1970	1971	1972
Value	2,428	2,431	2,555	2,742	2,841	3,137	3,097	3,380

Source: Junction People's Commune *Accounts 1949–85*, pp. 29–30. Figures are for total output value in the collective sector in agriculture, forestry, animal husbandry, fishery and sidelines.

pyramids, the Great Wall or any other previous human construction in scale and social purpose many times over.

The political movement at Junction People's Commune that was the impetus for these constructions, began in December 1966 when retired secretary Deng, who at that time was director of the commune, received a circular on the Cultural Revolution from the central committee in Beijing.[3] Not realizing what was in store, he started to implement the directive without delay.

The sun blinked through the clouds on a crisp December morning as Deng, accompanied by two young friends from the high street, set out by bicycle to make the rounds of the thirteen brigades. The trio were in good humour. In the fields on either side of them shoots of winter wheat and rape seed had already popped their heads through the earth and as they pedalled along the bumpy road the cry of the magpie, the bird of happiness in China, could be heard through the bamboo groves. The slack season had begun and the peasants were looking forward to the year-end income distribution.

When Deng and his comrades reached the first settlement they found no shortage of candidates for the Red Guards, especially as Beijing radio had announced that secondary schools, as well as colleges and universities, would be on vacation for the next six months so that students could take part in making revolution.

Not too clear on just what the central slogan, 'grasp revolution, promote production' meant, at least the first part, Deng could not explain it plainly or in detail to the young villagers. But in casting his eye over the central committee document he noticed some new things.

Red Guards could join the militia, it said, although it forbade armed struggle. The revolution aimed to transform the countryside into a big school for the study of Mao Zedong's Thought, and to foster energetically the new ideas and new habits of the proletariat such as participation in field labour by the cadres. This practice, if 'thoroughly enforced', read the directive, could help overcome the *old* habits of commandism and bureaucracy characteristic of exploiters. Hints for definite action such as this one were rare in central documents, since to have said more would contradict Mao's thesis that it was up to the masses themselves, through their own social practice and experiment, to discover the meaning of proletarian values and culture.

Deng's efforts led to the formation of an organization with the cumbersome name, Rebel Headquarters of the Big School for Mao Zedong Thought, which established its headquarters on Junction high street. It also formed sub-branches out in the brigades and production teams, calling them worker-peasant-soldier detachments.

A twenty-one-year-old by the name of Liao Moquan, a well-built youth who liked to create an off-hand, swashbuckling impression by wearing his coat jacket loosely thrown over his shoulders, became one of the main leaders of the Rebel Headquarters. He lived in MaGaoqiao village.

Seventeen years later, in 1984, it was not easy to arrange a meeting. He did not turn up for the first appointment and for the second his wife came running after him to drag him away, saying that he would only get into more trouble. A few minutes later, however, he did reappear and granted an interview.

'It's not that I am afraid to speak with you', he said. 'It's just that in thinking about my activity in the Cultural Revolution I feel some regret, there were many senseless actions without positive significance. Since then I have never taken up any leading position, not even in the militia.' Now he was in business on his own, driving a tractor.

In the light of hindsight, Liao said that, compared to the 'four clean-ups', the purpose of the movement was never very clear. But its novelty appealed to him and he did things by following others.

At first, since they thought the revolution in their brigade was too sluggish, a dozen of the worker-peasant-soldier rebels under Liao's leadership took Y200 from the collective and went off to other counties to pick up experience. After a week of staying in hotels and eating in restaurants their money had disappeared and they returned to report on the things they had seen and heard.

Following this they pushed aside the Poor and Lower Middle Peasants' Association, whom they called 'little crawling insects', and started to organize more basic study/criticism meetings. Snubbing the Poor and Lower Middle Peasants' Association, although politically indefensible, was for Liao Moquan already quite a daring repudiation of old Confucian customs, since cousin Wang, the chairman of that organization, was not only a relative (brother-in-law) but also seven years his senior.

To create the right atmosphere at their meetings the rebels purchased coloured paper, brushes and ink to make posters of Mao's sayings and militant slogans – 'leniency to those who confess their crimes; severity to those who refuse', and 'carry the Cultural Revolution through to the end'. Scores of people came to rallies wearing Red Guard armbands and carrying the little book of quotations from Mao which had been distributed during the 'four clean-ups' by the militia.

Since most of the villagers over the age of twenty-five were illiterate, the rebels conducted readings in unison of the 'three constantly-read articles' by Mao, *Serve the people, In memory of Norman Bethune*, and *The foolish old man who removed the mountains*, which illustrated some of the new values of the proletariat. And in their smaller study classes they read aloud some of Mao's analytical essays, such as *Analysis of the classes in Chinese society* and *On correcting mistaken ideas in the party*.

Many people were hearing complex texts by Mao for the first time, and the ability of the young rebels to present his writings considerably moved the older peasants, raising the prestige of the Rebel Headquarters in their eyes. This intellectual capital helped the rebels push aside the largely illiterate leaders of the Peasants' Association and enabled them to become something of a match for the party cadres.

The spearhead of the rebels' attack in No. 8 Brigade turned first against the brigade's leaders, especially party secretary Yao who had earlier got off so lightly for wining and dining visiting tractor-drivers. With shouts and chants they brought him to mass meetings crowned with a dunce's hat, and they put some former landlords on the stage beside him for further humiliation. They fired questions demanding to know where he got the grain for all his household sideline activities – raising hens and ducks and pigs and other items. They forced him to kneel on the stage and admit that the furniture and consumer items he had bought and the more than average amounts of liquor he drank were evidence of his love of a soft life. Had he taken any of the collective's money to buy these things? They weren't able to prove anything and therefore didn't draw any conclusions about him, but at the end of the meeting they would go up and hang a sign around his neck saying 'I am a capitalist roader'.

It was exciting to confront the top village official but the results were superficial and unsatisfying; the young people felt frustrated with their lack of success in combating the 'four olds'.

After this they started entering and searching the homes of those under suspicion of clinging to old customs and old beliefs. This was illegal, and expressly forbidden by central committee documents, but the other rebel groups were doing it and Liao said his group felt they had to prove that they were just as daring. When Liao's rebels had collected a cartload of old books and sent them to the commune, worried villagers starting pulling down their ancestor altars, getting rid of their classical books and burning anything else that might be thought of as belonging to the past.

Over on the high street in Junction where Liao was secretary of his Rebel Headquarters, rival groups of Red Guards with links to the provincial capital tried to outdo each other and were even more active than his organization. Every market day they pushed commune director Deng and other cadres out on to the high street, placed tall paper hats on their heads and forced them to shout out their mistakes and crimes while facing the people in the market. Red Guards organized strikes in some of the factories.[4] Other rebels wanted to pull down every cadre, even those they could not prove to be capitalist roaders. In opposing the 'four olds', these anarchists made a great sensation by publicly burning the valuable costumes of the local Sichuan opera troupe along with the yellow robes and red caps of the Daoist priests.

As retired commune secretary Deng recounted:

> At the hottest time we cadres had to hide ourselves like cats or else be hit. If we supported one rebel faction the other faction would beat us. But if we said that they were both revolutionaries we would be accused of eclecticism and of stirring the mud (blurring the line between right and wrong). Commune members had to eat so we quietly busied ourselves in directing production work.

According to Liao, his own group criticized the other rebels for going too far.

> The Cultural Revolution put people's thinking into disorder. It seemed people could disobey the rules and policies and serve their own self-interest. It was contrary to what we were reading in the little book of Chairman Mao's quotations but we could do nothing.

When it came to seizing power by taking over the seals of office in the brigades and communes, and even at the county level, the rebel groups became more violent and began fighting actively among themselves. In one mêlée in February 1967 the director of the personnel office of Shifang county was beaten to death. Similar events on a larger scale took place in other districts. As a result of the terror, the Chengdu Military Garrison went into action that month arresting the rebel leaders and suppressing their organizations as counter-revolutionary.

During this February reverse current, Liao became frightened.

> I knew that it was our turn to be dealt with. All of us rebels were worried. They caught Jiang Wenmao, son of vice-team leader Jiang Tenglin, and locked him up for a while. I ran off to my grandmother's on my mother's side and hid here and there outside the village. I didn't dare come home.

The reverse current of February 1967 virtually ended the rebels' confrontational activity in MaGaoqiao, although it sputtered on in the commune headquarters because no direction came from the upper levels on how to reorganize the administration.

In the cities and factories, Liao explained, the debates were more dynamic and the struggle went on much longer because the urban rebels continued to receive their wages whether they worked or not.[5] But in the countryside where the state was not paymaster the production team and brigade activities were the only sources of income. As Liao put it, pointing to the smokestack half a mile away:

For example in the Chemical Fertilizer Machinery Factory over there, they stopped production for a year to engage in the violent movement, and the workers still got their wages from the bank. But for us things were different, we got no wages from the state. So here only a few of us went out to make revolution and we came back and tried to make the production team give us work points. This made the commune members angry. The older generation wouldn't stand for this. Therefore the Cultural Revolution did not affect production much in the countryside. People had to work in order to eat. We had to be spare-time revolutionaries.

To help solve antagonisms between the rebels and the cadres a Mao Zedong Thought Propaganda Team came from the army to Junction in the first part of 1968. After six months of negotiations the Thought Propaganda Team established a fairly stable commune revolutionary committee with a standing committee of seven members. It included two women, three of the male rebel leaders — one from each faction — and retired secretary Deng as the chairman. This committee started to lead the commune's big development projects in 'learning from Dazhai'.

Before long, however, the new committee ran into trouble when it discovered that one of its rebel members was stealing — to the tune of Y20,000. For this corrupt activity and some sexual misbehaviour the court sentenced him to several years reform through labour.

Such occurrences were common enough in the countryside for the central committee in Beijing to launch another rectification called 'one strike, three antis'. Once again work teams came to the brigades to initiate a campaign to 'strike down the counter-revolutionaries' and 'oppose corruption, stealing and speculation' — called the 'three antis' for short.

In MaGaoqiao's No. 5 production team, where feelings between some of the families were already quite tense as a result of the previous political movements, the campaign had a tragic result for the team's vice-leader, Jiang Tenglin. He had been a team cadre, including a short spell as village head, for twenty years, but since he was not a party member he had escaped heavy criticism during the 'four clean-ups' and became part of the leftist group that took part in criticizing the others. This time, especially as his son had been such an active rebel, he was not so fortunate.

Sitting in wait for him was a woman who could not forget or forgive. She was Lan Guifeng, a modern-day Madame Defarge who, like Madam Defarge, watched and remembered everything. The day she told her story a broad, black velvet head-band secured by a jade-like pin shaded eyes that had a foxy look. Her main complaint was that her husband, who had been armed forces leader in the village at the time of Liberation, was later passed over for promotion. Also she could not reconcile herself to the fact that vice-leader Jiang had got off so lightly in the 'four clean-ups'.

Now she saw her chance and decided to go to the work team with her complaints. As they sat round the table in the brigade headquarters she told them that Jiang had been a member of his relative Jiang Beixiu's armed band and had taken part in robberies at the time of Liberation: since Liberation he had once taken a gun to threaten a peasant; when keeper of the collective storehouse during the Great Leap he had stolen some tobacco and grain and exchanged them for steamed cakes to eat; his son, the rebel Jiang Wenmao, who was a work point recorder had sold some work points to a team member in return for several yuan and the father had not reported it; more recently Jiang had cut down three of the collective's white sandalwood trees for his own purposes and she calculated they were worth Y30 each. Wasn't it time for this thief and criminal to be punished, she asked, her voice rising to a shrill pitch of indignation.

It seems that Jiang knew of Lan Guifeng's animosity towards him. Disturbed by the potential charges she would bring, he began to think out his defence. Anticipating the usual requirements for self-criticism, he realized that there would be some truth in the accusations. It was true that he had taken some things during the Great Leap when his family suffered from hunger, and he would now return Y20 for that. As for the trees, he had permission to cut them down to make a wheelbarrow, but if people objected he would return the three logs. If his son had made a mistake he should be responsible for that himself. About the gun incident, his sister had had an illicit love affair with a man and people were making jokes about this to his face. He became angry, so he took a gun and went to his sister's house where he caught the man. He just told the man not to come around any more. Finally, it was true that he worked as a cook for Jiang Beixiu before Liberation, but he had not engaged in any fighting, he was just a hired hand around the house.

Before Jiang had completed the confession that he planned to make the work team hauled him before a mass meeting of villagers. There he stood silent with his head bent low while all kinds of things, both true and false, were hurled against him, and he never offered to make the reparations which he had in mind. To stir him into action the militia leader, Huang Kaiyao, shouted at him, 'You must be honest. Your problems are serious. Jiang Tenglin, I tell you, you must confess! Think it over seriously.' This was the final straw.

Not used to receiving this kind of talk since he had always been on the other side handing it out, Jiang panicked that afternoon and went to see team leader Wang. 'I can't survive this movement, I can't keep my head up,' he cried. 'What shall I do? I can't explain myself clearly, especially about the Jiang Beixiu connection because the peasants won't listen to me.' He feared that he would be sent to reform through labour.

Wang tried to comfort him saying that his case was still only a contradiction within the ranks of the people, not one between the people and an enemy. He assured him that no decision had been made and pointed out from his own experience that at the stage of exposure people inevitably said all kinds of things. Jiang had been a valued leader of production for twenty years, which everyone knew, so for now he should just admit his wrongdoings and mistakes and listen to the people.

'I asked him not to take it too hard, not to worry,' said Wang, 'but he didn't believe me. That night after supper someone came running over to inform me that Jiang had taken a rope and hanged himself behind the brigade headquarters.'

Wang, greatly upset by this news, had snatched up a large kitchen knife and sprinted out the door. When he reached the scene of the tragedy, a quarter of a mile away, he slashed the cord. But he knew it was already too late. He carried the body of his friend inside and laid it on a table while he went to seek medical help and to inform Jiang's family.

Years later Lan Guifeng remained vengeful. 'He committed suicide to escape punishment', she said without any sense of pity. Wang disagreed. 'He met his death because of his inability to understand the movement properly; his corruption only amounted to Y150 and using the power the collective gave him to cut a few trees.'

The village was shocked at the news of his suicide and after investigation the commune leaders decided that his death was mainly their fault; they had not done their work properly. To mark this conclusion they did not exonerate Jiang, nor did they give him a public funeral because that would call into question the whole process of public confession and rectification. Rather, they affirmed that Jiang had been one of the people, not an enemy, and his problems were relatively small, and they gave his family money to buy a coffin and to help them through their time of grief.

Rectification campaigns such as the 'one strike, three-antis' were a method of forcing leaders to face up to their mistakes and of teaching the public by negative example. They constituted part of the arsenal of pro-letarian democracy to be used from time to time. But they were not the only or even the most important means 'to cut off the tails of capitalism'. More fundamentally the way to curb individualistic, self-serving behav-iour associated with capitalist thinking lay in arranging the ordinary processes of daily work and production in such a way as to encourage the co-operative, sharing attitudes of socialist proletarian ideology.

Two significant measures taken during this time in Junction involved hog marketing and experiments with payment for collective labour. The purpose of the experiments was to reshape and strengthen 'the iron rice bowl', a symbolic term for social security. Although such an objective may appear to be something quite ordinary and straightforward, in practice it proved to be a vastly complex undertaking. An unexpected result of the struggles and debates surrounding 'the iron rice bowl' was that a great cult of Mao took shape, sidetracking rational thought and harming the revolutionary process.

Pigs are vital to the villagers' economy. Except for a brief period during the Great Leap when policy resulted in all livestock being communized, pigs remained part of the family economy. In the family compound it is convenient to feed the animals and make good use of kitchen waste. Pig manure provides fertilizer for the family fields and the sale of full-grown animals brings in Y100 each to provide a major part of the household's annual cash income. The location of the pigs within each family compound also minimizes the spread of swine diseases.

During the Cultural Revolution, however, radicals viewed this system of pig raising as one of the 'tails of capitalism'. This view was not without cause. First of all, not all the peasants had sufficient capital to start raising pigs since it is a costly business. There are expenses in building pens, buying piglets from private breeders, purchasing the grain husks needed to fatten up the animals and gathering the extra fuel required to heat the fodder. About 20 per cent of the villagers could not afford this outlay. To forget about these poor families, said the radicals, would mean forgetting about the revolution.

Furthermore, households often tried to avoid delivering the precious manure to the collective fields; they preferred to use it on their family plots to increase their private income. Instead of 'serving the people', which Mao's writings put forward as a prime tenet of proletarian culture, they were serving themselves. And finally, the pig market engendered attitudes of cunning and deception considered unworthy of a socialist community.

Team leader Wang described how the free market worked.

There are go-betweens on the high street who are very knowledgeable about pigs, and they are able to talk up the good points or gloss over the negative points of a pig, depending on whether it's for the buyer or seller. If you are afraid that your pig might be a little sick and you want to sell it in a hurry, you try to find a go-between. He pulls money from his pocket and seems to be on the verge of buying – all the while bargaining loudly – this is what attracts the third party, who then may jump in and make the purchase just as you wanted, and perhaps at a higher price than you expected. That's the way the pig market worked.

As he dramatized the system Wang, in spite of himself, seemed to find it amusing.

By establishing a co-operative pig market and a published schedule of prices, the commune could eliminate the go-betweens with their questionable ethics and help the inexperienced pig breeders. The obvious place for such a market, in the minds of the commune cadres, was the spacious and not much used grounds of one of the temples on the high street. It would mean the desecration of yet another cultural symbol, but this consideration did not seem to trouble them any more than such matters had concerned a pre-revolutionary generation in these parts. An American missionary, V. H. Donnithorne, noticed this when he came to the area in 1933 looking for a Nestorian Christian stone thought to be dating from the Tang dynasty (900 AD). He observed that, along the fifteen miles of motor road being constructed to connect Shifang with the next county, sixty or seventy watercourses had been bridged over with old monumental stones from which the lettering had first been chiselled smooth. 'Nothing is sacred or precious because of its age or associations in this modern iconoclastic China', he wrote, and he lamented that before 'many of these destructive years have gone by we shall not have an ancient monument left in this country'.[6]

To locate a pig market on temple grounds seemed like a better alternative than using up some precious fertile fields for the purpose, and besides, was not religion one of the 'four olds' that the Cultural Revolution sought to replace? Thus the cadres irreverently decided to turn the Temple of the Myriad Lands and Waters dedicated to the Goddess of Mercy into a pig slaughtering ground.

The new pig market worked well but it still did not solve the problem of those families who could not afford to raise pigs, nor did it get the pig manure on to the collective fields.

The next short-lived experiment, therefore, was to change the system of ownership from private to public pigs. Each village discouraged private pig raising by constructing collective pig pens in which the manure automatically became collective property. Unfortunately these communized pigs cost more to produce. Deprived of the family kitchen scraps, they fattened slowly and epidemics of disease took a higher toll. In addition, the peasants, who lost a good part of their cash income, privately disliked the new system. Pig raising proceeded half-heartedly and soon people in the city had a hard time finding pork in the markets.

Faced with these problems, the government found an effective compromise combining public and private ownership with emphasis on the latter. Families received public grain and work points in return for delivering their pig manure to the collective fields. The boars and breed sows, on the other hand, remained under collective ownership and provided free piglets so that even the poorest families could get into the business. Then, in order to supply households with fodder, an increasing portion of the collective land was used to grow trumpet creeper and turnips. With this approach the state got pork to feed the urban workers, the collective obtained its manure, and the commune members received their cash income. As team leader Wang explained:

> Some narrow-minded commune members tried putting water into the manure they handed in to the collective, keeping their best fertilizer for their private plots, but most people were honest and the system worked well. Our county soon became a Dazhai-type county in raising pigs, with one pig for each *mu* of land as Chairman Mao requested. There was even a report about us in the *People's Daily*![7]

Apart from pig raising, the other matter vital to an 'iron rice bowl' was the creation of an appropriate system for rewarding labour. This was a more difficult and challenging task. The underlying issue here was the degree of egalitarianism and other programmes of a socialist welfare nature which were consistent with maintaining incentives to work productively.

Many structural factors influenced work morale, such as low procurement prices for agricultural produce, or the existence of a surplus labour force that could not migrate elsewhere to find gainful employment. The national development strategy of the government, including limitations on urban growth, imposed these restrictions and could not be changed by the villagers.

Given these constraints, the main contradiction in the village arose from the fact that for every able-bodied member working in the collective fields there were one or more dependant children or older persons. The uneven distribution of these dependants among the various families — some having two or three dependants while others had none — required a system that could meet everyone's basic needs and yet reward the able-bodied workers fairly for their labour. Equity and incentive co-existed uneasily in the village as a unity of opposites.

In the earliest days of the commune, in 1958, everyone received free food and medical care. These elements began to shape the 'iron rice bowl'. Those able to take part in labour earned, in addition, a small monthly wage in cash. The wages rose in seven grades — from Y2 to Y9 — according to work responsibility. But the collapse of the Great Leap undermined the free supply system as being too egalitarian and too communistic for China's level of development, and the search for a different system began.

The people's commune regime became more family-centred once again, but it still maintained an 'iron rice bowl' for it members. Every household received a guaranteed distribution of grain and other goods from the collective, irrespective of the number of work days that its able-bodied members managed to accumulate, but records were kept. If the family did not have enough work points to pay for the basic food grain it would have a long-term debt to the production team until such time as it became self-sufficient. In any given year about 20 per cent of the families went into debt to the collective (see Appendix, Table 9).

In spite of the existence of some household debt, the new 'iron rice bowl' of the people's communes was quite substantial. It included up to 80 per cent of the grain divided up within the village. In addition, there were other distributed goods such as cooking oil, salt, sugar and firewood that together provided the basic necessities of life. As Table 6 in the Appendix shows, the 'iron rice bowl' (basic grain ration plus other agricultural products) of No. 5 production team at MaGaoqiao in 1982 took up about 27 per cent of village income. When the more egalitarian policies of the Cultural Revolution prevailed, the guaranteed supply occupied as much as one-third of the total income.

This impressive system of social security – a guaranteed income through interest-free loans for those temporarily short of labour power – represented the egalitarian principle of socialism. Older villagers strongly approved and it was the pride of the Communist Party members. It constituted an assurance that nobody would have to beg from relatives or seek philanthropic benefactors in order to survive a time of accident, illness or other hardship.

Within the 'iron rice bowl' system of social welfare, incentives for the more productive members of the village were not neglected. The remaining village grain (from 20 to 35 per cent depending upon party policy) and all income from the sale of cash crops went as a reward for labour in the fields or for pig raising. Table 6 shows the fine tuning of payment for specific tasks. Grain rewards were allotted for each private pig, for manure handed in to the collective, and for each work day in the fields. The cash was similarly distributed to each worker according to five different categories of his or her labour.

In addition to a share of the collective distribution, there also existed the incentive of the private plot of each family. The produce generated here is entirely tax-free, creating an additional inducement for individual effort. At MaGaoqiao villagers estimate that 40 per cent of family income is derived from the self-consumption or sale of pork, vegetables, and other products of household sideline activity such as sewing, poultry raising or basket weaving that are based on the private plot.

An economy with a ratio of 60 per cent from the collective sector and 40 per cent from the private sector appears reasonable at first sight, an effective combination of social need and material incentives in the context of China's aim to build a socialist society. In reality, however, the collective sector proved quite difficult to administer. As the Communist Party groped its way along searching for solutions, several competing models of organization were tested. Prolonged and sometimes fascinating debates over the detailed workings of these models engrossed commune members for several years and as the struggle became more heated it lead to the creation of a hero-cult around the figure of Mao.

In 1962, after the Great Leap, Junction People's Commune adopted a system of labour organization called 'three contracts, one reward'. Under this system the production team formed several smaller groups of twenty to thirty farm workers (about twenty families) and allocated some land and equipment to each of them. Negotiated contracts with each group covered payment for labour, other costs and expected output. These were the three contracts. The reward took the form of work point credits or work days whose value was calculated after the size of the harvest became known.

Team leader Wang Daoquan gave an example to explain how this operated. As team leader he agreed to credit a work group with 400 labour days if they raised a ton of tobacco leaves within certain cost limits (usually 30 per cent of the crop value) on ten *mu* of average quality land. (The land was divided into three basic grades according to its quality.) If the group overfulfilled its contract, the reward was a credit of extra labour days. An underfulfilled contract resulted in the loss of labour days.

With an agreed quota of labour days in hand, the small work group then met to distribute these as work points (ten points constituted a full labour day, five points half a day) to its members on a piece-rate basis for preparing the land, sowing, weeding, spraying, irrigating and harvesting, according to the intensity of physical labour and skill involved. Those who took the harder jobs worth more points got higher pay. In this way incentives to work harder appeared clear enough.

However, since farm work, unlike a factory assembly line, requires an infinite variety of tasks whose results often do not become apparent until weeks or months later, the work group leader could not judge the quality or quantity of work done by each member with any precision. As a result, differences of opinion over entitlement to work points could lead team members into hours of argument in long meetings. One peasant summed up the attitude toward such meetings by saying, 'Doing a little extra work won't kill me, but this damn staying up all night will!'[8]

To avoid these complications some team cadres in Junction commune in the mid-1960s quietly made contracts with individual households. After agreeing to a contract the household, rather than the cadre, took responsibility for planting, nurturing and harvesting the crop. Following the harvest the household exchanged the contracted crop for an agreed number of labour days. Meanwhile the household could arrange its own schedule for work. The family could also tend its private plot during the work day and sell its surpluses on the market without interference. This method was simple and the benefits attractive. It was a version of the 'three freedoms and one contract' discussed earlier.

But the central leadership opposed such methods on the grounds of political principle and for practical reasons. In the opinion of Mao and others, the household contract system too much resembled the old landlord-tenant relationship, with the production team now taking the place of the landlord. Socialized agriculture aimed to replace that kind of relationship. Mao wanted a more public form of production where labour group members democratically elected their leaders, where leaders' rewards took no more than 1 or 2 per cent of the community income, and where they would be expected to participate in manual labour along with everyone else. He pushed for open account books which representatives of the commune could inspect at regular intervals as a check on corruption.

Apart from these ideological aspects, other practical drawbacks to the household contract system existed. Small-scale household farming would make it harder to mobilize the peasants for construction projects and for the mechanization of agriculture; it would be easy for families to under-report their harvest, conceal their surpluses and sell them privately, possibly creating an uncontrolled black market; and, perhaps most worrisome, the differences in family resources could lead to greater inequalities and a revival of class divisions. These were all questions of deep concern to the Communist Party. Mao believed that if a system of contracting of land to individual households gained momentum, it would represent a defeat for the agrarian revolution and would lead to the emergence of a new rich peasant class capable of exploiting others.

Mao discovered an alternative to this system which at the same time avoided arguments over work points. This was the manner in which the famous Dazhai brigade in Shanxi province rewarded its labour. During the Cultural Revolution Mao, through party channels as well as in the public media, urged everyone to learn from them.

Under this pressure Junction People's Commune sent a delegation to Shanxi to see how Dazhai operated. They found that Dazhai rewarded its labourers on the basis of a personal rating and time worked rather than piece-work. Although quite unfamiliar to the Sichuan peasants, they became interested since Dazhai looked as if it was prospering.

The name for the Dazhai system was 'fixed-rate flexible-assessment'. Through discussion production team members classified themselves into grades from one to ten on the basis of strength, skill, diligence and work attitude (political consciousness, willingness to shoulder difficult tasks). This fixed rating became a person's allotment of work points for the day's work, no matter what task he or she did. A young able-bodied woman could theoretically receive eight or nine points, while a male in the top category got ten points for a full day's labour. These personal norms could move upwards or downwards periodically according to self-assessment by each member and collective evaluation by the group. But rather than meeting at the end of each work day, such adjustment took place once every month or two when everyone could take the overall picture more objectively into account.

After the Junction delegation returned from Dazhai and popularized the concept, the commune adopted this work point system. It lasted for five years from 1967 to about 1971. At Junction the peasants called it the circle work point system. If a team member showed up for field work the work point recorder put a circle opposite his or her name for a full day or half a circle for a half day. At the end of the month the accountant multiplied the number of circles each member had by their fixed norm and this gave them their work point total. The system reduced arguments and simplified the accounting procedures.

To succeed, however, the 'fixed-rate, flexible-assessment' system depended upon a high level of social – or as the Chinese called it – political consciousness among the members. If group meetings were poorly led or ineffective, a lazy person could go out and stand in the field gossiping half the day without doing much and still get his or her circle, since rewards were not directly linked to results as in the piece-work contract system. An old man over seventy, according to retired commune secretary Deng, 'might get more work point credits than a young able-bodied man in his twenties because the former could be considered politically more advanced. In this case the young man would lose his enthusiasm for work.'

In these circumstances the cult of Mao grew in 1967 at Junction and elsewhere. Reference to Mao became a way of increasing everyone's political consciousness. As the Red Guards popularized Mao's teachings about self-reliance, hard struggle, aiming high and concern for the collective's welfare, commune leaders used his sayings to try to boost enthusiasm for production. They understood these qualities as the meaning of proletarian culture. Stimulated by the idealization of Mao as the 'great leader, great teacher, great supreme commander and great helmsman' in national newspapers and radio stations, local leaders elevated his *Quotations* into a kind of scripture. As retired secretary Deng put it:

At meetings, the Red Guards used the *Quotations* no matter what was being discussed. Rewards given at all levels were copies of the *Quotations* or Mao badges and they were handed out year after year. Chairman Mao's portraits and statues were everywhere, as well as a basketful of *Quotations* in every household whether people could read or not. We made Chairman Mao into a god, but how could he be aware of the minutest details of everything as he sat in his room in Beijing?

Ironically the apogee of Mao's deification came after he attempted to check its growth. Following a rowdy battle among students in Qinghua University in Beijing in 1968, Mao made a gift of mangoes to a group of workers and peasants who had gone there to curb the excesses of the student Red Guards. Like some Paris fashion fad, the mango fruit suddenly became a symbol of the latest twist in the Cultural Revolution.[9]

In Junction Commune veteran leaders, tired of all the haranguing by student Red Guards, seized upon the mango symbol to put them down too and to suppress their irritating behaviour. Retired secretary Deng led a solemn procession along the highway with flags and drums and portraits of Mao to pass a mango from brigade to brigade, from one commune to the next. With Deng cradling the sacred fruit in crimson cloth, arms outstretched, commune members lined the route shouting out slogans on the Chairman's latest instructions.

It was an incongruous sight. A cultural revolution that had been launched with the principle that 'the only method is for the masses to liberate themselves, and any method of doing things in their stead must not be used', resorted to the most archaic forms of emperor worship, calling upon people to offer their loyal hearts to one man acclaimed to be the source of all political and moral wisdom.

Although the statues of clay buddhas, ghosts and demons had been torn down and their temple grounds turned to secular purposes, the cult of personality that thrived around Mao showed that the embers of religious fundamentalism were by no means extinct in the countryside. Ancient rituals found a reincarnation in the guise of political fanaticism, often in the very same people who earlier had been such iconoclasts. 'If someone shouted the wrong slogan', said an embarrassed retired secretary Deng, 'he could be sent to prison.'

Such anachronisms surrounding the 'cult of genius' and playing on the superstitious habits of the peasantry were tolerated by Mao in his political struggles and were most vigorously promoted by Lin Biao, the defence minister who hoped to succeed him, but they were not a uniquely Chinese spectacle. As Karl Marx once wrote when commenting on the case of mid-nineteenth-century France under Napoleon III:[10]

At the very time when men appeared engaged in revolutionizing things and themselves, in bringing about what never was before, at such epochs of revolutionary crisis do they anxiously conjure up into their service the spirit of the past . . . to enact a new historic scene in such time-honoured disguise and with such borrowed language.

Eventually Mao himself put the damper on this new kind of buddha worship. The small statues of Mao were put away in 1970 and the wearing of Mao badges discouraged. According to retired secretary Deng:

In his talk with Edgar Snow, Mao joked about the large outdoor statues of himself 'in the winter evenings when it is frosty and the people are warmly sleeping in their homes I have to stand in the cold outside and in the summer when it is hot I have no shade'.

The practical effect of limiting the cult of Mao in the commune was the abandonment of the circle work point system. This happened in 1971 after Defence Minister Lin Biao, the principal supporter of the Mao cult, fled the country following a failed *coup d'état* and died in a plane crash on the steppes of Mongolia. The denunciation of Lin as an anti-Mao conspirator trying to usurp supreme state power came as a great surprise to the peasants. 'Only a few days earlier we were praising him and wishing him long life', said team leader Wang. 'We could hardly believe the news from the central committee.' Their confidence was shaken and, without the intense ideological pressure of Lin's ultra-leftism, the peasants quickly turned away from the Dazhai system.

Junction commune reverted to experimenting with its earlier 'three contracts, one reward' method, constantly searching for techniques to make people more responsible for the result of their work. To achieve this aim production teams formed smaller production groups so that members would feel more intimately accountable to each other for their productivity. In No. 5 production team at MaGaoqiao, for example, where the eighty-three families formerly worked in three parts, by 1980 they had seven labour groups. Each group sought ways to link individual payment to work done by offering more rewards and forfeits.

The social and economic results of the system can be seen in Table H which shows the pattern of growth and distribution of collective income to the households. In 1980, especially, a large measure of equality remained, consistent with the socialist values of the communes. The income of most families clusters around the team average of Y195 *per capita* and the gap between the best paid and the lowest is not much more than four times. By 1982, with output and incomes growing rapidly, it is noticeable that the difference between the top and the bottom had increased to about six times, reflecting a

TABLE H
Distribution of collective income by household
No. 5 Production Team, MaGaoqiao, 1980–2

| Yuan per capita | Income level | | | | | | | | | | Total |
	<100	<150	<200	<250	<300	<350	<400	<450	<500	>500	
No. of households (1980)	9	9	36	21	4	2	2	–	–	–	(83)
No. of households (1982)	–	10	10	15	20	14	9	5	3	4	(90)

Source: No. 8 Brigade, Junction People's Commune, list of 'Distribution of Income to Households in No. 5 Production Team,' 1980 and 1982.

new central party policy stressing individual incentives and criticizing egalitarian thinking.

In view of the argument which is being presented here about the strong commitment of the people's communes to distributive justice, one further comment on the information presented in Table H is in order. It is about the degree of polarization suggested by nine families receiving under Y100 in 1980. This is surprising and appears to undermine the argument. A close investigation of these nine 'deficit' households, however, provides a reminder of the limitations of statistical information in reflecting social reality.

Two of the nine are widowed grandmothers. They prefer to live on their own with a separate kitchen, but in addition to the basic grain ration from the team they receive subsidies from their married sons who live next door. By village standards these grandmothers live quite comfortably and are not considered as being in deficit. They are also more independent. The move to her own place was initiated by one in order to escape the family arguments as to which grandchild she would look after. Five other households are headed by women who have husbands working in industry with state salaries so that, although they may have deficits in work points, their household incomes are considerably higher than those indicated by the village accounts. The remaining two households in this bottom category are of bachelors. One of these married and moved away; since he received work points and income for only part of the year he appears in the statistics as a poor household. The other one is a 'poor' bachelor of fifty-four who is a puzzle to his fellow villagers. In the past he took part in field work irregularly, wore ragged clothes, and the production team paid for his medical care and helped him with his deficits. Then during the Spring Festival of 1980 he suddenly appeared dressed in new trousers and leather shoes, and he had bought a table and Y18 worth of dishes in the county town. 'He is a strange man', said team leader Wang Daoquan. 'Now we think that in the past he saved up and has several hundred yuan in the bank.' Team members suspected that while avoiding collective labour on various pretences he was actually engaged in private trading of some kind.

The failure of the Cultural Revolution to solve the problem of work incentives satisfactorily was clearly a major disappointment for the revolutionary committee at Junction People's Commune. Nevertheless, as we have seen (and will see further in Part III of this book), this lack of permanent success did not prevent the villagers from rallying to chalk up some remarkable achievements in community development and social change that reflected the values of a new proletarian culture as taught by Mao.

Using Mao's slogan of 'put public interest first, self-interest second', which is the reverse of bourgeois liberal values stressing individualism, these tangible results included the digging of the Red Cliff canal in 1968 and other major water conservancy efforts to create an area of 'high and stable yields' for grain; the building of tractor roads to every hamlet, and purchase of machinery to open the door to mechanization; the massive investment of labour in farmland reconstruction to wipe out the dreaded plague of schistosomiasis and to square the fields so that chemical fertilizer could be technologically applied; the improvement of the railway to bring lime and phosphorus fertilizer down from the mountains; the introduction of high-yield hybrid rice seeds after careful experimentation; the use of science to tame the tobacco blight and improve cash incomes; the construction of a primary school and a health clinic in every village; the electrification of the villages and the founding of several small industrial enterprises; and the shaping of an 'iron rice bowl' embodying advanced principles of social security and distributive justice. Such innovations and rapid advances, achieved by the labour of the peasant collectives in a self-reliant way, had never appeared in the village in two millennia since the unification of China under the Han dynasty.

When Mao died in September 1976 the commune turned the South China Temple on the high street in Junction into a memorial hall. On the stage potted evergreens surrounded a huge portrait of the Chairman and out on the street giant arches of pine boughs framed the pathway leading to the hall. Thousands of peasants and their children filed in fifty at a time to bow three times before his portrait. Many wept. They vowed that his memory would remain ever green; they would continue the revolution.

In spite of the growth of social awareness and the material progress made possible during the Cultural Revolution by Mao's political line and the search that he led for proletarian values, the fact was that at the time of his death the living standards of the peasants remained low, there was too much labour available for too little land, and the ability of cadres to exercise their bureaucratic power over the villagers continued to grow despite the mass campaigns of rectification. It was these conditions as well as the dubious ways of hero worship and ideological overload that Mao's successors set out to remedy.

11

FAMILY FARMING ONCE AGAIN:
AFTER 1982

Two years after the death of Mao Zedong the Central Committee of the Communist Party met to decide upon a strategic shift of direction. This meeting, in December 1978, turned out to be one of the most famous gatherings ever held by the party.

The party's decision for a 'new Long March' to modernization, including an opening to the capitalist West, was as bold an act as any ever contemplated by the late Chairman himself. From now on, said the new leader Deng Xiaoping, a man active in the communist movement for as long as Mao but ten years younger, there will be 'more talk about economics and less about politics'.[1]

Deng and his supporters planned to make the market place the centre of more social and economic transactions. They invested more capital in light consumer industries in order to raise the people's standard of living rapidly. Helped by a better world situation in which the United States had turned friendly, China aimed to quadruple its gross value of production by the year 2001.[2] These were the highlights of the government's general policy. Deng called it a 'second revolution'.

Agricultural changes came first. Under the reforms he had in mind Deng Xiaoping predicted that the peasants of China would 'lie awake at night so long as a single piece of land is left unplanted or a single pond unused for aquatic production, and they will find ways to remedy the situation'.[3] This attitude of the peasants would create much of the additional wealth China needed.

Step by step the reformers under Deng Xiaoping found themselves moving outside the collective framework of agriculture until for most purposes commune members once again became independent peasant producers as in the early 1950s. The new framework is called the 'household responsibility system'.

As change gathered momentum it went further than was at first expected. Put on the defensive by critics who suggested that the reforms opened the door to capitalism and were an admission that private enterprise is superior to a socialist system, the party centre decided that it would have to maintain greater continuity with the former regime of Mao Zedong. To achieve this impression it placed certain ideological limits on reform. Deng announced four cardinal principles to guide political life in China: the socialist road, the dictatorship of the proletariat, the leadership of the Communist Party and the ideology of Marxism-Leninism and Mao Zedong Thought.[4]

Although dogmatic-sounding, the broad generality of these principles actually allows considerable room for manoeuvre. Debate continues within the Communist Party between those who wish to extend further the economic reforms of 1978 and others who, fearing that the inroads of capitalism are fostering the worship of money and selfishness, favour giving greater emphasis to the social concerns implied in the four principles.

Villagers at MaGaoqiao did not seem eager to give up collective farming. Those interviewed as late as 1981 reacted negatively to talk of structural reform returning the responsibility for production to individual households. In spite of the fact they they knew about such experiments elsewhere in Sichuan, they were not anxious to follow suit.

Their objections to the notion of dividing the land once again into small household parcels touched upon such practical matters as access to water, different qualities of land, use of tractors for ploughing, families who were short of able-bodied labour. They feared that old quarrels over who would get the water first at rice-planting time, about the priority for ploughing, or over the best pieces of land might reappear. The collective system of farm management had resolved these practical problems in a fashion that disadvantaged no group.

In addition the Communist Party members had an ideological commitment. 'To be a communist', said one party member, 'means to support the collective, to defend the interests of the collective. We have pledged our lives to that. We believe in reaching prosperity together, not individual success.'

Apart from their basic attachment to the collective structure, however, the villagers warmly welcomed many other policy changes. Increased state investment in agriculture, for example, gave the village six times as much chemical fertilizer in 1980 as it had five years earlier (Appendix, Table 12) and a corresponding surge in the output and yields of grain and cash crops followed (Appendix, Table 11). The peasants were especially happy with the boost in prices they received for their farm products (Appendix, Table 13), a one-time windfall that was the gift of the state to get the system going. They had also been willing to experiment with the smaller 'responsibility groups' for field work linking payment more closely to work done. In these smaller groups they could accomplish the field work more efficiently and quickly, leaving greater time for leisure or other activities. With increased grain supplies the peasants developed more household sidelines such as raising hogs, chickens, ducks, and geese; they grew mushrooms, and created bamboo-ware for sale on the more frequent market days. All these activities increased their income.

Grandpa Deng, of No. 5 production team, summed up the good feeling after the collective accounts for 1980 were finalized:

> This year my family received almost 1,000 yuan cash from the collective in addition to our grain ration. Our household sidelines also increased. We raised four pigs which brought us Y400 and about Y100 of vegetables which we ate. We raised another pig which we slaughtered and ate ourselves. The total income for our seven-member family was over Y2,000. We bought two bicycles and I have Y200 in the bank. Before my family was a deficit family for ten years because we had small children and too few able-bodied. We've paid back our debts. This is the first time I have received real income.

By 1982, still under collective management, the village economy continued to move ahead. Its income from collective sources increased by almost 40 per cent above that registered in 1980, with gains coming mainly from field crops, collective sidelines and employment in the commune's rural enterprises (Appendix, Table 7). The share of wealth available for peasant consumption also increased remarkably. As shown in Table I, the commune collective system (not including the private plots and household sidelines) tripled or even quadrupled (in the case

TABLE I
Growth of per capita *net income 1963–82*
(from collective farming sources)
Junction People's Commune

Unit: yuan

	1963	1965	1970	1975	1980	1982
Junction People's Commune (119 production teams) Of which:	54	95	96	78	173	240
No. 8 Brigade (7 teams) Of which:	77	104	94	82	165	254
No. 5 production team	82	109	105	81	195	311

Source: Junction People's Commune, *Accounts 1949–85*, pp. 35–6; No. 8 Brigade, *Accounts 1949–85*, pp. 35–6.

of No. 5 production team) the individual peasant's spending power from 1975 to 1982. With success like that, what need was there to change the system?

But the change came anyway. With one stroke of the knife, as the Chinese saying goes.

In 1982, after autumn harvest, villagers heard rumours that the higher levels had decided to scrap the collective management system throughout Shifang county. County leaders confirmed the rumours when they visited MaGaoqiao and informed the brigade leaders that they had selected the village as an average unit in the tobacco growing region, to become one of the places for decollectivization to begin.

It would be difficult to exaggerate the psychological impact that this news had upon the local cadres and party members. Some of them, of course, took part in bidding for the collective assets and were able to get a buffalo or help a relative buy one of the tractors. They were less shaken up than those villagers who got nothing beyond land and a few tools. But the orders baffled many of the cadres at the village and commune levels. Had the instructions to decollectivize not come down from Beijing, there is little doubt that local party members would have considered them the product of confused thinking, a temporary loss of nerve, or even downright counter-revolutionary. As team leader Wang Daoquan explained:

> It was something like the situation in 1953 before the co-operatives were formed. Suddenly this policy came from above and was pushed through here. In September 1982 county Party Secretary Lo and the county governor came to ask if we would be willing to contract the land to households. We said, 'Yes we would like to try that.' We waited for the documents from above. Once they were here we did just as the documents instructed. Our county was one of the last to go this way. Some of the older peasants said, 'We should never forget Chairman Mao as we turn things over.'

Consultation was minimal. After thirty years of making revolution the style of bureaucratic commandism continued to thrive and ironically became an instrument to undo some of the revolutionary gains. The cadres, bound by party discipline to follow instructions from higher levels, went into action quickly.

The first point was to decide how to distribute the good pieces of land. Although a subsequent land survey showed that there were twelve different grades of soil, the villagers were content to divide it into six grades. On that basis they measured out the land. Good land could produce 700-900 *jin* of grain per *mu*, average land 500-600, and poor land 300-400. The cadres combined pieces of good, average and poor land into packages of more or less equal productivity and then invited everyone to express their views about the fairness of each package. Once there were no more opinions, the households drew lots on a *per capita* basis for the land nearest their own courtyards.

Following the distribution of the land, each household received small hand tools free of charge and private individuals took possession of the bigger items by auction – the buffaloes, hand-tractors, and rubber-tyred carts. The collective retained ownership of the two large tractors because nobody could afford to buy them and leased them out to the highest bidders. Likewise families able to pay the highest annual rent contracted for the small fish ponds and grist mills, the bean curd mill, restaurant, shop, agricultural machinery repair station and other brigade sideline enterprises. The barefoot doctors contracted for the brigade medical clinic as a business enterprise. In less than a month the collective property had been dismantled and an entirely new agrarian order inaugurated.

These sudden changes stripped the local leaders of much of their responsibility for running the economy. In a production team, for example, the number of cadres like Wang Daoquan eligible to receive subsidies for their administrative work fell from twenty-five to three. No longer needed were the work point recorders, the work group leaders, the warehouse keeper, the treasurer, the deputy team leaders – only the team leader, the women's leader and a part-time accountant remained, and even their self-esteem was impaired, their prestige battered and their political authority diminished. As township party secretary Yang Changyou put it a year later:

> Many party members do not feel comfortable and cannot adapt themselves to the new situation. Some cannot find the head nor the tail of their work. It's like trying to untangle a ball of string: you don't know where to start.

The county authorities foresaw this confusion to some extent and they had a well-prepared campaign in hand to guide the way forward and to entrench the new order.

First and most important was the actual contract signed between the production team and the household. This blueprint of the new regime came in the shape of a small ten-page booklet called the 'Contract for all-round responsibility of households in farming'. Mass-produced so that each agreement existed in triplicate – one copy each for the village, the production team and the family itself – the contract spelled out in detail the household's obligations to the state and to the collective for taxes and sales of grain, cash crops, and hogs and for family planning in return for the use of a defined amount of land according to the family's size.

It took long and difficult negotiations to decide how each *mu* of land should fit into the quota for state grain deliveries.

Anticipating some of the problems that could arise, a short preamble to the contract tried to give legal effect to certain duties of an ideological nature. According to this the household contractors had an obligation 'to develop the spirit of mutual help and friendship' and to support the poorer households or those who had difficulty with their work. They were bound to observe the guidance of state planning for agriculture as well as the regulations about birth control. The production team, which still owned the land, warned that it 'is prohibited to buy or sell, to lease, to transfer or to waste [land]. Planting of trees or bamboo, house building, digging out earth for brick-making or burying the dead are also restricted.'

In return for these undertakings by the peasant producer, the production team promised to have a plan and 'to do well' the 'organizing, distribution, purchasing, and supplying of hybrid seeds, draught animals, farm machinery, irrigation etc.' necessary for production. It pledged to support the poorer members and to popularize advanced agricultural science and technology among the commune members.

To allay the fears of the commune members about irrigation water and ploughing arrangements the village made other subsidiary contracts. During the crucial two months of May-June, for example, it hired a person to be in charge of irrigating every sixty *mu* of land. That person manned the pumps and each household paid .80 cents to Y1.20 for having one *mu* irrigated. As for those who had no draught animals, an official township price list itemizing the amounts a buffalo owner could charge offered some protection from profit-seeking owners. The fee for year-round ploughing was Y9 for one *mu*. Tractor owners, most of whom used their machines for transportation business, signed an agreement to be available for ploughing three times a year – once in October for wheat and rape seed, once in February for tobacco, and in May for rice. 'We also control them by our monopoly of diesel oil supplies', said village party secretary, Jiang Wenguang. 'If you don't plough you can't get oil.'

No sooner were the contracts arranged than the signboard of the People's Commune came down. Names changed. The commune became the township, the brigade resumed its former village name, and the production team turned into a village group. Internal reorganizations created a separation of functions between politics (the party), administration (the government) and economics (agriculture, industry and commerce). These arrangements and the new names on all offices, schools and public buildings had the effect of closing a door on the past. The old gate to the township (formerly commune) headquarters was torn down and a new, modern-looking one put up in its place – minus the red star. It was a deliberate policy. If the new era was to take hold, the forms of address, the symbols and the language of thinking itself would have to be different.

Either from force of habit or intentionally, however, the ordinary peasants at MaGaoqiao continue to speak of the production team and to refer to themselves as commune members. It is familiar, and politically it still feels more comfortable.

Hard on the heels of name changes, the county party committee issued yet another sweeping directive. It instructed the village party branches to increase the membership of a brand-new social category called the 'specialized households'. This category consisted of the entrepreneurs who had bought or contracted for the productive assets of the brigade. The idea was to stimulate individual initiative by increasing the number of 'specialized households' to 30 per cent of the population as quickly as possible so as to produce more commodities for the market.

This method of increasing production sounded strange to the ears of many party members, it sounded like 'the capitalist road', but they could not escape the demand. The party committee reviewed the village rolls and picked out the more capable households. It selected as candidates those who were thought able to generate 50 per cent more income than the average, and assigned each party member the task of counselling three or four such families to help them arrange loans from the Credit Union or the Agricultural Bank to start up in business. The campaign to create 'specialized households' thus became the central political task of the party.

Some peasants, fearing that they were being set up as targets for future criticism, refused to budge until village cadres also stepped forward to join those who were going to 'get rich first'. To offset the doubters the village committee pasted up large wall charts in the village headquarters with the names of the 'specialized households', their party adviser, their expected output and the nature of their enterprise – noodle making, poultry and hog raising, mushroom planting, carpentry, transport, cement block production and a score of other activities.

Within six months MaGaoqiao claimed 145 'specialized households', – 31 per cent of the total number of households in the village. The government advanced them Y15,000 in loans and by the end of the year some families grossed Y20,000 or more. With their net income suddenly ten to fifteen times that of their neighbours, ninety families (18 per cent of the village) built new brick and tiled houses to replace the pounded mud and thatch cottages that had been the common lot of peasants here since the Han dynasty two thousand years earlier. Some had TV aerials. In No. 5 production team members now owned fifty bicycles, where three years earlier there were only fourteen.

To offset criticism of the new policy by the majority who were being left out and to ensure that everyone got in on some part of the affluence, the county government took extraordinary measures that first year. It slashed the cost of production materials and postponed household contributions to the public accumulation funds for investment purposes, with the result that at MaGaoqiao the villagers received a staggering 78 per cent of the total output value as net income in 1983. This was unprecedented, up from 63 per cent in 1980 and never to be repeated again (Appendix, Table 17). 'We have been well satisfied by the results, especially this year', said Wang Daoquan, smiling self-consciously for he too had become one of the 'specialized households'.

The most talked of 'specialized household' at MaGaoqiao was one headed by a man named Wu Wanwu in neighbouring Yinfeng township. It became a kind of scandal.

Mr Wu was a former party secretary who had been overthrown for 'following the capitalist road' during the 1960s. Together with his wife and three sons he had begun following it again and this time, with the blessing of the party, he contracted for the village distillery, noodle shop, and starch factory (with a son in charge of each) as well as for three-and-a-half acres of land on which they raised fodder for eighty pigs, which in turn they slaughtered and made into sausages to sell at three shops they had established. The family's gross income reached Y240,000 in 1983. To do all this they hired seventeen people. Still not satisfied, Wu continued to look for unused buildings or warehouses of former collectives with plans to turn them into new enterprises – a veritable merchant prince!

This man's story and rumours about other such entrepreneurs shocked party activists in Shifang. They felt that some people were going too far in getting rich. It was not only that private individuals were exploiting labour once again. That was bad enough, but equally disquieting was the wheeling and dealing, the under-the-table bribery and corruption that had to be involved in amassing that kind of fortune in such a brief period of time. The party secretary at MaGaoqiao said he hoped Mr Wu had some good bookkeepers so that if some day he landed in gaol for his activity 'at least he will have very clear account books on which to rest his head'.

The Sichuan provincial authorities soon found themselves embroiled in controversy over the 'specialized households'. When the head of the People's Bank arrived in Chengdu from Beijing to check on all the loans that had been handed out the provincial head of the bank committed suicide. The provincial party committee hushed up this incident because, having won fame as the national pace-setter for this kind of reform when Premier Zhao Ziyang (later General Secretary of the Communist Party) was its first secretary a few years earlier, it wanted to press on.

It criticized those who were being held back by 'the invisible rope'[5] of leftist egalitarianism. To demonstrate its determination the party invited Mr Wu to come to the provincial capital where he sat on the public platform with provincial leaders and had his picture and story printed in the *Sichuan Daily*. 'I felt very glorious,' said Wu, 'I got rid of my feelings of fear and am prepared to go further.'

The dramatic reduction in the number of rural cadres as a result of the household contract reform has already been mentioned. The remaining cadres soon received instructions to organize their work, wherever possible, in the form of business contracts. Contracts, contracts . . . they were all the vogue. As in the case of the land, contracts with cadres linked specific political tasks and social objectives to direct material incentives. With cadres trying to win points which could be translated into money, their work became increasingly divorced from political values and motivation. This trend is well illustrated by the comments of Huang Kailan, leader of the Women's Association at MaGaoqiao and deputy head of the village:

> The township sets goals for our activities and at the end of the year there is a check on results. People doing this work no longer get the same amount, payment is according to work done. For example, one of the targets is to develop 'specialized households' from the woman's point of view and if you haven't fulfilled the plan then you lose some points. There are twelve points for having a full-time nursery school; if you only have a part-time one you lose six points. If a woman is abducted by force or fraud from the village and sold into marriage elsewhere then you lose three points. If a woman gives birth to a second child you lose one to six points according to circumstances. If your village reaches the goal for late marriages set by the township (males at twenty-five years, females at twenty-three) then you may get some extra points. This year I had 90.07 points out of 100. I don't know why I lost some points, I didn't go to ask. I was second highest in the township. Some of the lowest got only 52 points. If you do not lose any points and get 100, and each point above 70 is worth Y8.50, then you'll receive Y470. My income from the collective was about Y400.

If the accounting for cadres' incomes is stricter and more defined under the new contract responsibility system, the opposite trend is evident in the case of ordinary villagers. Their incomes have become more fluid and market-oriented, and public knowledge of what people earn is less certain.

The upward turn in production and in personal income established before 1982 under collective management generally continued after the contracts to household. To what extent this trend would have continued under collective management without the return to private household management is a question of great political interest and ideological sensitivity in China.

Some party theorists, in reconsidering the long-held idea that, to be socialist, agriculture must be organized into collectives, argue that it is precisely private management that allows the peasants to work more efficiently to increase farm production. This conclusion may be questioned, at least in part, from the experience at MaGaoqiao. Although it is true that many peasants use their free time to do non-farm work, it is not the case that private management has greatly increased their agricultural income.

At first sight the village accounts all across China give the impression of a great leap in farm income as a result of the first year of privatization. These figures are sometimes given to unsuspecting foreign journalists and visitors. At MaGaoqiao too, the statistics show that disposable income in the hands of villagers increased by over 60 per cent – from Y494,000 in 1982 to Y815,000 in 1983 (Appendix, Table 17, col. 14).

However, this result is entirely misleading because the rural accounting system changed after 1982 and the figures are no longer comparable. If one wishes to learn the truth about trends of social life and living standards in the countryside one must be prepared to push away the branches and penetrate a little into the thicket of Chinese agricultural accounting. The experience is not too painful, even amusing at times.

One major difference in the current system is that the income from the private plots, private pig raising and other household sideline activities is included in the public accounts for the first time. As a result the figures after 1982 are greatly inflated compared to those of previous years. To make them equivalent the accountants at MaGaoqiao suggested that the post-1982 figures should be scaled down by 40 per cent. When this is done it turns out that the peasants' income from farming in 1983 was actually 1 per cent *less* than it was the previous year under collective management! Even after a few more years of experience in Junction township when disposable farm income increased by as much as 4 per cent per annum, it was still a far cry from 60 per cent and not enough to demonstrate a claim about the superiority of private over collective management.

Another difference in the accounting system from 1983 onwards is that, since there were no longer any production team records on crops, marketing and income distribution, a sampling method had to be devised to collect information on these subjects. In the beginning the sampling methods were far from scientific. The county statistical bureau (which reports its results to the State Statistical Bureau) simply asked the cadres at MaGaoqiao to choose nine typical families. They selected three rich, three average and three poor families without regard to the proportion of each type in the village. This resulted in an upward distortion of income levels since poorer families are more numerous in the population than rich ones.

By 1985 the authorities had refined the system considerably and changed to a 'random sample'. In preparing a method to determine peasant income the accountants selected three characteristics – family size, labour power and amount of contracted land – and weighted them according to a formula. They excluded those families who had members working outside the village in commercial or business activities because their incomes would be much higher. Then they drew up a list of the remaining families and chose nine sample households at equidistance from each other on the list. They paid these nine families a small amount to keep detailed daily accounts of their income and expenditures as related to production. Once every ten days the village accountant went round to collect their accounts and he filled in the county statistical bureau report at the end of the year.

While this system appeared to be a great improvement over the 'typical sample' method, some questions remain as to its objectivity. The 'Records of the Economic Situation of Sample Rural Households' at MaGaoqiao, for example, show that the nine sample households in 1985 included the village head, the village party secretary, the village accountant, and the former village party secretary (who had since been promoted to a higher position in the township administration). Thus out of 505 families at MaGaoqiao, four of the nine chosen 'at random' to form the basis of sampling were, in fact, the main village cadres. Whether this distorted the statistical result cannot be determined. But it provokes a suspicion, at least, that there may have been strong political pressures at work to make sure that the village made a good showing in terms of income levels.[6]

By the autumn of 1985 the Central Committee of the Communist Party began to have its own doubts about the reliability of reports of peasant prosperity coming in from the rural areas. At a special national conference in Beijing, Chen Yun, one of the outspoken veteran leaders of the party, castigated the press for its exaggerated reports of 'specialized households' that were making over Y10,000. 'Their number is extremely small,' he said, 'our media's reports are divorced from reality.'[7] After that more sober press reports began to appear saying that 80 per cent of the peasant population remained poor or of average income and that about 20 per cent were not able to make ends meet. In private conversation at MaGaoqiao the village head, Liao Wenfang, indicated that he thought this situation also prevailed in Junction township.

As income gaps widened and people felt themselves left behind or exploited by others, signs of destabilization appeared. In a speech in Beijing in February 1986 Vice-premier Tian Jiyun referred to 'unhealthy tendencies' surfacing within the party and society – the result of a yawning gap in income among people working in different units, inordinate price increases, blind competition and exorbitant profit-taking.[8]

Resentments increased on the plains of Sichuan too. Since the Poor and Lower Middle Peasants' Associations collapsed after the demise of the Cultural Revolution, there was no organization where people could go for help outside the ruling party.

'In a big village like this there is always something happening, every day', said Liao Wenfang, who became village head at MaGaoqiao in 1983 after five years as chief accountant. He said that mediation of civil disputes took most of his time. People quarrelled over little pieces of contracted land, over the boundaries of their private plots, over who should use the land along the edges of the fields, over chickens and ducks and farm animals wandering into the fields of neighbours to eat the crops; there were disputes over occupying burial ground for new house building, and quarrels over the younger generation not wanting to look after their parents. As team leader Wang Daoquan said:

> Quarrels must be solved carefully, otherwise someone might try to commit suicide, especially by drinking the pesticide 'rogor'. It's almost becoming a habit. As soon as they drink it they become unconscious. During this past month there were two of our people who drank 'rogor' and we had to send them to the hospital for emergency treatment.

The subject came up because Wang and Liao as well as the village women's leader, Huang Kailan, had just returned from several hours of strenuous mediation in the open air. The case was like a miniature soap opera involving some chickens that had escaped into a rapeseed field and eaten the plants. As thirty-three-year-old, former rebel leader Jiang Wenmao returned from the high street with a bottle of cooking oil he saw chickens in his field and ran after them. He threw a stone at one bird, knocking it into a manure pit and killing it. As soon as the owner, Chen Guoyuan, learned of this he came running out of his house shouting at Jiang. He claimed Jiang had no reason to kill his chicken and denied that it was his chicken who had eaten the plants. 'There are so many chickens in the courtyard, how do you know it was my chickens in your field?' he yelled. In anger Chen picked up the bottle of cooking oil, broke it and splashed it on Jiang's new winter padded coat. Jiang then said he would replace the chicken, but Chen must buy a new coat, which cost over 20 yuan. That would have been a heavy burden for Chen who was not well-off. Amidst swearing and threats of castration the village leaders were called in by worried neighbours. 'In our presence they continued to shout', said the village head Liao. Chen said he would pay for the rapeseed plants if it was decided that his chicken had eaten them. Jiang said he would pay for the chicken, but Chen must pay for the new coat. 'We tried to reason with them and calm them down', said Liao. Finally it was decided that the chicken and the oil cancelled each other out, and Chen would pay 5 yuan for the stains on the coat. In the mêlée surrounding the chicken, the oil and the stained coat, the rapeseed plants were conveniently forgotten and the disputants went away muttering.

'We did not have many quarrels like this in the collective time but now they are frequent', said village head Liao. When asked about the difference, he referred to the fact that under the collective there was sometimes a lax attitude toward productive property. If your chicken ate a few leaves from the collective fields nobody took much notice. In team leader Wang's colourful expression, 'If you "plucked a few feathers from the rooster's tail" nobody would run after you.' But now that most things were privately owned people were ready to fight over their profits and losses.

Even more unsettling than the unpleasant civil disputes was a developing crime wave, especially among the youth. By the summer of 1983, according to village head Liao, the state had to begin a 'comprehensive and vigorous' policy of bringing criminals under control. Theft, corrupt business dealings, robbery by small gangs, as well as arson, rape and murder were on the increase. In September of that year the public executions in Shifang county referred to in Chapter 1 took place. Lesser criminals had their photographs placed on public display in front of the Law Courts in Fangting. Officers from the public security bureau bundled convicted law-breakers, their arms bound behind their backs, on to open trucks and took them to propaganda meetings at the various market towns. Included among these were the three leaders of the Building Construction Team of Junction Township. According to party secretary Jiang Wenguang, 'they took advantage of the contract system to act recklessly and get rich'. After concluding that they had embezzled over Y20,000, the county court, in 1986, sentenced the trio to seven, five and two years in gaol respectively.

At MaGaoqiao nothing startling occurred but there was uneasiness. The village cadre in charge of security rounded up several youths thought to be thieving and gambling and sent them to a county re-education centre for two weeks. Another lad disappeared and was presumed to be engaged in illegal activity in some other county. Someone stole two large electric irrigation motors which were never recovered, but the village has not had anyone actually sentenced for criminal acts.

Reasons given for the change of spirit among so many of the people always included a reference to 'the chaos of the Cultural Revolution'. But that time of disorder was more than fifteen years before and no longer really relevant. The Youth League secretary referred to recently imported films and TV programmes produced in the West and in Japan, saying that they set bad examples of lawlessness and violence. Others pointed to the increase in card-playing and gambling in leisure time. But the most important cause of slippage in social behaviour undoubtedly related to the stirring up of long dormant individual acquisitive motivations following the privatization of village economic life. Under the household contract system community moral values began to shift away from the ideal of upholding the collective interest in favour of celebrating individual success.

The fate of the local militia organization illustrates this weakening of social commitment. For twenty-five years or more the volunteer militia played a central part in the life of the village. It had concurrently been a youth organization conducting sports and cultural activities, a force for basic farmland construction, and a pathway to promotion as well as a reserve for the armed forces that could play a role in maintaining social order. Thus members of the militia had a special sense of themselves in the community. During the movement to learn from Dazhai the militia commander of Junction People's Commune called them 'the vanguard in class struggle, a strong, fresh army in the battle for production'.[9] They responded to natural disasters, floods or other difficult tasks and had a high sense of social responsibility.

Stemming from Mao Zedong's military writings in the days of the civil war when 'war, like work, was integrated into the pattern of daily life',[10] the militia organization paralleled that of production – a platoon in each production team, making up a company in the brigade and a battalion in each commune. Everyone, both male and female, could apply to join at the age of sixteen and most were accepted. From then until the age of twenty-eight they were members of the 'basic' or 'backbone' militia and had twenty days of training, including political and ideological education, each year. Within the basic militia there was a small armed group. Depending upon the situation, MaGaoqiao village had three to nine rifles which would come under the command of the commune battalion commander in the event of a crisis. From the age of twenty-eight to forty-five the young people became part of the 'ordinary' or reserve militia.

As late as 1980 at MaGaoqiao there were 690 in the militia, 320 of them backbone members. But as collective production tasks faded and were given over to individual households, militia activity reduced itself to marching around occasionally doing military drill. Enthusiasm waned. Young people found they had more interesting and profitable things to do with their time and by 1983 the militia organization virtually disappeared at MaGaoqiao.

With everyone turning to ways of making money, the Communist Party members were placed in a distressing, if not impossible, position. They had the task of promoting socialist doctrine and morality, summed up in the phrase 'Serve the People', while simultaneously opening the door to more and more private commercial enterprise. As the situation became more unstable the party centre started a corrective ideological campaign in the winter of 1983 calling for the creation of 'a spiritual civilization'. This effort to offset profiteering and greed did not penetrate far into the countryside; nevertheless, the party cadres were expected to do something about linking the material and spiritual worlds.

One solution to this dilemma was to publicize successful rural entre-preneurs who used some of their profits to benefit the community. The favourite project was to open a cultural teahouse. These establishments usually had a colour TV set, library, chess boards and storytellers to entertain the general public. According to the head of the county cultural bureau, such teahouses proliferated rapidly, and over 100 of them had sprung up in the county by the end of 1983. The new dispensers of 'noblesse oblige' were praised by a leading cadre as 'standing high for not forgetting the cause of the party or the people'. However, the motivations of 'specialized households', handing out old-fashioned, self-serving philanthropy in the tradition of the Confucian gentry, did not impress many peasants even as they sat in their cultural centres spitting melon seeds on to the floor and drinking tea.

Some villages, including MaGaoqiao, preferred to establish their own collectively owned cultural centres and have retired cadres run them. The county Cultural Bureau also began training backbone personnel for the arts – music, dancing, creative writing and painting. Young people between the ages of fourteen and seventeen, who were no longer in school, went to the county town for several weeks to be trained as catalysts for the village cultural centres. In one case, for a training class of Sichuan opera in classical and modern themes, there were 1,300 applicants. This was in spite of the fact that students had to bring their own bedding and food. For the forty-five successful candidates the state supplied a place to live and practise and an instructor for three months.

Another way of promoting desirable ideology was a campaign to discover model households in each village. These moral exemplars, nominated after discussion by village groups and elected at a village meeting, were judged by five standards. The head of the Women's Association summarized these as: i) studying Marxism-Leninism well and observing social discipline and the law; ii) loving the country and society while working hard to become productive and prosperous; iii) observing family planning and helping the children's education; iv) being conscious of public health and safety; v) being good at respecting the aged, daughters-in-law and in helping neighbours.

While these criteria for the 'five good' households are broad enough to include almost any possibility, in 1983 the villagers at MaGaoqiao pointedly ignored the rich 'specialized households' in their choices; most models were poor families seen to be struggling, as one woman said, 'by honest labour', to succeed in spite of a lack of able-bodied members or other handicaps.

Yet another means of rekindling community involvement is through the electoral process. After a lapse of four years Shifang county held general elections in 1984. The election at MaGaoqiao took place on Sunday, January 15th:

It is sunny, unusually warm for a winter's day and the Dragon Gate mountains shimmer through the early morning haze as the villagers at MaGaoqiao crowd into the village headquarters for the election meeting. The day has been declared a holiday throughout the county and there is a festive stir as patriotic music pours into the courtyard.

Inside the hall the national flag unfurls from a strong bamboo pole, its red and gold fabric attached to the front wall, and before it a long table is flanked with potted shrubs, flowering cactus, spruce, miniature orange trees and chrysanthemums. Strung across the barn-like room are colourful banners stating that 'the secret ballot is the method of' expressing the opinion of each voter in a democratic way' and announcing that this is the tenth general election for both the county and the township people's congresses. Another banner reminds that to advance the four modernizations 'we must persist with the four basic principles, the socialist road, proletarian dictatorship, leadership of the Communist Party and Marxism-Leninism, Mao Zedong Thought'.

As usual in China, it is an election concerned with finding good people, with personalities rather than issues. But there is something new. This time there will be more names on the ballot than people to be elected. This has never happened before. It will be possible for some of the leaders to be defeated. Democracy may teach bureaucracy a lesson. As it turns out there are no upsets in store but the possibility adds excitement to the proceedings and suggests that the party centre is serious about political reform.

Things are done in an organized fashion. The 1,149 electors, out of a possible 1,189, sit together on benches in units according to their production team (now called 'village group').

Party secretary, Jiang Wenguang, calls the meeting to order. Unexpectedly he begins by telling how the toilets are arranged. People find this amusing and there is a ripple of laughter. Special pits have been dug outside the back door, says Jiang. He thinks this information is important since everyone will be staying until all the votes are counted and if insufficient candidates receive 50 per cent of the vote the first time round, there will be run-off ballots, which could mean a long meeting.

Following the national anthem Jiang starts off again rather stiffly. He states that the election is a chance for the masses to pass judgement on their leaders and an opportunity for the leaders to hear the heart-felt opinions of the masses. Then he proposes names for an election arrangements committee and scrutineers and asks the people to applaud if they agree. There is scattered applause led by himself and the prospective committee members. Grandpa Deng, team leader Wang Daoquan and several others are chosen to count the votes. Cousin Wang Youming, former head of the Poor and Lower Middle Peasants' Association, is supervisor for the county election, while poor peasant Liao Wenping, recently reinstated in the party and one of the more successful 'specialized households', is chosen to do the same for the Junction township election. Jiang then retires from the scene and the committee members take their places around the head table.

Cousin Wang starts to explain the election procedure in detail. 'It is a secret election', he says through the microphone. 'For the county there are three names on the ballot and only two names are to be circled. If three are circled then the ballot will be spoiled.' He points out that there is an empty space on the ballot where voters may write in the name of someone else they wish to elect. 'Apart from that,' he warns, 'you must not make any other distinguishing marks on the ballot.'. . . Poor peasant Liao presents the ballot for the township People's Congress on which there are eight names, five of them to be elected. His task is more complicated because he must make it clear that among these eight there are three women, two of whom must be elected and five men, three to be chosen.

Meanwhile the election committee ceremoniously breaks open the red-sealed packages on the table and invites the production team leaders to help them distribute the ballots to each elector. The younger people, who can read easily, stop listening to the repeated explanations coming through the loudspeaker, and pick out for themselves the important points of instruction printed on the ballot. Soon there is a quiet hum of conversation as others stop listening too and begin exchanging opinions on who to vote for. They fill in their ballots and drop them into boxes that are passed along the rows of benches. The count begins at the table in full view of the assembly.

The weeks of preparatory work for the election – drawing up the voters' list, issuing voter identification cards and the nomination of candidates – centred on the orderliness and openness of the procedures and on ensuring a balanced list of candidates. Young and old, male and female, professional people and field workers, cadres and ordinary commune members – all should be fairly represented. Each village received suggestions about social categories that might be included on the ballot. In all this out-pouring of energy it did not seem to matter what particular candidates thought about public issues, or even that they should be publicly introduced to the voters before election day. This strange phenomenon is explained by Wang Changyun, the incumbent county governor.

Mr Wang's name is on the ballot as a candidate for the county people's congress at MaGaoqiao. Although everyone seems to know that he is a candidate, many of the younger voters have never heard him speak and do not even recognize him in their midst on election day. Governor Wang thinks this is quite normal.

> It would be unseemly for me or other candidates to come along before the election asking people to give us their votes. That would be a type of individualism on our part. They know what we stand for. They can decide for themselves if we are doing all right or not.

He seems quite confident that he will be chosen by the villagers as one of their representatives and he is not mistaken.

The tabulation of ballots is finally completed and the county results are given to cousin Wang to announce. Governor Wang heads the list with 2,448 votes, which is the combined total from MaGaoqiao and neighbouring Cool Water Well village that form a single constituency. The other winner also has over 2,000 votes, and the loser has 600. By now there is also a fourth candidate. Cousin Wang reads out the name in the same dramatic fashion and the fact that this one has two votes. There is a brief moment of silence and then the crowd, recognizing a prank, burst into laughter. A couple of people had written in the name of a friend on the ballot. After this moment of levity, the victors are called to the front and are solemnly given a certificate of election. They bow as school children pin to their chests a large red paper flower – the symbol of glory and trust.

The business of the morning is not yet completed. Party secretary Jiang comes back to the stage wearing his red flower. Although he has only managed to come fourth out of five for the township people's congress he does not allow any disappointment to show. He says that a further order of business for the day is the election of the village committee. There are five people to be elected – the head, deputy-head, accountant and two others. Jiang reads out the names of the five people who have been nominated and then suggests that the seven village groups meet separately for a few minutes to decide on procedure.

When the assembly reconvenes Jiang announces that there are no further nominations. In view of that he proposes that a secret ballot is unnecessary. The vote is conducted by show of hands – those for, against and abstentions. The only one to receive a noticeable number of negative votes and several dozen abstentions is Huang Kailan, the women's leader who is running for deputy-head. She is also in charge of the family planning programme and her result is interpreted afterwards as a mild protest vote about the one child per family policy of the government.

The meeting adjourns. As the people drift out into the courtyard a roving reporter from the local radio station is there conducting interviews.

Compared to the political campaigns of the past, especially the 'four clean-ups', this general election was a mild, self-controlled affair, hardly ruffling the surface of village life. It did not become an occasion for expressing discontents and hopes or even a forum for clarifying public policy or for popular education. This result was predictable given the passive role of the leadership, from Governor Wang down to the village party branch, and given the absence of a catalytic work team from outside able to mobilize public participation.

The election episode, however, pointed to something significant in at least one respect. By offering a choice of candidates to be selected by secret ballot it introduced an element of creative uncertainty into village political life. So far nobody seemed quite sure what this opening might mean. But if village voices find new ways to become articulate periodic elections may yet evolve into a less chaotic means than the mass movements of the past as a way to have cadres 'pass the gate'.

In spite of the difficulties experienced in trying to find ways to link spiritual goals with the material realities of village life, there is no significant movement for a return to large collectives. But as time passes it is also clear that small individual farming, lacking sufficient scale and funds for capital investment and further mechanization, will prove less effective for the long-term modernization of agriculture. Experimentation has begun, therefore, with amalgamations, with voluntary contractual agreements and small co-operative joint ventures in an effort to cope with some of the continuing stubborn realities of rural life.

PART III

CULTURAL CHANGE

12

BAREFOOT DOCTORS: THE VILLAGE CLINIC

An unpainted door opens into a room that is like many others in the brigade headquarters. From the earthen floor rise the tamped clay walls, which in turn support the roof rafters where, amid cobwebs, the fire-baked grey tiles slope to the eaves. The austere white-washed walls, without windows, carry some old posters and reflect the bluish light of a neon tube.

It is the furniture that makes this place different: a high counter divides the room in two. In the front part a bench by the door can seat six or eight people waiting for their turn, while nearby, without any privacy partition, is a plain table surrounded by several chairs where one of the barefoot doctors interviews patients.

Beyond the counter are dusty bins and a long, low cabinet with fifty or more small drawers where medicinal herbs are stored; here another barefoot doctor moves about filling prescriptions. Below the counter, out of sight, there are bottles of pills, alcohol, bandages, syringes, acupuncture needles, moxibustion cups and other paraphernalia of both traditional and Western medicines. This is the medical clinic at MaGaoqiao village, 1981.

The creation of village clinics has already been cited as one of the positive accomplishments of the Cultural Revolution. The success of these 'new-born things of socialism' as they were called in Shifang county was, in fact, so widely recognized that in 1981 the government of China chose the county as a place for the World Health Organization to carry out experiments for preserving the potency of vaccine during mass innoculations for the prevention of childhood diseases. According to a report in the national media the county was 'remarkable for the extensive medical services' its population enjoys.[1] Life expectancy is now 66.7 years.

Thirty years earlier, at the time of Liberation, this corner of Sichuan was a most unlikely candidate for high rating in the field of public health. The use of opium was widespread and the life expectancy of the peasants averaged out at thirty-three years. Smallpox took the lives of so many children that it was common to see little coffins tied among the trees since folk tradition held that those who perished from this disease could not be buried in the ground. Parasitic diseases were endemic, with the majority of the rural population suffering from hookworm, snail fever, roundworm or other debilitating conditions. The county town had only one private medical clinic.

Western 'miracle' medicines were not entirely unknown. 'I heard about penicillin when the Americans were building the airbase in Guanghan', said one peasant. 'It was very effective – a pill the size of the tip of your little finger could bring the fever down.' Nevertheless they were rare and expensive, and few people could afford them even if they were available.

Out in Junction township traditional doctors dispensed medical care on the high street through private medicine shops. Since the shop owners also gave the doctors meals, the conflict of interest was inescapable: in return the doctors prescribed medicines which patients could then buy in the shop. 'If you wanted a doctor to come to your house', recalled another peasant, 'you had to hire a sedan chair to fetch him.'

The hold of private medical practice continued until Beijing launched a national public health campaign in the context of the Korean War in the 1950s. Things started to change.

The township cadres brought together eight doctors of Chinese medicine to create a 'unified clinic'. In the communization movement of the Great Leap Forward they expanded this effort. During the medical crisis caused by the famine, apprentices enrolled for training in Chinese medicine and the department of public health assigned a paramedic in Western medicine to the clinic, a man who had picked up his knowledge while working around hospitals formerly run by Canadian and American missionaries in Chengdu.

Preventive public health measures developed with the 1958 national campaign to combat rats, flies, mosquitoes, and sparrows, all of which, except for grain-eating sparrows, were vectors of common diseases such as typhus, polio, malaria, and encephalitis B. As team leader Wang recounted:

> During the campaign against the four pests, we wiped out the rats by stirring them out of the straw piles and baiting them with poison. For the sparrows we used baskets to catch them; we let off firecrackers and the people came out on one day in the whole prefecture to make such a noise so that the sparrows had no place to rest and they fell from exhaustion. We put lime and tobacco stems in the manure pools to kill the fly larvae; later we used chemicals to kill the mosquitoes. This campaign brought the pests under control.

Not until 1968 did a high tide for public health really gather. At that time millions of former Red Guards, some of whom had become a problem in the cities, creating unrest, or who were unemployed, went down to the countryside on Mao's orders to gain experience and to contribute to the modernization of the rural areas. The influence of these energetic and often idealistic young people awakened villagers to the possibilities of getting better health facilities.

The educated youth took as their guide in this activity a document of Mao's called the 'June 26th directive on public health' which demanded that the focus of medical and public health work should be transferred to the countryside.[2]

Like a trumpet blast to dozing listeners in some draughty concert hall, Mao shook up the medical profession and the Ministry of Health, criticizing them for their narrow concerns. He dubbed the Ministry 'the department of city gentlemen's public health' and made proposals for sweeping changes in favour of the rural areas where 85 per cent of the population lived.

He proposed that city hospitals keep doctors who had graduated 'after one or two years and are not very good' and the rest should all be sent to work in the villages to educate peasant youth in medical knowledge. Physicians trained in this fashion, he said, 'might not be very competent but far better than fake doctors and witch doctors [and] furthermore, villages can afford them.' An important point about these 'barefoot doctors' was to raise their standards during practice. As for the allocation of resources, to spend the largest sums on penetrating research of difficult diseases was to 'aim at the peaks and detach medical work from the masses', according to Mao. The 'peaks' would not be abandoned but the lion's share of resources from now on should be allocated to prevention and cure of the common, frequent and widespread diseases.

The popularization of this directive signalled the start of a stormy decade of struggle in which the rural cadres of the Communist Party, encouraged by the arrival (in some cases the return) of educated youth, pitted themselves against the doctors and professional administrators in the county department of public health to establish a new medical system centred in the villages.

Under the pressure of Mao's directive, the county bureau of public health in Shifang allotted substantial resources to upgrading the commune hospitals. At Junction a grant of Y20,000 allowed the commune to purchase land for a new twenty-bed hospital equipped with an X-ray machine, and to recruit staff for various departments in traditional and Western medicine – surgery, obstetrics, paediatrics, internal medicine, orthopaedics, ophthalmology, haemorrhoids as well as dispensaries for Chinese and Western medicines. This brought minor surgery and treatment for fractures and other common ailments within the range of the villagers.

Another result was a crash programme to find barefoot doctors, midwives and medical orderlies for the production teams and the rudimentary medical clinics established in most of the 256 brigades in Shifang county. In three-month, sometimes six-month, courses, qualified doctors, sent down to the countryside by rotation during the Cultural Revolution, trained 658 barefoot doctors in basic first aid, Chinese medicine, acupuncture, the use of thermometers, the dispensing of vaccines by injection and drugs for influenza, stomach upsets and other common ailments. The total number of medical personnel in the county rose from 592 in 1965 to 3,420 a decade later.[3] As one barefoot doctor explained:

> We decide on what medicine to use according to the patient's condition. For chronic diseases and gynaecological problems, abnormal menstruation, we use Chinese medicine; for infections or pain we use Western medicine. For colds or flu we can use either traditional or Western medicine depending on the patient's choice. When there is a flu epidemic we cook up a large brew of Chinese medicine and send it to the field for everyone to drink a bowl.

The director of the commune hospital highly appreciated the role of the paramedics. 'Without them and the village clinics', said Dr Yang Zengli, a man trained in Western medicine, 'we wouldn't have been able to cope with the situation because the peasants would crowd in here even when they had minor problems. And the barefoot doctors did most of the preventive medical work as well.' It was a good start on creating an accessible, experimental, non-élitist public health system biased in favour of prevention.

Perhaps the greatest success of the new rural medical system lay in its victory over schistosomiasis, otherwise known as snail fever. This disease is caused by a microscopic worm that lives part of its life-cycle in the liver and intestine of warm-blooded beings and the other part in an amphibious snail. The connecting link is the water in the irrigation canals and rice fields where the peasants become infected as they transplant seedlings or wash their clothes.

Symptoms of the disease in humans are intestinal inflammation causing bleeding, malnutrition, fatigue, hardening of the liver and flow of fluid into the abdominal cavity; the belly becomes distended from this fluid and from enlargement of the spleen which may expand until it weighs up to twenty pounds instead of its normal seven or eight ounces. Affected children do not mature in height or sexually and women cease menstruating; if left to run its course, the disease is fatal.

The first systematic checks in Junction People's Commune in 1959 revealed that one in four commune members had the infection. The campaign against schistosomiasis in the people's communes of Shifang county followed a national pattern that included both medical and political dimensions. The strategy concentrated overwhelming forces and applied the 'mass line' concept that Mao Zedong had worked out and tested during the revolutionary wars. This concept rests on the belief that the common people have inexhaustible strength and wisdom and that when their energy is given full play they can accomplish great deeds; the task of the leadership is to learn from the people, summarize and systematize their experience and with this knowledge decide on policy.

By means of posters, radio broadcasts, films, exhibitions and mass meetings the peasants learned the nature of their ancient enemy. Once they became aware of the sources of schistosomiasis they joined in making plans and in forming a public health army to defeat it. As barefoot doctor Tan put it:

> We were carrying out Chairman Mao's instruction to do away with the 'god of the plague'. It was a people's war against disease. It was a life and death battle; if we didn't get the snails, they would get us. When the masses understood this, then the teams were willing to contribute the necessary labour power to wage the people's war.

Each production team appointed a medical orderly and organized groups of seven or eight people to gather the snails from the banks of the irrigation ditches. 'The people had to be young and healthy and not afraid of wading in the cold water', said Tan. Teachers mobilized their pupils to go out after class to look for snails.

After initial successes in the 1950s and 1960s the disease reappeared. This prompted an even more concerted effort in 1975 during which the county mobilized 50,000 people.[4] They dug new irrigation ditches and filled in the old ones to eliminate the snails' habitat. Because of the difficulty of finding every snail the brigades tried to interrupt the life-cycle of the worms at another point by preventing faeces containing live eggs from contaminating the fields. This could be done by making cement-lined pits to store the excrement for several weeks until the heat generated by the ammonia killed the parasites. (The process also created methane gas for cooking and lighting. At the end of five years 55 per cent of the families in No. 8 Brigade had such methane gas pits for curing fertilizer and also for creating inexpensive fuel.)

Next to prevention, treatment became the prime objective of the campaign and this meant case-hunting. From 1959 until 1981 in Shifang county they did a general inspection for schistosomiasis each year.

'Everyone had to hand in a sample of their faeces three times', said the director of the hospital at Junction People's Commune, 'and we checked each sample three times.'

The huge scale of this effort could only be accomplished by local people using simple, improvised methods with a minimal dependence on outside experts. Each general inspection took about two months. Each brigade set up a temporary headquarters with about ten staff – one trained person from the county hospital, one person from the commune and the rest from the production teams. These groups of ten, each responsible for about 2,000 people, lived and worked on the spot for the two months. 'We had a list of all the names of the people and we checked them off as we went along', said Tan.

After years of hard work the commune reached the criteria of the central authorities. The number of people afflicted by the disease after 1959 was 5,700 and by 1982 it was down to four. In the county as a whole, where there had been 70,000 sufferers in the same period of time, there were now 2,000. But any slackening could lead to a renewal of epidemic conditions since the worms and host snails breed easily. 'Even if there is only one infected person,' said commune director Yang Changyou, 'it is enough to have the disease spread quickly again. We do sample checks each year.'

While the campaign against snail fever yielded success, not all was smooth sailing with the new medical system. Sometimes through mismanagement of the public welfare fund, or limited supplies of medicine, or the questionable professional competence of some barefoot doctors, village clinics had difficulty winning and keeping the confidence of the peasants. The clinic at No. 8 Brigade often found itself in this situation.

The brigade leadership assigned Tan Qijun, a trusted poor peasant and party member, to help get things started. He had only one year's formal education and could not read fluently but he became interested in the work of the two barefoot doctors in his clinic – a young man and woman in their early twenties – and managed to attend classes to qualify himself as a medical practitioner.

'On the first night the clinic opened there was much confusion', said Tan. 'Many people came, about fifty, and we weren't familiar with the location of the various medicines. We had no tables so the boxes were all on the floor and we really got backaches from stooping to read the labels while the people waited impatiently.'

Tan also made house calls and when he spoke of the way some people came to believe in the clinic it became obvious that inherited unscientific ideas of folk medicine were as valid to him as the materials in his barefoot doctor's kit:

One day I was returning home after visiting an old woman with heart trouble in No. 2 production team. The deputy team leader, Zeng, stopped me, saying that his wife was having a miscarriage and could I help. I told him I had nothing left in my kit except three acupuncture needles, but he begged me to come, so I agreed. When I saw her she was very pale and the padded trousers she was wearing were soaked in blood; she couldn't even speak. So I used the three needles – two on her feet and one on her upper lip, just below the nose.

Zeng told me that during his wife's miscarriage the womb had come down; he had just washed his hands with soap and pushed it back up. I said, 'How could you do that, in such a simple way! It may cause serious infection.'

I asked him, 'Do you have any hair? If you don't I can cut some of her hair and burn it.' Zeng said he had some, and got it from his room. Then I asked him to get a copper coin. I wrapped it in cloth, burned the hair and then rubbed the coin in the ash. Then I put the remedy into her mouth.

At that moment the person who was helping me whispered, 'This thing is too serious, better send her to the commune hospital.' I said, 'Don't worry, we'll see. If it doesn't work in five minutes we'll send her.' Within three minutes some colour returned to her cheeks and the bleeding stopped. It was more effective than a blood transfusion. Then she began to speak again.

Zeng was immensely impressed and pleased, and hurried to cook a few eggs for us to eat. I said I had just had my lunch but he insisted. Then I prescribed three doses of Chinese medicine for her.

A few days later their daughter came and said that her mother was ill again and wanted me to come. I asked, 'What's the problem?' She said, 'I don't know, you'd better come and ask her.' How could I take proper medicines? So I just took my kit and went.

When we got there she wasn't ill; it was just a pretext to invite me to dinner. As a result of his wife's cure, Zeng believed in the clinic and joined the co-operative medical insurance and persuaded the rest of his team members to follow suit.

The peasant barefoot doctors and the medical orderlies in the production teams, in spite of their shortcomings, were no doubt the essential element in the success of the public health campaigns. Trained by the professional doctors sent out from the cities, they were, as Mao predicted, something that the villages could afford. The brigade paid them in the form of work points which they exchanged for grain and cash in their production teams in the same way and at the same level as the other commune members received their income. This covered between 200 and 400 work days each year. They also worked part-time in the fields. These methods of operation solved the medical workers' living expenses and kept them close to the peasants they served.

But apart from this basic support from the collective's public welfare fund the finances of the clinic remained a constant problem because of the costs for supplies and medicines.

Faced with economic difficulties the commune leadership, again using the 'mass line' process, began searching for new ways to support the co-operative clinics beyond the annual Y3 fee *per capita* shared fifty/fifty by the collective and the individual. They received proposals from the peasants in No. 6 Brigade that commune members should begin growing medicinal herbs to help the clinics. The suggestion seemed to have several merits: it could alleviate the shortages of medicine; families short of cash could pay their premiums in kind; surplus herbs sold to the state would provide cash to buy Western drugs; the herbs could be grown on odd bits of land around the houses without occupying arable land, and, perhaps most important politically, it would rally the people in self-reliant support of socialized medicine.

As a result of these considerations the commune adopted the plan and a cadre went to the brigade to help create a pilot project. Following a year's effort of cultivating such items as root of gold thread, peppermint, bark of eucommia, red-root salvia, root of Zhejiang figwort and peony the results were positive and the experiment spread to the other brigades in the commune. After some time the commune claimed that 3,914 of its families (out of 4,492) were growing from five to twenty different types of herb medicines around their homes and that the thirteen brigades had a surplus of Y26,000 in their co-operative clinics.[5]

The party press popularized this experience and as a result of an article in the *People's Daily* the clinic in No. 6 Brigade became a famous model, with delegations arriving from all over the province and beyond to learn from its experience.[6] The brigade could not cope with all the visitors and in desperation appealed for help. The provincial government responded with some investment funds for an auditorium capable of seating 600 people and the provincial press stepped up publicity. The *Sichuan Daily* of 19 June 1973 wrote in an editorial:

> Co-operative medical care is a new-born thing during the Cultural Revolution and it has met the hopes of the poor and lower middle peasants . . . to prevent illness and to cure the sick by depending on the collective strength . . . by taking the socialist road.

To drive home the political lessons of No. 6 Brigade, the paper declared in high-flown language:

The people are the real heroes and there is no limit to their wisdom; since co-operative medical care is created by the people, the people can eliminate all obstacles during practical struggle on their march forward. The critical question is how to strengthen the leadership, how to trust the people completely, how to discuss with the people when they confront problems, how to go among the people to discover, summarize and spread experiences that grow among the people.

But as it happened, many peasants in the commune grew tired of growing herbs. Some of the 'heroes' lacked the necessary skills and their plants never flourished. Then, too, there was the bother of using Chinese medicine since you had to have a special pot and use fuel to cook up the brew; any left over could not be easily stored and was wasted. The pills of Western-style medicine were much more convenient to use – if they could be obtained.

Several of the city-educated youths in the commune, struck by the inconvenience of using herbal medicine in the traditional way, pitched in to do something about it. They set themselves the task of discovering means of extracting the essence of some common herbs in order to make pills. Starting on a small scale on the high street in a shop that they called the 'Junction People's Commune June 26th Traditional Medicine Factory' in honour of Mao's famous June 26th directive on public health, they built upon the experience of the 6th Brigade and eventually their efforts blossomed into an operation of great importance for the commune. By 1979 with the help of a Y30,000 grant from the county they moved into new premises over the reclaimed land at the White Fish River. From the original five workers they grew until there were 106 employees with an output of Y4,000,000 in 1985 and markets throughout the province and in other parts of the country.

Although spectacularly successful, the medicine factory could not rescue the co-operative medical clinics from their difficulties. There had been exaggerations and boasting that led to false impressions. 'For example, people said that the co-op medical clinic had money to spare at the end of the year,' said commune director Yang Changyou, 'but it was not true.' Some of the production teams were in debt to the clinic because they could not afford to support every needy person from the public welfare fund. Therefore although the account books of the clinic recorded the total figure owing as an asset it could not be collected. 'It looked as if we had a surplus,' said Yang, 'but it was only on the books.'

Yang also maintained that the ideological level of the peasants fell short of the needs of a co-operative system. Chronically ill people had to go to the clinic frequently and used as much as Y100 for medicine per year; when others saw this they said, 'I've also paid my money and should get my share out' so they went to get medicine even when they were not ill and sold it on the market.

A few years later, in 1983, after decollectivization the clinic in No. 6 Brigade looked forlorn like a faded summer dream. The doors of the empty auditorium swung on rusted hinges, on the walls were old posters and graphs showing the triumphs of past years. A distillery had contracted for part of the complex and on the clinic door, scrawled in chalk, were the pathetic words, 'People must have a conscience. Please pay your credit account as soon as possible! signed: Barefoot doctor Liu.' The same situation prevailed in most of the other clinics.

With the abandonment of the commune and its work point system for rewarding labour, the social basis for paying the barefoot doctors disappeared. Along with the land and other means of production, the villages contracted most clinics out to barefoot doctors who were forced to operate them as business enterprises with fees for service.

As the pressures to become cost-efficient under the reforms introduced by Deng Xiaoping begin to break down the tradition of social health care, the ideological debates heat up. A peasant in No. 8 Brigade laments the change.

> Before under the co-operative health system, we used to say, 'when one is ill thousands come to help', but now the saying is 'when one is ill one pays' and the more ill you are the more you pay. Isn't this a little backward?

The preventive work by the barefoot doctors continues with a subsidy from the township government but the leadership of this vital area is weakened. The barefoot doctor in No. 8 Brigade explained:

> We no longer take any measures to cure the manure or sanitize the cesspools. We leave them uncovered and there are many flies in summer and early autumn. This is because people claim that manure from the methane gas pits is not as good and that it takes more time and labour to get the manure out of the pit than from an open cesspool.

The professionals in the county department of health say that these problems are temporary. They justify the collapse of forty clinics and the reduction in the number of medical workers in the county from 3,739 in 1982 to 1,828 in 1985 as a lessening of waste and an improvement in the quality of personnel by weeding out the incompetent. It is called scientific management. Now that the barefoot doctors are responsible for their own profits and losses, it is argued that they will work harder to cure illness, otherwise nobody will come for treatment and their income will be affected.

Although the voices in favour of socialized medicine are muted in the post-Mao era, they are not entirely absent. One of the former barefoot doctors at No. 8 Brigade, Zhou Zhizhu, maintains that when she worked in the clinic they didn't have serious financial problems in funding the co-operative plan.

> We grew some of our own herbal medicines beside the railway tracks. Basically we made ends meet. We didn't take any medicine from the clinic for our own use, not even if our pigs were sick.

She says that the public accumulation funds are quite high and should be used to support co-operative medical insurance.

And one of the villages in Junction township, formerly No. 5 Brigade of the People's Commune, stubbornly continues with its co-operative clinic. This is in spite of disapproval of the head of the county public health bureau who says it gives a poor quality of service. The local party secretary disagrees:

> The people in our brigade like the co-operative medical system. We are running a cement factory and other enterprises and we use some of the surplus in our public accumulation fund to give Y2,500 for medical care. Next year we shall increase that amount.

The tradition of social responsibility for medical services has one other strong advocate in Junction township in the person of Ran Shengxiang, the burly young man who helped found and continues to direct the June 26th Chinese Medicine Factory. Ran maintains that his enterprise is resisting the upsurge of backward capitalist ideology among small peasant producers.

> The rate of profit on medicine is quite low, because it is a kind of social welfare product, a humanitarian enterprise. We emphasize the social results. The most important thing is to explore the treasury of Chinese medicine.

As for relationships between workers and managers, Ran was proud of its socialist character.

> We are all jointly masters of the enterprise, there is no such thing as giving bad treatment or beating workers. We have a workers' congress and a women workers' committee that join us in making plans and regulations.

The financial position of the factory is posted on the wall at the end of every month for everyone to see.

Ran's salary is Y120 per month, while the average among the workers is Y80 – not a large gap. Ran explained that wages are conditional.

Each month I take Y48 which is 40 per cent of my wage. This is for living expenses. The other 60 per cent will be linked to economic results. If the targets are fulfilled I can take it all; if there is more I get more, and if we fall short I get less. It is the same for everyone who works here.

In this way, he claimed, everyone works with a sense of responsibility and unity.

This is not some individual's enterprise, it is a socialist organization belonging to the collective. That is what we tell the workers and this is what we believe.

The polemics continue. The professionals, who receive their salaries from the state and are mainly unshaken in their belief that political mobilizations are a hindrance to good medical care, have reclaimed their positions of leadership. The head of the county bureau of public health pours scorn on the peasants' co-operative health clinics as 'a pauper's pipe dream'.

But this reversal does not obscure the result of the mass movements in transforming the level of public health in Shifang county. And to judge from the experience of other modernizing Third World countries, had it not been for the energy of politically motivated change set loose in the Chinese villages, the most elaborate and well-intentioned plans and budgets of a national ministry of health could well have had little effect. Many of the party members at MaGaoqiao continue to believe that co-operative, socialized medicine will be the wave of the future.

13

PART-WORK, PART-STUDY: THE SCHOOL

There are three types of school in Junction township in 1986: government, private and voluntary schools.

The government operates a middle school and a central primary school on the high street; the teachers here are fully paid by the state and the library and other teaching resources are more plentiful. Generally, the pupils with the highest standing get admitted. The provincially-owned Chemical Fertilizer Machinery Factory runs a private school for the children of its workers; its teachers are paid out of the profits of the enterprise. The rest are voluntary or people-run schools located in the thirteen villages of the township.

These include primary schools, combination primary and lower-middle schools and an agricultural technical middle school which is a part-work, part-study school that equips young farmers with scientific knowledge for modernizing agriculture. The majority of these voluntary schools, which were created during the Cultural Revolution (1966-76) where none had been before, still face a shortage of qualified teachers and have few learning resources.

'Ours is a large country and we can't rely on the state for everything', explained the county education director, Zhang Shitai, an urbane man with grey-streaked hair who sported two pens in the breast pocket of his black wool cadre's jacket.

> So we have state schools and schools run by the people. In 1983 the townships and villages raised about Y800,000 for the running of their schools. If we were to look for such a large amount of money from the state, we'd have to wait for fifteen years. We have to walk on two legs. Every year the state gives us about Y40,000 to help in running the schools. The state is trying to increase this figure, but it takes time.

While the voluntary village schools receive modest financial subsidies from the state it is the responsibility of the village committees to raise the necessary funds, to recruit the teachers and to organize the administration, the curriculum and textbooks in accordance with the directives of the ministry of education.

The voluntary school at MaGaoqiao opened in 1972. This was during the Cultural Revolution when Mao sent down educated youth from urban centres to work in the villages. A number of them came to MaGaoqiao where they acted as a catalyst to expand the school facilities and some of them served as teachers.

The school building, erected on the feed lot of No. 5 production team, consists of six single-storied classrooms that are furnished in a rudimentary fashion. Except for the blackboard across the front of each room, the white-washed walls are mainly bare and there is little sign of teaching materials, most of which are kept in the school office. The windows are without glass and the desks and benches, made of stone and cement, are on the dry but cold earth floor. The school is enclosed in a small compound with an imposing red star over the front gate symbolizing a commitment to the Communist future.

Before the construction of these buildings the teachers held classes wherever space could be found. Some of the luckier children went over to the central primary school on the high street, while others studied in makeshift rooms in the brigade headquarters. Many did not attend school at all. In those early years when the village was in the throes of rapid social changes, including the Great Leap Forward, schooling was intermittent and teachers were often villagers who themselves had had no more than a primary or lower-middle school education.

The head teacher in MaGaoqiao school, Shi Zhengfa, was a typical example. Born in the village in 1948, two years before Liberation, he attended primary classes at the Wang Family Ancestral Temple, followed by three years of lower-middle school in a neighbouring town. After this he returned to No. 3 production team in the brigade to do farm work.

In 1965, at the age of seventeen and without any normal school training, the brigade leaders asked him to be a teacher. Within a year the Four Clean-up movement came and then the Cultural Revolution closed the schools for a year. He spent that year at public expense, along with all the other teachers in Fangting town, learning, as he said, 'what it meant to have education serve proletarian politics'.

When I returned from the county town, I taught the children Chinese language for a year and then I gave up the job and went back to my production team to farm. I was not satisfied with teaching. The work points for me as a teacher were less than for those who worked in the fields. And besides, I didn't have any textbooks for my students. It was not easy to do a good job in teaching so I gave it up.

From 1969 until 1975 he threw himself into the farmland construction campaigns. He joined the Communist Party and took charge of youth work. Meanwhile the primary school expanded and was short of hands. 'So I was persuaded to come out and pick up my teaching job again', he said. He learned some teaching methods by working alongside the urban educated youth and when they left the village in 1978 he found himself head teacher at the age of thirty, in a school with 290 pupils and seven other teachers.

The school year has two semesters, the first beginning in September and the second, after the Spring Festival in February, which lasts until July. The school operates six days a week with time off for a few days during the busy agricultural seasons so that the pupils and teachers may help with the farm work. This arrangement is part of what is meant by having education serve proletarian politics.

Children enter grade one when they are seven years old and graduate into lower-middle school at the age of twelve. According to the school committee 98.7 per cent of the children between the ages of seven and twelve were in school in 1986 and over 80 per cent complete the requirements of the primary curriculum. The crowded classes, which are mixed, have up to fifty pupils who sit in pairs at the desks.

The weekly timetable provides for twenty-eight periods – three in the morning and two each afternoon, except for Wednesday afternoon which is reserved for teacher political study or professional development. A long, three-hour noon break which allows time for pupils to help their parents with gathering pig fodder and other household farm chores is another illustration of the way that the school timetable is closely related to the needs and rhythm of village life. The weight given to the various subjects throughout the primary school years reflects both the difficulty of learning to read and write in the Chinese language and the need of the collective economy for record keepers and accountants trained in mathematics:

Chinese language	12 periods
Arithmetic	10 periods
Music	2 periods
Art	2 periods
Gymnastics and Sports	2 periods
	28 periods

There is a detailed syllabus for course content and the standards to be achieved for each grade. The outline for Grade 3 is as follows:
Chinese language including composition: consolidate knowledge of

pinyin (phonetics) using standard pronunciation, learn 800 new characters (for a total of 2,500), take dictation, recite and be able to read texts aloud fluently and with feeling, and read children's stories silently and retell them; write paragraph describing a picture, short stories, 'My Mother', 'New Year's Day' . . .

Mathematics: use of abacus to add, subtract and multiply; multiplication and division of large numbers; finding areas of squares and rectangles; initial recognition of fractions; mastery of decimal notation; practical problem solving.

Music: theory of beat and rhythm, basic musical signs and notes; choral singing and children's songs.

Art: drawing, perspective of simple objects, sketching vegetables and fruits.

Gymnastics and sport: basic knowledge of physical health, marching, running (60 metres in 12.3 seconds for boys, 12.7 seconds for girls is the pass mark), jumping, throwing, skipping, ping pong, other games.

While this syllabus provides a clear idea of the skills that pupils are expected to acquire, it does not reveal the moral-political dimensions which have always been, and continue to be, fundamental to Chinese education. In part, this aspect is developed outside the regular curriculum through the Young Pioneers organization which all children between the ages of nine and fourteen are eligible to apply to join.

At MaGaoqiao the majority of pupils are members and one of the teachers is assigned to give leadership. The pioneers have their own red banner and each one wears a red scarf. Their activities are designed to foster good study habits, teach members to help in the home, encourage physical and mental growth and develop initiative and creativeness. They use the *Children's Newspaper* to which the school subscribes, as a source of ideas. Around such holidays as International Children's Day they prepare singing, dance and drama groups for a cultural performance. Their initiation ceremonies have the type of rituals that children enjoy – a pledge of allegiance, a flag raising at sunrise, planting a tree or some other socially useful action. According to one Chinese source the organization

> enlightens children on communism and trains them to be a new generation that loves the motherland, the people, labour and science, that takes good care of public property, is healthy, active, courageous, honest and creative in spirit.[1]

Apart from the extracurricular activities there are classroom practices which help to train leadership. Each class elects two representatives who assist the teachers to maintain discipline, keep the classroom tidy, and plan sports and other activities.

Physical punishment is not allowed but it is not entirely absent either. 'If a pupil's behaviour is very bad,' said head teacher Shi, 'the most serious step is to ask the pupil to go to the teachers' office and there he or she will be criticized.' The teachers keep contact with the parents by visiting the homes and also by speaking about school affairs at brigade membership meetings. Some parents still spank their children if they hear unfavourable reports from school. 'That's fair, all right,' said one teacher, 'but it's unfair for teachers to do so. From two directions – parents and teachers – the pupil's behaviour can be improved.'

A major way of influencing and shaping the moral-political outlook of village youth is through the texts used for teaching Chinese language. Apart from relatively non-political factual information, the readers contain certain values respecting personal beliefs and social behaviour.

During the time of Mao's leadership the core values included such matters as devotion to the new China in all its aspects, rejection of the evils and superstitions of the old society, thrift and hard work, the superiority of solidarity and co-operation over individualistic behaviour, altruism, especially towards the aged and those less fortunate, good behaviour has its own reward, improper behaviour to be attended by bad consequences for the individual, the primary social role of the worker-peasant-soldier, and latterly glorification of Chairman Mao as the 'great teacher and helmsman'.[2]

In the post-Mao era new readers replace some of the older values with stress on the goals of modernization, individual responsibility, openness to the outside world and the positive role played by scientists and intellectuals.

Within the texts there are contradictory messages such as the themes of hard work and achievement vs. the themes of sacrificing personal ambition for the benefit of society, or the themes of ingenuity in solving problems vs. themes of obedience to the rules and to authority, or themes of the evils of old China vs. themes of the achievements made in China's past. In the hands of the most able teachers such matters become the subject of classroom discussion and debate, with the teachers aiming to clarify what a 'proletarian' standpoint would be in each case and promoting discussion to train students to handle contradictions as part of the Marxist dialectical way of thinking.

Many teachers feel that students in the 1980s are not as good as those they taught earlier. Too much time is spent watching TV programmes with cunning villains and other negative models. 'Students now are more selfish than before', said one teacher. 'They lack knowledge, are without any great or definite aims and are afraid of hardship', said another. 'Sometimes they don't believe what you say. What can you do with them?'

It is customary to blame such traits on 'the ten years of turmoil of the Cultural Revolution'. While there may be some truth in this view, the turmoil ended before many of the present generation of students were born.

Another explanation is the shift of emphasis in society generally from attention to revolutionary ideology and developing social consciousness as proposed by Mao Zedong when these teachers were students, to the present policy of motivating people by material incentives. Mao had argued that even if the importance of material incentives was recognized it could never be the sole principle, there was always another principle, 'namely, spiritual inspiration from political ideology'. Every person entering school to study culture and technology in a socialist society, said Mao, 'should recognize before anything else that they are studying for socialist construction, for industrialization, to serve the people, for the collective interest, and not above all for a higher wage'. He wanted people to have some consciousness and not turn to the principle of individual interest 'as if it were some magic wand'.[3] What the teachers at MaGaoqiao decried about their students' attitudes was the result of the weakening of such socialist politics upon which they themselves had been raised. After the decollectivization of 1982 it is difficult to avoid the consequences of emphasis on material incentives and private ambitions to get ahead.

When the commune was abandoned at Junction in 1982 the financial support for education also had to be reconsidered. Tuition fees from individuals remained the same: with the exception of children of revolutionary martyrs, dependants of army members or families with a single child, parents pay a fee of Y4 per year for pencils, notebooks and textbooks.

Most of the funds for the voluntary schools, however, are provided by the production teams. Originally under the commune system, this happened in the form of work point credits given to teachers. By 1976 the teachers received an income equal to an average able-bodied brigade member of their own sex. Gradually after 1977 teachers began to be better paid and by 1980 they earned substantially more work points than the average brigade member – 3,130 points (worth Y165) compared to 2,410 points (worth Y126).

After the contracting of land to households and the disappearance of the collective work point system, the village began supporting education through several taxes on the households, called 'subsidy for teachers in voluntary schools', 'fund for adult education', 'education fund', 'school tuition fees to single child families', 'fund for repairing school houses'. By 1984 these taxes amounted to Y11.81 per household which was more than double the value of contributions under the old system.[4]

Part of this startling increase was the result of price inflation which had begun to creep into the Chinese economy. But the main source was pressure from the Ministry of Education through the county education authority to seize a moment of change in the economy in order to introduce various reforms in village schooling.

One positive result of the new financing arrangements was equality of salaries for teachers. 'All of us teachers are now equal in our basic income', said head teacher Shi. Formerly salaries depended on the value of the work day in the teacher's home production team and could vary by 10 or 15 per cent. Women teachers, especially, benefited by the change because work points for women on the production teams were only eight per day, two less than for men. 'So although they taught the same classes as men teachers,' said head teacher Shi, 'they got 20 per cent less pay. Now we are paid equally, the new system is good.'

More controversial is the introduction of a merit pay system. Under current policy about 10 per cent of each teacher's salary is withheld and is called a floating salary. This becomes a pool that is distributed at the end of the year according to the results of teaching. 'If you do your teaching work well,' said Shi, 'you will get more pay, but if you have not been doing well you will be at the minimum.'

In order to decide who has done well the ministry has introduced examinations at all levels. 'Even the seven-year-old primary school pupils have to take part in a year-end examination,' said Shi, 'so that the quality of teaching can be evaluated.' And there is an external county examination for graduating students conducted on the same day throughout the county, by which teachers are ranked. Shi referred to the negative effect of the merit system upon teaching methods.

We have to think of ways to help the students pass the examinations. We give them more dictation and writing practice and more memorization of texts. If a student fails a dictation I keep that student after school. It is a kind of spoon-feeding. We do not have much time for talking with parents or visiting the students' families as before.

The township has the name list of all the candidates in order to prevent teachers from weeding out the poorer students in their classes and discouraging them from sitting for the examinations. Shi explained:

Under this kind of pressure, you can only get the students to do their work well for the moment. They memorize the things they are supposed to learn and they are not encouraged to use their brain to think about the things they are learning. Once they reach the higher levels they will crash. Our methods are not a good way to open up a young person's intellectual interest.

Other pitfalls of the bonus system were hinted at by Shi, including fraud in the examinations.

When some teachers whose level of consciousness is not so high are in the county marking papers they may recognize their students' handwriting and give them higher marks, or lower marks to others. If the average mark of a teacher's students is only one point higher than others, that teacher might get a bonus. Also teachers in some schools put their good students at the same desk as poorer ones and encourage the latter to copy from the clever neighbour. The teachers exchange places to supervise the examinations (we go to the school in No. 9 Brigade and they come here) but who knows whether you have arranged the seating plan a few days before the examination?

In an effort to raise teaching standards every rural teacher in the county will have to pass a qualifying examination in the next three years, in which 30 per cent of the content is on teaching methods. If after three attempts a teacher fails to meet the standards he or she will have to give up teaching and transfer to some other field of work. To assist teachers' professional development the township designated several schools as keypoints in which better qualified teachers with normal school training are concentrated and from which the others may learn. Shi explained:

We sit in on other classes to observe good teachers, and on Wednesday afternoons we talk over these matters. We are encouraged to use the method of enlightenment, of drawing our students out, but how to put this into practice is another matter. Mainly we have to find our own path but as to whether the way we are doing things can be called a teaching method or not I don't know.

In another part of the educational reform Junction township improved access to middle school. Many farmers complained that of the almost 500 primary school graduates each year only about 170, or 40 per cent, were able to go further. This demand led to the establishment of two new lower-middle schools and this allows 60 per cent of primary graduates to have higher education. One of the new schools is in MaGaoqiao. It is a two-storey combination school paid for out of the profits of the rural enterprises. Students with lower averages, 65 per cent in Chinese language and mathematics, may enter compared to a 75 per cent average required for the keypoint middle school on the high street.

Although there is a sense of pride and enthusiasm for the advances in educational opportunity at the township-sponsored lower-middle school in MaGaoqiao, relations between the teaching staff and the local village cadres are cool. This is a noticeable feature of the local scene. Peasant cadres have always needed the active assistance of the rural intellectuals for conducting propaganda work but since many of the intellectuals come from the more privileged class backgrounds they were also the targets of class struggle during the mass movements. Teachers and cadres remain mutually distrustful. Although mass movements have ended for the time being, memories fade slowly.

Just such a rural intellectual is teacher Zhang Gufu, aged forty-four, of rich peasant background and headmaster of the lower-middle school. He is a survivor of the class wars, bruised but unbowed.

A gentle-mannered man with a long, rectangular face, a full head of hair tinged with grey, metal-framed glasses of 1950s vintage to correct a left eye that looks to the left, he wears a green cotton jacket with blue arm protectors held by elastic at the wrist to prevent chalk powder from falling up his sleeve.

'Life was difficult for me,' he said, 'I had all kinds of disasters, some natural and some man-made.' The difficulties of the Great Leap Forward led to the closure of the normal school before he could get his teacher's certificate, but in spite of this shortcoming he was the best qualified person available in the commune. The commune leaders therefore put him on the state payroll in charge of the twenty-four teachers in village-run schools and with five classes to teach.

'To run schools well you had all kinds of problems in the 1960s,' he said, 'conditions were poor.' After receiving complaints and making investigations he would write reports to the commune leadership.

> Their attitude was not good. The cadres at the commune level liked playing cards and Chinese chess. Sometimes they ignored me when I went to them with questions. They only turned to me after they were tired of playing cards.

Upset by this treatment, Zhang developed migraine headaches.

During the Cultural Revolution the cadres often asked him to write articles about model workers or to make broadcasts. He did this and managed the editing and printing of a small newspaper for the commune. Once he wrote a short play about the way his production team learned from Dazhai that was highly praised by the prefectural revolutionary committee.

I felt glorious. I studied some works of Marx, Lenin and Chairman Mao, and once gave a lecture on the *Critique of the Gotha Programme* by Marx which the county organized. The reaction to my lecture was good and the party secretary of our brigade praised me. Our party secretary was such a person: he praised me on the stage and kicked me under the table. To be a teacher I have tasted all kinds of bitterness. There was always someone to make trouble for me.

The cadres may have given Zhang a hard time but to judge from essay topics he assigns he is not without indirect means of hitting back by influencing his students' ideas about cadres. The following student essay, picked from a pile that Zhang was grading in 1983, reveals some strongly-held opinions.

Since the contract to households every family in our production team is happy. It is only those who are officials who are not so happy, why is this?

We have to start from the beginning: formerly the official of our team, that is, our team leader, did not play a leading role, did not carry out the business of the collective, he just looked after his own pleasure. Everyone said he was a dog official. As soon as the collective got some money he went to drink wine and eat meat at the restaurant until the cash was spent. Then he would take collective grain and tobacco to sell and use the money to satisfy his appetites. He brought the collective to the verge of collapse. Long before the next crop was harvested commune members ran out of food to eat. They would go to look for the flustered team leader. He would have to go elsewhere to borrow food grain. When the next crop was reaped there wasn't much left after the debt was repaid . . . from year to year our living standard was going down. Just at this critical point when we could not sustain ourselves the party sent down its policy that the land should be contracted to the households. The team leader reluctantly distributed the land to everybody. Why wasn't he happy? He could no longer take advantage of his free ride. He could no longer take what belonged to others, couldn't bully the commune members. He was very unhappy.

As soon as the commune members contracted for the land they were jubilant, everyone was full of vigour, because those who worked more would receive more, nobody could exploit others. Very soon after the contract was made, the harvest was collected and after taxes and quotas sold to the state there were still piles of grain at home. Once the commune members had money many of them built tile-roofed houses or even two-storey buildings. Not short of food, or clothes, or even money, they could buy radios, television sets . . . In this way the commune families became rich households within a year. ('Rapid Changes', by Xu Dingju (female), aged fourteen.)

In the post-commune period with the power of the peasant cadres curbed Zhang seems more relaxed. 'When I look back at the footprints of my life I feel happy and contented in my heart', he said. Although disappointed that he had not done as well as some of his contemporaries who had gone on to college or university in the latter years of the Cultural Revolution to become teachers or doctors on the state payroll, or even his third brother who is an engineer and has been elected as a representative to the county People's Congress, he is philosophical: 'I believe that to be a man I should make my own contribution to the people, to my country. If I do that in my life it will do.'

The school system at MaGaoqiao continues to grow and change under constant pressure from the higher levels. In 1986 the Ministry of Education raised the standards requiring that there be six years of primary and three years of lower-middle school education.

To meet the challenge the village education committee makes co-operative arrangements with a neighbouring village to increase the accommodation.

The search for more and better qualified teachers continues and so does the friction between teachers and cadres. Although none of the teachers at MaGaoqiao have completed normal school training, their salaries, bolstered with subsidies by a state that is determined to raise their status, have risen greatly to an average of Y600 per annum. In addition, like everyone else in the village, the teachers contract farm land and the additional income which this generates puts them in the top bracket ahead of most of the villagers.

It is not easy for veteran rural party cadres to accept this new balance between intellectuals and peasants.

14

THE POLITICS OF
WOMEN'S EMANCIPATION

In January 1981, during Spring Festival time, the village meeting hall at MaGaoqiao is brightly lit for a celebration. Behind the front table piled with fruit candies, calendars, packets of cigarettes and other small gifts, a striking-looking woman of medium height, with short bobbed hair and in her late forties, speaks eloquently into the microphone.

'In the county's campaign to establish three-member families,' says Wang Dequn, leader of the county Women's Association, 'this village has become an advanced unit, a model for others to emulate. Here today are sixty-one more couples with one child who have pledged to keep their family to that size.' She congratulates the large, smartly dressed audience of two hundred or so young men, women and children as the village party leader prepares to hand out certificates of honour to these couples.

Gathered outside, peering through the windows, are a cluster of older men and women looking less than enthusiastic. They are uncertain whether the government's drive to control population growth is in their best interests.

Many questions relating to women's emancipation have cropped up on the agenda of the Women's Association over the years, including equal pay for equal work, job opportunities for women in the rural enterprises, free choice of marriage partner, adequate day-care nurseries, husband participation in domestic labour, the right to divorce and remarry. On these matters some uneven progress has been made, but for the most part fundamental breakthroughs remain to be achieved. However, for reasons that relate to the survival of the community itself, the central focus of women's current struggle for a better life has clearly shifted to the gains that can be made through family planning and winning more control over their reproductive functions.

In the past a woman's ultimate worth was judged by whether she could produce a son. And in a male-oriented society where a family's fortunes, including security in old age, depended upon its own labour power, the more sons the better since daughters always married out. Even after the collectivization of agriculture daughters-in-law were expected to fulfil this expectation, and through proverbs such as 'more sons means more blessings', the village patriarchs and the mother tigers (as some mothers-in-law were known) never let them forget it.

The result of an ideology that placed such a high premium on male heirs was the creation of social pressures that often forced young women to have more children than they wanted or their health could bear. And the results for the community were equally serious. When the demand for sons was combined with improvements in public health it brought an alarming increase in population growth in the mid-1950s and again after the Great Leap Forward. At MaGaoqiao the rate of population increase soared as high as sixty per 1,000 population in 1969 in comparison to the world average of seventeen per 1,000.[1] In a single decade after 1963 there were 550 new people added to this village of 1,300. Thus within one decade 48 per cent more people have to be fed and housed on the same overcrowded 345 acres. Clearly the village is headed for disaster unless the trend can be permanently reversed.

The reversal process began in 1971 with the commencement of a national campaign for later marriages. Although the constitution then allowed Chinese women to marry at eighteen and men at twenty, the local authorities in Shifang county set the ages at twenty-three and twenty-five respectively. In addition to late marriage the county government made great efforts to spread birth control information, and to provide free services for contraception. When contraceptive methods failed, induced abortions became more common. Ultimately in 1979, when it became evident from population surveys that China would still not be able to stabilize its population at 1.2 billion by the year 2000, the call went out for the present generation of new families to have only one child per couple. It is this policy, especially, that makes the older generation uneasy: if the single child is a girl and moves away at the time of marriage, there will be no one left to help out.

The single-child policy is, no doubt, an infringement on a woman's control of her reproduction process because many women, while perhaps not wanting to have to go on until they have one or more sons, do wish to have at least two children. Therefore women have regrets about the policy too. They are gaining only partial control of reproduction. However, limitations on their full emancipation in this respect is dictated, not by men, but by the general interest of a community that is faced by a crisis of over-population.

Based upon acceptance of this reasoning and as a result of determined efforts, especially by the Women's Association, the rate of natural increase (births minus deaths, immigration minus emigration) in Shifang county fell from thirty-two per 1,000 in 1971 to just over two per 1,000 in 1978.[2] In Junction People's Commune, after a surge of population growth in 1970 when several hundred urban educated youth arrived to settle in the countryside (Table J), the rate fell from twenty-six per 1,000 in 1971 to 2.1 per 1,000 in 1978, and in MaGaoqiao village it declined further to 1.5 per 1,000 in 1980.

This is a rare achievement. It has not gone unnoticed in the annals of the United Nations as a success story of the 1970s.[3]

In addition to the organization and ideology evident at the Spring Festival celebration in MaGaoqiao village hall, the decline in birth rates was accomplished with the help of material inducements to encourage young couples and older people to accept the loss of potential labour power. The incentives were substantial. For the young couples: a larger private plot, more grain, more work points, free nursery care, free primary and secondary schooling and free medical care, priority consideration for factory recruitment. The value of these incentives over the child's first fourteen years is estimated to equal an income of Y1,600,[4] a sizeable sum when it is remembered that the annual *per capita* income from the collective in Junction People's Commune in 1980 was Y173.

For the old people who had retired and lacked family to help them: the 'five guarantees' from the collective – food, clothing, shelter, medical care and burial expenses. According to the party branch secretary, Jiang Wenguang, the three existing families in this category at MaGaoqiao are supported at the middle level income. They get 600 *jin* of grain, Y9 per month (Y18 if they are unable to work their private plot), free electricity

TABLE J

Rate of population growth 1950–79
Junction People's Commune
(per thousand people)

Year	1950	1951	1952	1953	1954	1955	1956	1957	1958	1959
Rate	15.2	10.1	9.6	13.3	25.1	56.2	36.7	27.8	−43.6	−69.8
Year	1960	1961	1962	1963	1964	1965	1966	1967	1968	1969
Rate	−61.7	23.6	−17.1	57.4	30.5	33.5	50.2	34.6	38.2	38.2
Year	1970	1971	1972	1973	1974	1975	1976	1977	1978	1979
Rate	52.3	26.9	27.8	17.8	15.1	16.6	6.6	5.2	2.1	7.5

Source: Junction People's Commune, *Statistics 1949–85*, p. 1. Note: For a discussion of the drop in population 1958–60 see Chapter 6.

and cooking fuel, free medical care worth about Y60, one set of clothes each year, and every third year a set of winter padded clothing. They may raise chickens, cut bamboo and do other activities to augment their income if they feel strong enough. In nearby Democracy People's Commune similar experiments in establishing a type of farmer's pension had been started.[5]

There were also disincentives, a schedule of fines for any couple having a child beyond the plan, although at MaGaoqiao these have reportedly never been used. 'Generally speaking,' said the head of the Women's Association, 'our villagers are reasonable and conscientious about this matter; no one has gone and hid themselves in order to have an extra baby.'

The whole programme reflects an impressive commitment of resources and energies by the rural community. It is an effort that will probably have to continue into the twenty-first century because even if birth rates and natural growth rates fall close to zero, the absolute number of people will still expand for some years since the large base population, half of it under the age of twenty-one, has yet to enter its period of fertility.

In speaking to the village meeting Wang Dequn has a shrewd sense of occasion. She knows what a tough time the small handful of women party members in MaGaoqiao have had in promoting the 'one couple, one child' concept and she wants to bolster their prestige, and encourage them to keep active. Therefore she goes beyond the topic of family planning to raise awareness about the role and position of women in society generally.

Her talk is of a kind she must have given many times but it keeps its lustre because she has a warm and magnetic personality, an openness that draws people to her. Raised in poverty by a widowed mother who made a living by sewing for others and by seasonal farm work, Wang sets the tone for her remarks by referring to the importance of the party's leadership. She declares that 'if there was no Chinese Communist Party and Chairman Mao, my family would not be alive today. That is why I respect Mao Zedong and the party.'

As Wang moves into her main theme of women's emancipation, people at the meeting, both men and women, recall at the back of their minds how not so long ago, during the Cultural Revolution, this vigorous woman's daring and her quick mind propelled her to head the revolutionary committee of the whole county. She was, in effect, the county governor during that time. She is someone who can help make things happen.

More and more women are participating in government and political affairs, says Wang.

If we compare the situation for women now with that in the old society, it is just like the difference between sky and earth. Before Liberation the women of China were under the suppression of three big mountains weighing on the people – political authority, clan authority and religious authority, and women were also under the oppression of patriarchal power. There were locks and chains around the legs of women. In the old society it was said that it was virtuous for women to be without any knowledge; in the past there were only male towns and female counties.

The countryside people used to say, 'The girl is born like a flower, but she will soon be busy in front of the stove scooping burnt rice; the boy may be born with a lame leg, but he can do business on the high streets.'

In other words, according to Wang, no matter how capable a woman was she had to run around inside the house doing domestic chores. She had to obey her father when she was young, her husband after marriage, and later her son if she was widowed. These were the three obediences. Only men could move about freely.

The four virtues also controlled and limited women's activities. Women were only asked to do needlework and weaving, and were expected to be dressed up and made up for the pleasure of men. Women were not allowed to speak in the presence of men, especially strange men. When women smiled, they weren't supposed to show their teeth.

That was before Liberation. Women in New China are quite different. We are now allowed to participate in government and political affairs, we can join the men in socialist construction and we can do all kinds of work. At every level women comrades at conferences are 20 per cent or more of the delegates. This still isn't enough, more would be better! We have to fight harder for our emancipation.

Wang quotes 'elder sister' Deng (national women's leader Deng Yingzhao) to the effect that 'the emancipation of women is first and foremost the business of women; it is important that the full realization of our rights depends upon our own struggle and can never be bestowed upon us by others.' Wang urges women to participate fully in public life.

She gives a thumbnail sketch of women's historical struggles in the county: women organized to battle with the landlords, to confiscate their properties during the land reform, to take part in the armed forces; they made propaganda among the women to carry out the new Marriage Law of 1950 to get rid of the old system of one husband with several wives and replace it with the new policy of one husband, one wife. Sometimes rough men and rough mothers-in-law were sentenced to reform through labour or gaol. Women left the doors of their homes and took part in construction and production work by forming 'iron girls' fighting groups', 'red sisters-in-law fighting groups' and 'red grandmothers' fighting teams'. 'We had 1,000 such groups in this county', said Wang, 'and this actively led women to love the collective, to do farm work actively and at the same time increase their own income and become more economically liberated.'

Wang then touches briefly on some of the things that have been done to lighten the domestic chores of women.

> Now we can use coal briquettes; before we had to use wood or straw for fuel and that fire needed constant attention. This coal gives a long, steady heat and has really made it convenient. We can leave the stove while the rice is being steamed and it will be ready when we get back. Some people have sewing machines and they are willing to help their neighbours with their sewing. A machine has been invented to make the soles of cloth shoes which saves much time and effort. Now many families have pumps, hand pumps for drawing water from the wells which saves having to lift heavy buckets by hand. With the medical clinic in each village we don't have to take our children all the way to the hospital on the high street for every little problem. There is the nursery school in most brigades, so when we go to work in the fields or go to a meeting we have no worry. Now we women have more free time.

As for future tasks, apart from family planning, she singled out equal pay for equal work. Although the principle is written into the constitution, Wang notes that it is not yet carried out well since women, no matter how strong and able they are, only get eight work points per day, while the men can get ten. This is true not only for working in the fields but in all areas of work where there is remuneration. She mocks male cadres who receive more than women cadres for attending the same meetings saying, 'Why do you men get ten points for attending this meeting while women cadres only get eight? Is it because you have an extra ear, one more than women? Do you hear more about the content of the meeting?'

Speaking off the cuff, without notes, it is a brilliant presentation that provokes outbursts of laughter and wins appreciative applause from the audience. Wang is dedicated and she raises important feminist issues. She speaks of the need for consciousness-raising to 'clean up the old feudal ways of looking down upon women', of the necessity to safeguard the legal rights of women and children against 'bullying, despising and ill-treatment'. She looks at the village party secretary and cites Engels' remark that 'the degree of women's emancipation is the natural standard by which to measure a people's liberation'. Seldom has the cause of women's dignity and equality had more inspiring advocacy.

From what she says there is clearly no room in her mind for the notion that women should organize politically to pursue feminist goals outside of or independently of the party's leadership. If the struggle for women's liberation is not combined with the party's central task for each period, then she believes that victory for women is impossible. At the same time, if the party's struggle for socialist modernization, including population control, does not have women's active and willing participation then victory on that front is also impossible. After all, women 'hold up half the sky', and have a large role to play. It is a somewhat elusive, semi-autonomous, critically supportive relationship between party and women's organization in which party leadership is central that she is advocating.

In MaGaoqiao village, according to the 1982 census, there are 977 females and 971 males. An equal proportion of each sex (about 580) are registered as full or half-time agricultural workers in the commune and are eligible to receive work points for their labour. Such an achievement of numerical equality with men in the workforce is in itself a change in the sexual division of labour and a significant victory for women. It indicates that as a collective group they have broken into some of the customary male preserves and established their right to work in the different sectors of the rural economy. The common saying among the more militant women is, 'Whatever men comrades can accomplish, women comrades can too'.

However, while gaining work for wages in certain jobs outside the home, mainly the lower-paid ones, women generally continued to perform most of the domestic chores – cooking, washing, mending, carrying water, cleaning, gathering fodder and child care – and thus are saddled with double work, a condition that is all too common in other parts of the world as well. The common saying was not made reciprocal, i.e. 'Whatever women comrades can accomplish, men can too'.

During the heyday of the people's communes, especially during the Cultural Revolution when revolutionary theoretical perspectives were more prevalent, the party advocated that men should share the household chores with women,[6] but the practical advances were not consolidated.

After the dissolution of the people's communes in 1982, pressures on women changed as the centre of economic activity shifted back to the household unit. As noted in an earlier chapter, women as well as men welcomed the chance of organizing their own work timetable. But in other ways the structural change is proving unfavourable to women's emancipation because it reinforced the sexual division of labour. The tendency is for the married women to handle the domestic economy once more, while the men and perhaps the unmarried daughters go outside in search of factory work or other employment.[7]

Since patriarchal views about the proper role of women in child rearing remain deeply entrenched in the country, and are shared by many of the women themselves, the women's leaders tread softly and act indirectly on this aspect of the domestic economy. They speak of educating men and women to deal properly with the problems of love and marriage in order to have a democratic and peaceful family; they urge the production teams to establish nurseries and kindergartens, laundry and mending units so as to socialize housework and reduce the burden of women.[8] It is mainly among some younger couples, especially those who have urban contact or who have served in the army, that the men actually share freely in the household chores, including child rearing.

The village women's leader, Zhong Tingyin, a strong, articulate thirty-five-year-old who was a school teacher in a neighbouring township before her marriage to a Junction man, went to the party secretary one day to report a disturbing incident and to ask for support. A fellow villager had come up to her and said, 'You are very happy because you have two children, one boy and one girl. Maybe some day I'll kill your son, then how would you feel?' This was on top of another incident a few months earlier when her son was almost pushed into the canal. By 1983, after five years of limiting new couples to one child, tensions were definitely running high at MaGaoqiao.

The result of her complaint, when it came before the party committee, was unexpected. Instead of a vote of confidence and a move to curb those who were threatening her, the committee decided that Zhong should resign as leader of the women. The party branch, which was dominated by men, forty-two of them to six women, reasoned that if she stayed on she would continue to have that kind of problem and that tactically it would be better to find a younger woman who had only one child, preferably a girl, to take up the unpopular task.

The six women members of the party branch found this decision hard to accept; it seemed like a rejection of their efforts, punishment for having loyally carried forward the tasks of the party. Some of them felt like quitting.

If Zhong Tingyin was being forced out, then sister Zhang of No. 1 production team said she didn't feel like continuing to work in the women's organization. 'How can I continue doing this work when I already have three children and the present policy is to have one?' she asked. Sister Li of No. 6 production team, who had four children, expressed similar thoughts. In fact, none of the six leading women of the village could qualify for the post that Zhong Tingyin was giving up because they all had started their families before the present policies were adopted and they had more than one child.

In due course the party secretary found a new leader for the Women's Association. She was Huang Kailan, a barefoot doctor, fourth child in a family of ten in No. 5 production team. Huang, aged thirty, and her husband, a cadre in the township tobacco factory, had a little daughter and they had agreed to be a three-member family. But Huang was not really interested in taking on political leadership. When the party branch invited her to apply to join the party she declined. 'I only want to work for a few years in my present post', she said. 'There are many things to do for my own family, so I don't wish to join the party.'

The six women party members were disappointed, and felt somehow affronted at this result of the search for a new women's leader. Through all these years they had found it important to have the party as a venue for working to advance the women's cause. By being party members, they had more self-esteem and had felt able to carry on their work more confidently. Nobody could be forced to join the party against their wishes and an unwilling member would not be a good member. Huang would probably do her work conscientiously, they felt, but something would be missing. Perhaps she would change her mind later.

Most of the six women had joined the party in 1966, during the Cultural Revolution when there was an upsurge in women's consciousness. As they met now to take stock of their position in the new situation, they spoke of their past commitments and tried to strengthen each other's resolve to continue in public life. Sister Zhang said:

> When I joined the Communist Party I raised my fist and pledged to give my whole life to its cause. So my thought about giving up is not right. A party member should carry on with the revolution until the end of her life.

Sister Li agreed.

> We should keep ourselves moving forward. Since we've grown up under the red flag, things are easier for us than for the older generation of communist women, such as Liu Hulan. They joined during the hard times before Liberation. They laid down their lives for the revolution. (Liu was a revolutionary martyr in Shanxi province, who died at the age of eighteen and about whom a popular movie was made. When Mao heard of her case he wrote an epitaph: 'a great life; a glorious death'.) We should also win honour for the party; we must publicize its policies and carry them out. As women we must do the party's work among women and still take part in the responsibility for family planning and birth control.

The oldest member of the group is sister Shi Zengyu, born in 1937. She is married to a farmer, has borne five children and is the only one of the group to be native to Junction township. At the age of twenty, in 1957, during the campaign to form co-operatives, she had joined the party and although almost illiterate, held the post of leader of the village Women's Association for the next eighteen years.

> When I was young I had a very good memory and could remember what was discussed at meetings clearly for several months. I didn't have to make notes.

Although sister Shi handed over the top post in the village Women's Association to the better educated Zhong Tingyin in 1976, she continued on the committee and the others listen respectfully to one who is older and ripe with experience. She said emphatically:

> To join the party is to work to liberate the people of the whole nation. No matter how difficult the work may be, we must take up the tasks and overcome the obstacles.

She stresses the importance of continuing with family planning:

> There are too many people in our country. One year our village had over 130 births. Since family planning was begun, especially one child per couple, there are only ten births each year. I remember when there were only 1,400 people in our village; now there are nearly 2,000. If we don't carry out family planning and birth control the high street will become too crowded during market days – even now its over-crowded.

To encourage the others sister Shi tells a story about her own earlier timidity to show that everyone can make progress in their thinking.

> When I joined the party we learned about Marxism-Leninism, Mao Zedong Thought, to be loyal and brave, and to persist in carrying out revolution. But actually I was quite nervous and still worried about ghosts and gods.
> Our party group was set up in the Temple of Rebirth. When I went there I had to pass a spring and people said, 'Aren't you frightened, you're such a young woman?' It was said that an old woman drowned there and during the night you could see her sitting by the spring smoking, you could see the glimmering light of her tobacco as she smoked. I did see a pulsating light there, so the next night I decided to use a flashlight to see what it was. It turned out to be a fire-fly! There were other things that made me nervous. The trees along the canal were just about the height of a person and at night sometimes they took on the shapes of a person. It was a bit scary. I kept two words in my mind: be brave and you'll fear nothing; there are no devils. But when the dew dropped off the leaves of the trees it sounded as if a ghost were creeping up behind you – di di, da da . . .

Of course our party is atheist, so gradually I learned that we party members are not fearful of ghosts and gods. From this small example and from the films we have seen about revolutionary heroes, we know that the most important thing in our lives is to make revolution, to follow the path of the Communist Party.

These thoughts helped put matters into a better perspective for Zhong Tingyin, and she carried on with the same train of thought.

The Communist Party is the vanguard of the working class. It is an advanced guard. Compared with the working class we peasants are not so forward, but compared with the ordinary people in the countryside we party members are advanced elements. So we should be more active than the ordinary people; we've received more political education. We won't let the bitter life of the past return, male superiority and female inferiority. As living human beings we women should be full spirited and use our rights to speak out.

Class loyalties and gender solidarity are closely aligned in the talk and thinking of these women. This is a result of their experience and the political training they have received. But in their daily life difficult contradictions constantly arise between their role as party members and as women's leaders.

It is one thing to speak out when the oppressor is a class enemy or at the time of a mass movement as during the 'four clean-ups'; the women of MaGaoqiao contributed their share along with the men during those times of upheaval. But in ordinary times under the prevailing male domination of village political structures, it is difficult for women, even with the help of the Women's Association, to criticize bad behaviour publicly and hope to effect change when the target is husbands or male workmates from favourable class backgrounds. It is even more difficult if the male is an 'advanced element' by virtue of being in the Communist Party.

There was, for example, the case of villager Zhou Zhizhu's grievances. She had a second baby in 1976 when it was permissible to have two children, but she could not get her child put on the village register in spite of many appeals to the party secretary. This was a serious matter because without that registration she could not receive the additional private plot, basic grain ration and other necessities for the child.

The party secretary, Yao Shengwan, disliked her because when she was a barefoot doctor she had criticized a fellow barefoot doctor for taking the medicinal alcohol from the clinic and going on drinking bouts with his friends, including the party secretary. This was at a time when alcohol was rationed. Zhou finally left the clinic when things were made too uncomfortable for her, and went to join her husband who was in the army. Upon returning home to do farm work she announced that she was pregnant with her second child.

On hearing this party secretary Yao said it was too soon after her first child; the brigade would plan for her to have a child the following year but in the meantime she should have an abortion. He hinted that if she went ahead there might be difficulty in registering the birth.

She was defiant and refused his request as unreasonable, pointing out that her first child was already four years old and that party policy permitted a second child. When she gave birth the brigade refused to put the child on the household register.

After a year of delaying tactics during which sister Zhong, who was women's leader and on the brigade committee, could make no headway on Zhou's behalf, the brigade leadership said they would register the child if Zhou's husband had a vasectomy operation. Her husband, who was then on duty a thousand miles away from his wife, near Beijing, complied with the request but the brigade did not keep its word.

Another year passed before she could get redress. According to prevailing political practice the Women's Association avoids any open confrontation with the party, but with its quiet support Zhou wrote to the Ministry of Public Health in Beijing asking what the policy was for someone like herself. The ministry replied in a friendly manner and sent a message to the provincial bureau of public health which was passed on to Shifang county. Even when he knew about these letters the brigade party secretary passed the buck and said it was a matter for the commune.

It was not until the commune party secretary personally rode over on his bicycle to talk with Yao that Zhou's problem was solved. By then every woman in the village was getting the message that, even if they had a just cause, anyone venturing to rock the boat in defiance of secretary Yao was headed for a lot of aggravation.

Another area of contradiction with the men in the leadership of the party branch is over the attitude to be taken towards women who are trapped in unhappy marriages. Divorce is legal, but it is rare. In 1983 two women created a stir in the village by running away to Anhui province without trying to get a divorce.

The men will admit that there are some cases of husbands mistreating or beating their wives, but they think it is very rare compared to former times. They believe that women who leave their husbands are either simple-minded or are deceived by abductors who promise money and a better life in Anhui. As team leader Wang Daoquan put it in a common male reaction:

The two women who were abducted are both around the age of thirty. I think they are foolish women, slightly simple-minded, and they are easily diverted. Abductors come to find victims.

The men think life is better in Anhui than in Sichuan. According to Wang:

They have more land than we do but they seem to be short of women. The abductors give them some money, then the women are told to wash their faces, brush their teeth, comb their hair, put on a new suit of clothes and high-heeled shoes provided by the abductor. Someone from our village recognized Zhong Quawa's wife at the railway station in Guangyuan. The abductor gave her a lot of money, perhaps Y800, and told her to meet him at the station. Once a person disappears it is difficult to find them.

Village head, Liao Wenfang, recounted:

Dai Minghuai's wife went away with her little daughter. She was an honest, straightforward person who was tricked by a widow from here who had remarried legally in Anhui and came back for a visit. Once Dai's wife's departure was discovered we reported this to the police station and we told Dai that we would help get his wife back. But Dai refused. He learned where his wife was and went to Anhui but found that she had remarried there. His wife refused to recognize him. He had to come back alone, otherwise he would have been beaten.

The attitude of sister Zhong and the Women's Association leadership is that these women fled to escape from bad relations with their husbands or mothers-in-law. In all, six women moved to Anhui from Junction township in 1983. The Women's Association thinks that an attempt should be made to contact them and if they wish to return, then the township should send someone to meet them and help them come back. But if they are not willing to return, if they have settled and remarried and are happy, then they see no reason to try to get them back.

The phenomenon of Sichuan women moving to Anhui province is common enough to have received notice in the national press. A survey in 1983 showed that 60 per cent of the Sichuan women reported to have been sold or abducted into Anhui province had actually run away 'seeking a better social (not economic) life or the right to marry freely'.[9]

If the Women's Association at MaGaoqiao has not altered many patriarchal attitudes about free choice of marriage and patrilocal residence after marriage, at least the young women have a model of struggle for such independence in Zhong Tingyin, their leader for seven years. Zhong turned down a match arranged by her parents and found a sweetheart over in neighbouring Junction township through her own go-between. Her courtship and marriage were also unusual and reflected her revolutionary temperament. Then, after marriage she braved her husband's displeasure and her relative's taunts in deciding to keep on living in her parent's home so that she could continue with her teaching career:

I joined the party in 1966 when I was eighteen and I met the young man who later became by husband. He worked in the Red Star coal mine in the mountains to the north, though his paternal home was in MaGaoqiao village in Junction township. At first I didn't think much of him because he was so polite, the kind of person who tried never to offend anyone, a person of few words. I thought I should try to find someone more suitable to me. Since I had refused the man my parents wanted, my mother said, 'Girls in the countryside should not be so nit-picking. No matter how pretty you are you have to work around the stove, scour the burnt rice from the pot.' I was annoyed by her statements.

There was a shortage of teachers so I decided to exert myself in the teaching profession. Before giving me a job my brigade in West Cloud People's Commune asked me whether I was going to marry out or not. I told them I would not leave. I would stay in my home brigade and teach for ten years.

But my friend was a persistent fellow for all his politeness. He was a member of the Workers' Mao Zedong Thought Propaganda Team at the mine. In 1968, during the Cultural Revolution, such teams took over the leadership of all schools in the county. One day when I was with about a hundred teachers gathered in the county town for a conference, he was there and went around giving out candy kisses and announcing that we were going to be married. In a few weeks we got our marriage licence and he trumpeted this fact around too.

When the leaders of my brigade heard about my engagement they were furious and gave me a talking to, saying I had gone back on my word. I denied this and I said I would keep my contract. But by now my mother was upset and did not want me to stay in the house. My uncle on my mother's side said, 'You are very choosey but the one you've got is not any different from the others and you are not so special either.'

We got married in 1970. It was a travelling wedding. I went to his place of work. We invited some of his comrades over and served them tea, sunflower seeds and candies. There was no dowry or gifts, I just went there myself. The party secretary of Red Star said, 'You've come to visit the mine on National Day and you have got your marriage certificate. Let us welcome this new couple.' Everyone applauded and that was considered to be my wedding. That's the custom in state industries and in the army, it's the simple way of holding weddings.

After our wedding I did not move over to my husband's home village to stay with his parents. In 1971 I had my first child, and the second in 1973. At that time my husband came and said we should move over to his family's place, but I said it would be hard to get along with his sister-in-law. I couldn't stand her. Besides I had promised by brigade party branch that I would not leave my teaching post. How could I go back on my word to them?

In 1975 he brought up the subject again. He said he had talked to the people in his unit and that it would be possible for me to teach up in the coal mine district and then we could live together. Some teachers from there were going to be transferred so there would be an opening for me. But first, his plan was that we move over with the children to his parents' place so that the children would have a place to take root. Once we occupied some rooms there, then later, when they got a little older and became 'educated youth' sent down somewhere else in the countryside, they would have a place to come back to, some place to call home. It seemed like a good idea.

He showed me a document saying that veteran workers could bring their families to live at the work unit. He had been up there since 1958 so he was considered a veteran. I read it and I believed him. I was convinced by his plan. Also my uncle was still cursing me saying, 'A girl once married is like spilt water. Why did you stay at your mother's? Your mother has sons! You weren't needed at home. They don't need you to keep the rain out!'

My parents heard all this and so did my brothers. They urged me to leave as soon as possible. 'Since you have a place to go, you should leave', they said in chorus.

I had not said anything to the leadership of the brigade or to the school. I didn't dare. I asked my husband to do that, but he refused, so my mother went. I don't know what the discussion was but later I went to the head of the school and said I was leaving. He said, 'How can you leave just before a new term is starting?' I stayed another term and then moved in early 1976 to the 8th Brigade in Junction People's Commune.

Three months after I moved a new policy came down. It said that veteran workers' families could move their units, but only if the family was already on the state-supplied grain system. I was in the collective supply system, so I could not move to the coal mine district after all.

When this result became known a representative of the party branch in No. 8 Brigade came to ask me to be in charge of women's work and medical care. I accepted. I am a party member and when you join the party you pledge to give your whole life to the party, so I felt I should accept the party's request. I really did not want to teach anymore, I was a little tired of teaching. Shortly I was elected head of the Women's Association in the brigade, a post I held until April 1983.

As sister Zhong concluded her self-revelations the other five women comrades started to laugh, especially when she bent her head over the sweater she was knitting and said that she had left the post of women's leader because she was getting old and could not keep up with the situation. 'It's true I am only thirty-five', she said, a bit flustered. 'But we need to involve younger, more capable, keen-witted people. We should take turns serving the country and the people. We have to train some successors.' There was no one who could spin ideas through their brain as rapidly as Zhong. The role of the male comrades in removing her from the village leadership in favour of a more manageable type is diplomatically not mentioned.

'If it turns out that the young people find difficulty in their tasks or are over-worked,' she said, 'then I'll be glad to come and help them. That's my outlook.' Sister Zhong's attitude in defeat is admirable but no one is convinced that she is giving the real reason why she lost her job as women's leader. She is not too old and it is not because she has two children. That is no crime. Many families have two or more.

The real reason is the lack of understanding among the men and women of the party branch. The men are not prepared to accept the consequences of having a strong woman in a position of power. Instead of taking the problem posed by the threats to Zhong's children and raising it as a political question for the village to discuss in the context of family planning work, they dropped sister Zhong to avoid any unpleasant confrontations.

Sister Zhong gave in because she accepts the discipline of being a Communist Party member. But in doing so she and the men and women she had been helping to lead all know in their hearts that they have missed a chance to raise the level of struggle for women's emancipation.

15

FESTIVALS AND LIFE-CYCLE CELEBRATIONS

When missionaries arrived in China from Western countries in the nineteenth century some discovered much of permanent value in the ideas underlying Chinese festivals. They noted that themes of family thanksgiving, prayer for a fruitful season, feeding the hungry, hygiene and exercise compared favourably with Christian ideals.

But they also saw much 'superstition and idolatry' and they wondered whether it was worthwhile trying to separate the grain from the chaff, since they believed they taught the same positive values in other ways. They did not wish to encourage customs of 'heathen' ancestors nor did they want to ignore them. To let the festivals go by unnoticed, they thought, might be 'to neglect opportunities for the spread of truth . . . and for the uplift of Chinese society in general'.[1]

When the Communist Party of China came to power it also faced the problem of what to do about 'superstitious' and 'harmful' customs. It wished to eradicate them, while still allowing 'healthy' festivities and 'legitimate' religious observances.

The party eventually decided that religious freedom meant the right of Buddhist and Daoist temples, Moslem mosques and Christian churches to conduct services, to preach, to print tracts and bibles and make other objects, and to advocate theism provided these activities were done within their buildings and did not attempt to oppose the policies, laws and decrees of the party and the state. Although they were atheist, the Communists recognized that 'religion is a longstanding, complicated matter' involving 'millions of people of various nationalities'.[2] They declared religious toleration to be a long-term policy.

Apart from religion so defined, the party tried to make it a criminal offence for sects or sorcerers to perform fortune-telling, divination, exorcism of evil spirits, or planchette writings. In the privacy of their own homes individuals could more or less keep up many old practices since the authorities drew a distinction between 'the masses' who took part in superstitious activities and 'the sorcerers and witches spreading fallacies to deceive people [and] harm them'. But Chinese authorities described sacrifices to spirits, holding demonstrations to pray for rain or magic cures as 'offensive to heaven and reason'[3] and banned public offerings because they alleged that the fortune tellers swindled people out of money and property.

As noted by the missionaries earlier, it was these kind of superstitious activities that were most prevalent in the countryside.

One way to foster change after 1949 was to adopt new festival days such as International Women's Day, May Day, Children's Day and National Day. These events, when added to the traditional New Year Festival and the Mid-Autumn Festival, offered a new focus of attention, lessening the emphasis on some of the other highlights of the lunar calendar. In an earlier chapter the active efforts of the Shifang county government in 1983 to promote cultural and recreational activity for the new holidays has already been described.

As for the older traditions, the New Year Festival, renamed 'Spring Festival', continues to be the most important holiday occasion at MaGaoqiao village. People are free from most farm work at that season and it is a time for family gatherings and visiting friends.

On the last day of the lunar calendar (end of January or early February) families, if their economy can afford it, plan to have a large midday meal with nine plates of fried dishes and ten bowls of steamed meats and soups. Parents give their children some money wrapped in red paper for good luck, they paste poetic sayings on the doorways and in the evening people let off fireworks. The next few days are spent visiting others or inviting guests for a meal. The festive season ends with the coming of the full moon on the fifteenth day of the year and people hang up paper lanterns. This is a kind of Chinese Valentine's Day, the most popular time for young couples to announce their engagement or to get married.

After Spring Festival comes the Clear and Bright Festival in early April. Before Liberation people in MaGaoqiao went to the tombs of their ancestors on this day to tidy up the graves, to burn some symbolic paper money and place a bamboo stave on the top of the grave mound with more paper money attached to blow in the wind. In front of the tombstone they set out plates of cooked meat, chicken and a cup of wine for the dead. After a short stay the relatives put the food back in a basket and returned home. This activity has mostly disappeared because most of the graveyards became fields during the farmland reconstruction. In its stead there is a commemorative dinner when a place is laid at the table for the dead parents.

After the early rice is transplanted comes the fifth moon called the Dragon Boat or Flag Festival. It is in the month of June. The family has a special meal of glutinous sweet rice wrapped in bamboo leaves and jellied eggs, and red (orpiment) wine that is thought to ward off disease. The older people put a drop of red orpiment (a Chinese herb that is also used for making gunpowder) on the foreheads of their small children. The emphasis is on hygiene and exercise. People hang the stems of the sweet flag, or a bunch of grass, from the doorway; according to a village woman, Lan Guifeng, it is supposed to ward off mosquitoes, snakes, ghosts and devils. In the summer mothers take the grass down, boil it and use the resulting mixture to bathe the children in the belief that it cures them of rashes. Lan Guifeng recounted:

> Sometimes we have dinner ourselves, or if we are feeling especially happy and sociable we invite our daughters and sons-in-law back home to join us. After dinner we go for a walk together, down to the Junction market to see a movie or to Fangting for a Sichuan opera.

If one of the young men of the house is engaged, he will pack a gift basket with seasonal foodstuff augmented by some meat and four bundles of noodles and call on the woman's family. He leaves the basket and brings his fiancée back home for dinner and to stay over for the holiday. In former times the norms of segregation for unmarried people of both sexes required that an engaged couple be accompanied at all times by another family member.

The other traditional festival is at mid-autumn, after the harvest at the full of the eighth moon (September). This time daughters and daughters-in-law are guests and the family eats moon cakes as a special delicacy. Once again an engaged youth takes a gift basket for the woman's family and brings his future wife back to stay for two days.

Many of the villagers no longer remember why they eat moon cakes or how it was that a bundle of grass hung in a doorway could have such miraculous powers. As a Canadian missionary noticing the same phenomena once observed, the customs of a nation linger, at least in a partial way, long after the religious views of the majority of people have changed. 'Witness the many curious customs that survive in England and Scotland from pre-reformation times or even earlier,' he wrote, 'such as hot cross buns, Hallowe'en, and even Christmas.'[4] Like the black cats, bats and jack-o'-lanterns in Western culture, the Chinese equivalents did not pose any harm in the eyes of the Communists and they let them be, joining in the festivities themselves while seeking to create new, more proletarian occasions. The mix of old and new continues to evolve, subtly intermingling past and present values.

Apart from introducing new festivals, the party sought to change 'undesirable' habits by reforming the customs associated with birth, marriage, funerals and burial. This has proved to be an arduous undertaking.

As philosophical materialists, the Communists believe that, with the changes involved in building an industrial economy grounded on socialist principles, many of the ideas and customs which brought China to where they found it in 1949 will tend to disappear. If the process is left to happen naturally, however, they feel the leftovers of feudalism could continue to damage people and hinder the emergence of the New China they wish to see. With this in mind they have tried, with varying success, to change the prevailing habits related to the life-cycle of forming a family, giving birth and old age.

Parents in China have traditionally taken control of marriage negotiations, especially in the rural areas. The marriage of a child was a time when family fortunes could be greatly influenced for the better. A good bargain could include improved social status, financial gain for the bride's side through a handsome bride-price, and for the groom's family increased labour power and potential grandchildren to continue the line and provide security in old age. The size of the gifts required and the scale of feasting that accompanied such bargaining and status-seeking was enough to put many a peasant household into debt for years.

In this scheme of bargaining, there was no room for courtship. As in many Third World countries, marriage was considered too important to be left to the vagaries of falling in love. Three grandmothers at MaGaoqiao, in recalling their marriages, said that they had not set eyes on their husbands until the day of their wedding. Everything down to their delivery in curtained sedan chairs to their husband's home had been negotiated by their parents through go-betweens.

When the Communist Party came to power in 1949 it was determined to abolish such feudal marriages and to curtail their mercenary aspects. According to the new Marriage Law of 1950 the arranged marriage system was to be replaced by freedom of marriage. The law defined free choice of marriage as 'the provision of full rights for the individual to handle his or her own matrimonial affairs without any interference or obstruction from third parties and without regard for social status, occupation or property'. The new law was a 'weapon for releasing the people, especially the women, from the suffering caused by feudal marriage'.[5] The government also tried to promote later marriages as a way of slowing down the population growth.

By all accounts the young people have had a difficult time asserting their rights provided under this new law. The modern ideas, supported by political associations such as the Women's Association and the Youth League, are pitted against traditional rituals and ceremonies. The old sense of filial duty and family loyalty is maintained by a network of relatives, neighbours and friends who spread gossip about anyone who breaks with tradition.

In addition to village gossip there are also the realities of economic and social functions still held by village households. Even under the commune the policies of collective life left many sanctions in the hands of parents which they could use to prevent their offspring from going their own way. This power came from control over private housing and restrictions on land for new buildings, family responsibility for care of the aged and infirm, the pooling of wages through family accounting, and limits on migration. Since the introduction of the 'household responsibility system' in 1982 the temptation of parents to supervise the marriage plans for their children is increasing once more.

All this is not to say that there have been no advances toward free choice of marriage partners, at least if the changes at MaGaoqiao village are any indication.

In the old days at MaGaoqiao marriage negotations had a strict and drawn-out ritual. In the case of villagers Zou Jingfu and Lan Guifeng in the early 1940s the negotiations began with an exchange of horoscopes. A match-maker wrote eight characters denoting the hour, date, month and year of Lan's birth on a piece of red paper and took them over to Zou's house to see if they fitted his characters. Since no combination denoting an iron broom or bronze basin occurred, the result was auspicious. The male side had to make a decision within three days and if the decision was negative they returned the red paper. But in this case Zou's mother took pork and noodles over to have lunch at Lan's home to settle the terms of the engagement with her parents.

Following the engagement, at important festival times, Zou's side took a gift basket of food, clothing and money to Lan's family, all wrapped in red paper. As Lan recalled:

> Ten days before the wedding my relatives carried my dowry over to my future husband's home. That is where we would be living. My dowry was quite large although not much compared to those of wealthy people. It included a wardrobe, cupboard, table, chairs, bed sheets, pillows, quilt and mosquito nets.

After carefully calculating the cost of these pieces the Zous sent back about 60 per cent of the value in cash. In the meantime they prepared several suits of clothes, including padded winter clothes, for the bride.

On the day of the wedding Lan said that her fiancé's relatives and friends came over to her house carrying with them not only their gifts but all the items of her dowry as well. This was a matter of show. The more material goods, the higher the status of the families. It was a serious business and to complete the deal the Zous brought with them the final payment of the bride-price – 300 *jin* of rice and several hundred yuan in cash. Lan continues:

After some tea and cigarettes and letting off firecrackers, we formed a procession to start back again. I was quite excited as well as a little anxious about leaving the home of my parents. A flag bearer led the way followed by my flowery sedan chair, then trumpeters, more sedan chairs for members of my family, and they were followed by people carrying all the gifts again! I peeked through the curtains of the sedan chair and saw people along the way. Attracted by all this pomp they came out of their houses to stare and see whether it was a bountiful wedding or not.

When we arrived Old Mr Zou paid off the sedan chair carriers and I stepped out onto a carpet in my red coat and short bobbed hair. I felt a little embarrassed.

The old man led her into the living-room where she saw her husband for the first time. 'I hardly had time to glance at him before the bowing ceremonies started', said Lan.

On a command from Old Mr Zou the couple stood side by side, bowed low to heaven and earth facing the open door of the living-room, then turned around bowing and falling to their knees three times to the family ancestral tablet containing the names of Zou's father, grandfather and great-grandfather. They continued bowing as names of other senior relatives were called out.

Then my betrothed took a wooden peck filled with rice and placed two red candles in it symbolizing himself and me. When he lit them it meant we were married. After that I was led away to the bridal chamber where I stayed for the rest of the day. I had nothing to eat but two boiled eggs.

She grimaced at the memory.

Everyone else joined in the nineteen-course wedding banquet. The reason for excluding the bride was that if she spotted her dress with meat or oily dishes on her wedding day then, according to local myth, she would never again be able to wash her clothes clean.

In the evening after further eating and flushed with wine, the guests wandered in to see the new chamber and to tease the bride. 'They told stories, sang arias from operas and made rude jokes trying to make me blush. It was not very pleasant. After I gave them a cigarette and lit it for them they left', said Lan. Around midnight the bride and groom were left alone to begin the nervous process of getting acquainted.

The wedding was thus a humiliating, perhaps barbarous, occasion, especially for a woman who was being prepared for a life of submission to patriarchal authority. Treated as a chattel, sex object and servant, there was no escape. The local saying was 'If you are married to a pig you live with a pig, if you are married to a dog you stick with a dog, if you are married to a tree trunk you will be a widow waiting by the side of the tree all your life.'

The first important attack on this archaic system came with the revolutionary government's promulgation of the new Marriage Law in April 1950. It prohibited 'the exaction of money or gifts in connection with marriages', it raised the marriage age for men to twenty years and for women to eighteen; marriage was to be based upon the complete willingness of the two parties, no third party being allowed to interfere; it gave both men and women equal rights to the possession, management and inheritance of family property; it gave husband and wife the right to use his or her own family name, and set out the conditions for divorce. Perhaps most important it gave the local people's government the sole right to issue marriage certificates, thus establishing that marriage was a matter of public and not just family interest.

Once the local political organizations understood the provisions and intent of the Marriage Law they began educational campaigns to popularize it among the people. Gradually they started to experiment with new rituals and ceremonies to replace the conservative, patriarchal ideas. To oppose bride-prices the Youth League organized young women members to return the coloured gifts that came with engagement. One of them accompanied the return with a verse that received wide publicity:

> Returning the gifts,
> Keeping the engagement,
> Feelings of love deeper than ever,
> Hold high our hands for the revolution![6]

The Women's Association began to organize a new, lively way for weddings by having group celebrations. On one occasion at Spring Festival in the 1960s eighteen couples were married in one ceremony in the county theatre.

'This made a big impression on the people everywhere', said Wang Dequn, leader of the Women's Association. 'Every commune began to arrange group weddings in its own area.' At the marriage ceremony the party secretary gave a speech of congratulations and good wishes, hoping the couples would remain together until their hair turned white. There were songs and, amidst much laughter, the young couples were asked to tell the story of how they got to know each other, how they fell in love. The various organizations, youth league, women's federation, gave them some gifts – books, or cooking utensils – they pinned red paper flowers on the couples and issued a certificate praising them for having their wedding in a new revolutionary way. After the taking of pictures, relatives and friends organized a reception serving peanuts, fruit, candies and tea. Compared to the old custom it was all quite modest and simple.

During the Cultural Revolution matter-of-factness sometimes went to extremes. Radical peasants in Junction Commune wrote a verse in 1970 which to most people in the community bordered on the satirical:[7]

> Wedding ceremony in the morning,
> No special dinner at noon,
> Shoulder the plough in the afternoon,
> In the evening attend night school.

Perhaps more typical of marriage practices at that time is an account given by Huang Tianshou, the father of ten children in MaGaoqiao. When his eldest son was ready to be married in 1971 he said that the engagement and wedding procedures encouraged by the Communist Party had already made some headway.

Although the Huangs still used a go-between, the son and his mother went together to a restaurant on the high street to meet the girl and her mother face to face. 'If both sides liked each other, then the man's side ordered a meal', said Huang. 'If they did not hit it off, then they had some cigarettes and said goodbye.'

In the two years between his son's engagement and marriage the boy and girl were able to meet each other frequently at the market or go to the cinema. The girl came over to help her future mother-in-law do some housework for a few days each year – the washing, cutting pig fodder and other work. At this point she could still break off the engagement if she wished. The boy also visited the girl's house and stayed overnight with her father or brothers.

On the wedding day, said Huang,

> my son and his bride went together to pick up their licence at the commune headquarters. The rest of us carried the smaller gifts over to the bride's house. Their side treated us to breakfast and after the bride had dressed up in the wedding outfit we brought, we formed a procession for the return trip. We carried the gifts from both sides – clothes, dishes, thermos bottles and bedding – on five or six shoulder poles.

Then as if a little embarrassed, Huang added that there was no sedan chair available. 'My son', he said, 'gave her a lift on the back of his bicycle.'

Everyone attended the wedding banquet, including the bride, and an exchange of toasts and brief speeches, and the pinning on of red paper flowers replaced the former ceremonies.

The new ideology of free-choice marriage wore its way uncertainly all through the years of the People's Commune. It did make possible marriage based on love, although·village customs continued to place strict limits on courtship. The leader of the women's group in No. 5 production team at MaGaoqiao, Chen Guofeng, who married at the age of twenty-three in 1980, explained the prevailing relationship between generations.

> The old people still like to hold the celebration of these events in traditional ways with dinner parties and banquets and exchange of gifts when young couples get engaged. We still have to listen to the opinions of our family elders.

In practice though, the young people found ways to establish their personal choice before asking their parents for a go-between to make the engagement known. Those who had graduated from school might become special friends by passing notes or writing letters to each other. Others became acquainted through working together in the fields or on construction sites. As Chen recalled:

> Sometimes when my friend's clothes were torn I helped him mend them. Others laughed and teased us, but we did not mind. We were already open to each other about our love before we got a go-between. With most of our friends it is this way.

After the engagement, according to Chen, the older people are strict with both the young men and women and try to prevent them from doing anything that would cause their parents to lose face in the community. A broken engagement means loss of face too and probably explains why some young people commit suicide. Chen explained:

> We never stayed together overnight, even after we had our marriage licence. Young couples are not supposed to stay together until after the wedding ceremony. Sometimes we walked around shoulder touching shoulder but that is the most we did. I think it is a common expectation that young couples should not live together until after their wedding. I think everyone obeys this. In recent years we have heard that some young couples in the city live together before they get married and that in some factories this happens. We take this as a source of gossip. I think that such young couples are breaking with tradition because there are new birth control medicines that are very convenient. But even in the cities I don't think it is very common. So for our young couples, if they have a date in the evening to go to the cinema or theatre on the high street, they first get their parents' approval and they usually take a younger brother or sister along as company.

Chen and her husband had a group wedding celebration with several other couples and they limited the exchange of gifts to several hundred yuan, mostly things that were needed for setting up housekeeping. 'We grew up together and understood each other before we were married, so we did not waste our money on unnecessary things', said Chen.

But when the ideological pressure for change is relaxed as in recent years there is a tendency to slip backwards. Under one pretext or another the bride-price lives on. In MaGaoqiao it is called 'needle and thread money', and may involve hundreds of yuan.

In a slight reversal of the earlier custom, the bride's side prepares the bedding for the new couple while the groom's side makes the furniture. This reduces the element of status-seeking since the furniture never gets paraded along the village roadways. But according to local opinion in the late 1980s an inexpensive wedding will cost Y1,000, while many will cost Y2,000 or more. At the time of the engagement it is said that the girl's family is likely to ask for costly consumer items – a watch, sewing machine, bicycle – as well as clothing. Extravagant weddings involving as much as Y7,000 were reported in 1986 in some provinces.[8]

The Communist Party leaders at MaGaoqiao believe that until further economic and social reforms can be introduced into the rural areas – old age pensions, more village planning and houses with separate cooking facilities, freedom of migration and other changes so that the young people can more reasonably escape the pressure of their elders – the new ideology of marriage will continue to be contested by the old customs and rituals.

Customs surrounding childbirth are less controversial. In the past after a woman gave birth she stayed in bed for only three days and then had to get up to do the housework and feed the pigs. Since the 1960s the period of release from other work is forty days, with pay for time lost coming from the collective. This change is the most dramatic but other customs have shifted too, not all of them to the liking of village grandmothers. Wan Jinxiu, aged sixty-eight, recounts:

> In former times we killed a chicken for the goddess and a woman who had just given birth was not supposed to go across a bridge or walk around the fields, otherwise people said she would be insulting the Earth God. Nowadays some of the young women pay no attention to this, they seem not to care about our customs and they go about as they please.

Except in the case of Caesarean births, which are done in the county hospital, all deliveries are at home, under the care of the village midwife. The midwife comes to supervise the birth, cut the cord and wash the baby. She also saves the placenta which is either eaten by a family member or else is sold as a much-sought-after cure for poor health.

The family invites relatives to a midday dinner ten days after the baby's arrival. The guests from the grandmother-in-law's side bring a basket with clothes for the baby — shoes and socks, pants and clothing, little cotton quilts — and everyone brings eggs for the mother. There is a fetish about eggs. Widow Liao said:

> I collected about 800 eggs when my daughter-in-law gave birth. What do we do with so many eggs? We feed as many as possible to the young mother and then we also sell quite a few. You have to recover some of the cost of the luncheon and the cost of the midwife or other medical treatment. My daughter-in-law had to stay in the hospital for two weeks for a Caesarean birth which cost Y80. Then I used Y100 to set up the dinner for the guests. From the eggs sold I recovered about Y50.

Widow Liao and the other grandmothers agreed that this kind of custom is more popular than ever before, because each family is to have only one child. No matter how short of money the relatives are at the time, they will find some money to buy gifts and to visit the mother and baby. After this first occasion birthdays are ignored until a person is thirty; the big celebration is at fifty or sixty. 'At other birthdays', said widow Liao, 'you might get a pair of shoes or socks. That is all.'

Compared to other social customs, burial practices and funeral rituals at MaGaoqiao are the terrain over which tradition and revolution remain most at odds with each other. As of the mid-1970s, tradition has mainly lost out to revolution in its resistance to cremation as a form of burial but funeral rites remain a lively source of contention.

Since 1975, as the result of government pressure, cremation has become all but universal. This is true on all the plains area of Shifang county. There are heavy penalties for any family that insists upon disposal of the body by burial. According to team leader Wang Daoquan the cost for a small plot of land is Y200 and the son responsible for burying the parent must pay Y20 annually for the rest of his own life. As incomes rise, this amount will increase.

The government's case is that cremation is necessary to save timber and land. Forests have been heavily over-cut and the national average for cultivated land is down to a quarter of an acre for each of the one billion population. Every year about six million people die and if only half the dead were buried more than 35 million cubic feet of timber would be needed for coffins and 5,000 acres of land would be occupied by graves. Traditional burial customs required the choosing of an auspicious site according to the omens of the wind and waters as determined by Daoist priests. Most often it was on good farmland near the family home.

According to some authorities cremation was quite popular in China until the Ming emperors (1368-1644) forbade the custom as being contrary to Confucian beliefs. Their decree lasted until the 1950s. Beijing did not have a crematorium until 1957. At that time Mao proposed that Central Committee members of the party should be cremated after death and he was the first to sign the resolution.[9] Several important revolutionary leaders, including Zhou En-lai and Liu Shaoqi, had their ashes scattered on the rivers and seas of China but when Mao died the government decided to place his body in a memorial hall. According to Deng Xiaoping, this was against the Chairman's wishes and unfortunately it revived the feelings of those opposed to cremation.

At MaGaoqiao, team leader Wang reports that a few families still get a coffin to comfort the older people and keep it by the bedside of the dying person. Afterwards they usually return the coffin and send the body for cremation.

In 1984 the following conversation took place between team leader Wang and widow Liao:

> Widow Liao: I am not afraid of ghosts and devils. During the land reform I went about at night doing the work of the Peasants' Association. I don't believe there are spirits. But at my death, I would like myself to be buried in a coffin, that's true!
>
> Wang: Look here, grandma, when you were young you painted your cheeks and danced the revolutionary 'yangko' through the streets! You are in good hands. At your death I'll be the one to hitch up the tractor and take you along with your family members to your cremation. Premier Zhou En-lai was cremated and his standing is much higher than yours, so what have you got to worry about? He did not even bother about a box for the remains, but had his ashes scattered over the mountains and rivers of our homeland.
>
> Widow Liao, laughing: Yes, and at that time who knows anything? When you are dead you don't know anything anyway. But when my husband died I bought a coffin, and I keep feeling that for my generation it might be safer.

In spite of the feelings expressed by widow Liao and people of her generation, cremation has become the standard procedure. However, ideas about the appropriate rites and ceremonies to accompany a funeral are still in a state of flux. They enter the realm of freedom of religious beliefs vs. superstitious practices.

The ideal that lingers in the hearts of many families at MaGaoqiao, if they can afford it, involves an extended funeral liturgy especially if the death is of a family elder. Some of the grander funerals before land reform lasted the better part of a week and are recalled with nostalgia by older villagers.

For such an elaborate funeral the family invited half a dozen Daoist priests who came dressed in flowing yellow robes and red hats to lead a vigil in praise of the dead. The family hired a cook and spent large sums in feeding scores of extra people. They decorated the courtyard with white paper flowers and colourful pieces of cloth, while over the dragon gate apprentices of the priesthood set up a music tower where they beat drums, blew trumpets and let off firecrackers at inspired moments.

The coffin rested in the sitting-room. Each daughter made a quilt three feet wide and six feet long to cover the body. If the dead person had three daughters then he or she would have three quilts. 'Even in the summer when the weather was hot and the body began to smell,' said one seventy-three-year-old woman, 'you were supposed to keep the coffin in the house – this showed proof of your filial obedience to the older generation.'

An important part of the programme was to 'invite the waters'. The family members, relatives, friends and hired mourners, all dressed in white sack-cloth, lined up behind the priests who led a noisy procession in some roundabout way to a spring-fed pond or stream. There in front of the crowd that had gathered the Daoists blessed the water and declared it pure, whereupon the sons and grandsons filled a bottle to take back for making Chinese ink. A scribe then used the ink to write scrolls about the deceased's life – describing the hardships and difficulties he or she had experienced and any contributions and good deeds accomplished for the younger generation.

The night before burial the family organized a memorial meeting. As the priests murmured more chants, recited the classics, and read out the memorial scrolls in dramatic fashion, the relatives knelt on the ground while many people stood round to witness the spectacle. The next day another public procession took place in which the direct descendants held a long white ribbon tied to the coffin to lead the way to the grave. Hired mourners who wailed loudly carried a 'spirit house' made of paper and bamboo and bundles of symbolic paper money to be burned at the graveside.

So important were the funeral rites that even a poor family tried to arrange these ceremonies on a modest scale, going heavily into debt for the purpose if necessary.

After the land reform in the 1950s the Communist Party tried to relieve the poor from such financial burdens by convincing them that the customs were a form of feudal oppression. They sought to do this by linking funerary customs with prevailing superstitious and mercenary practices.

Retired MaGaoqiao village party leader, Zhang Jinghe, explains:

My own grandmother was a spirit woman or witch-magician. What she used to do for people who were ill was pure superstition. She would put a handkerchief on the top of her head and light some incense sticks. Then she pretended to speak in tongues. As she sat there murmuring something, it was said that she was talking to the spirits from Hades and saving her client. People paid her money for this.

Another type of sorcerer, known as 'duan gong', would light a torch in the house and go about shouting or beating a drum. He would shout that the devil had come out of the sick person and he then chased it out over the fields. Shortly he came running back with a small figurine in his hand. It was actually made of wheat flour, but he would say that it was the evil spirit and he swallowed it, thus preventing the patient from being recaptured.

Before you buried the dead you had to get the Daoist priest to check on the direction in which the dead person's feet should be pointed. If the feet of the dead were not in the proper direction according to the horoscope of that year, then it was believed that someone else in the house would die soon after, or the pig would get ill, or some other relative would have some disaster. These were commonly held beliefs, and poor people paid heavily for ease of mind. That is why we did a lot of propaganda work to persuade people to get rid of all the old superstitious ways.

Although the local government took measures to prohibit sorcerers and tried to limit funeral rituals by closing down the shops that made 'spirit houses' and paper money, the Daoists, acting as lay priests in their spare time, still exist. People hire them for ten yuan a day to help conduct their memorial services or to assist them in deciding on the direction for the dragon gate of a new house.

The oldest Daoist in MaGaoqiao is Xu Wenqin, a man of seventy-five who is troubled by a bronchitic cough. He lives with his wife and son's family in No. 2 production team. On a cool December morning in 1983 he protected his shaved head by a big fur hat and kept his hands tucked into the sleeves of his fur-lined coat. Broad of forehead and missing several lower front teeth, his adam's apple bobbed up and down as he talked.

He described the three-year apprenticeship to become a priest in his youth – putting on yellow robes to 'invite the waters', practising the use of large and small cymbals, bells and drums, and learning the scriptures by chanting. 'The scriptures are in a kind of ancient Chinese and if you are not in our profession you cannot understand the meaning', he said. He also learned how to use a wooden Ouija board that had a compass in the centre and various combinations of Chinese characters around the edges arranged according to the sixty-year cycle of the Chinese calendar, also known as the heavenly book. The priests used the board to decide auspicious days for burial and lucky orientations for graves.

One of the most important rituals is called 'freeing the soul'. For this the priest prepared a passport for the dead on silver paper. The passport contains personal and family details, place of earthly residence, drawings of gods and spirits and the words *E-mi-tou-fu* (May Buddha preserve us). The priest sets fire to the paper, thereby allowing the dead soul to use the passport to board the ferry at the ford of mercy and to cross the river into the spirit world.

There are several schools of Daoist priests. 'Some are mixed with Buddhism, that is my kind', Xu said. But for Xu his Daoist business was in the past. He said flatly that he gave up his practice after the land reform when the government began to organize small businesses into co-operatives in 1953. At that time the seventy-two trades, as he called them – butchers, barbers, blacksmiths, shoe polishers, other service businesses such as his own – 'each had its own hardships and bitter story'. He did not wish to become part of a co-operative.

> I was determined to stop, I didn't do it any more. Even if my neighbours in the same courtyard invited me to perform rites for them, I refused. I sold all the equipment and I burnt anything that could not be sold. I burned my scripture books. Someone said, 'Why did you do this? Others might be interested in reading them.' I said, 'No. I don't want to keep any copy of them.' I burned them all. I burned two Ouija boards; they were pretty new ones – I burned them.

His words betrayed a deep-seated anger. But it was an anger that appeared to speak less of religious freedom than of the loss of a business. He said that he could have kept going on a part-time basis and that he had missed the pocket money which would have come. 'Life would have been easier; I have been a little short of money, but I've got through.'

When pressed, Xu gave the other reasons for giving up his profession. In the first place he had decided to make a living by farming. In addition, the people's beliefs were changing, interest had fallen off and the practice of cremation made some things obsolete. 'It is useless to check the orientation for the burial', he laughed, 'because with a box of ashes you don't know what is head and what is feet. Now the Daoists just make things up.' But it also seemed clear that underneath it all heavy pressure over the years from the government and the Communist Party against old beliefs and customs and superstitions had played a part in this decision. Referring to some activities he said, 'No one dares to do them any more, at least not openly.'

In spite of his own resentment Xu indicated that in response to continuing needs of a religious nature, the Daoist and Buddhist professions remain active.

> Take the Women's Association leader in my team, for example. Her mother-in-law died a few days ago. She invited the Daoist, Li Yingke, from No. 13 Brigade to come over, the one who is called Li Dang Dang because of the sound of his cymbals.

On the invitation of this woman cadre the fifty-year-old Daoist priest, Li Dang Dang, and his apprentice had openly conducted a memorial service. They had 'freed the soul' of the mother-in-law by burning the paper passport and chanting scriptures; they had checked the place for burial of the ashes and had brought along two trumpeters to make sure that everyone knew what was going on. As Xu said:

> What Li Dang Dang does is very simple compared with what we did in our professional business before. He does not have enough people or equipment to do big things such as 'inviting the waters'. Anyway, the people often do not wish to do things in the old way any more.

During the time of the People's Commune, before 1982, when someone died the production team leader took the responsibility of going to the deceased's home and helping the family arrange the funeral and hold a memorial service. In this way the neighbours could show their sympathy. But this was only an interim solution since some team leaders were unsuited to such a role and perhaps had even been in conflict with the family over matters of everyday production.

The local leadership of the Communist Party is still searching for ways to respond to the psychological needs of people at the time of bereavement. Since they are not satisfied with the existing priesthood they are talking about inventing a new one – a person or two in each village responsible for conducting funerals. 'They should be literate, capable of writing a memorial paper,' said party secretary Yang, 'and thus able to help the peasants to have a meaningful, comforting funeral gathering.'

More probably there will be a compromise since Daoist and Buddhist liturgies remain popular among the villagers.

In January 1984, the party committee called the half dozen active Daoists in Junction township together for a meeting.

'We should consider the old customs in a practical way', proposed Junction township party secretary Yang Changyou. 'Why not have trumpeters and music and firecrackers and memorial scrolls?' he asked rhetorically. But Yang linked other activities with harmful superstition.

'Sometimes wizards or sorcerers or witch-doctors are invited by people whose relatives are ill', he said. 'They burn papers and mix the ashes in water and ask the patient to drink it. There have been disastrous results. We must oppose this kind of thing.'

The party is seeking a mourning liturgy more in keeping with a scientific age; the Daoists are considering their options now that private enterprises are permitted once again.

EPILOGUE

When I returned to MaGaoqiao for a third visit in the summer of 1986 I found the village continuing to prosper. The *per capita* annual disposable income at 500 yuan had about doubled since 1980 and almost half of the families had built new brick and tiled houses. With living standards rising the majority of peasants were clearly satisfied with the current policies.

It was time to reflect on the extraordinary changes that had occurred in the village since I first arrived in the winter of 1980 and to consider what the implications of these changes were for the future.

During my first visit the village was known as No. 8 Brigade in Junction People's Commune; the people worked in collective groups under the production teams and were proud of the co-operative medical clinic, the school, the electrified grain processing mill, the big tractors, the methane gas pits by the side of every house and other tangible achievements. The socialist collective period clearly had been a time of qualitative change in productive capacity, highly successful in turning surplus labour into capital for economic growth. The value of the capital construction – the roads, railway, waterways, reservoirs, fish ponds, reclaimed wasteland, new orchards, levelled fields – went unrecorded in the account books; statistically they did not exist, but they were there, nevertheless, for the eye to see. They had helped turn the whole township, the entire county into an area of 'high and stable yields'.

There was also evidence that the collective period had dealt strong cultural shocks to old ways of thinking and behaviour. Not sufficient to consolidate socialist values in an irreversible way, but enough to have an on-going impetus for equality, social justice, women's emancipation.

Collectively the community found itself with much improved educational and medical services and the healthy appearance of the population was noteworthy. No more drug addiction, no more extended bellies from snail fever.

By 1980 overcrowding on the land was exacerbated. The birth rate had been checked but the large youthful cohort under the age of twenty-five meant greater population pressures were yet to come and it already created surplus labour power. The search for more gainful employment for about one third of the labour force had become a major preoccupation of the leadership. Individual living standards, in terms of housing and available consumer products, had not changed much in two decades. But the people seemed to understand this disappointment as a consequence of their contribution to the industrialization of China under conditions of external threats from imperialist powers. They had had to 'tighten our belts to help our brothers and sisters in Korea and Vietnam'.

When I returned to Shifang county three years later, in 1983, sweeping changes had occurred. The signboard of the township replaced that of the People's Commune, while No. 8 Brigade had reverted to its former name before the land reform of 1952 – MaGaoqiao.

People no longer worked in collective groups for work points. The family household acted as the basic accounting unit and contracted land from the production team. Mao's dogged opposition to individual farming had finally been overcome. Under the new system each family worked the land, fulfilled its obligations to the state and to the collective, and then kept the rest of its production for its own use or to sell on the market; the labour group leaders, work point recorders and warehouse keepers were no longer needed. The security of the basic food supply, 'the iron rice bowl', was discarded.

Individuals had bought the tractors and buffaloes belonging to the collective and the barefoot doctor ran the medical clinic as a business operation. Now the subject on everyone's lips was the 'ten thousand yuan' entrepreneurs who enriched themselves by raising poultry and rabbits for the commodity market, or through making furniture or tailoring, or by offering transportation services or contracting the shops and processing workshops still owned by the collective.

The village showed signs of a new prosperity. Eighteen families in No. 5 production team had built new houses; there were more bicycles, even a few private television sets. One of the cadres dismissed the former commune structure as 'an empty framework', a remark that would have been unthinkable in the area two years earlier.

It bought one up with a jolt. Why, I wondered, did the Communist Party which had laboured so hard for a generation to bring individual peasant families into co-operatives, now seem bent on doing the opposite? Why the wholesale flight from collectivism?

Conversations with local cadres showed that there were no clear answers; they had not made up their minds about the implications of the new policies. For four years, until 1982, Shifang county resisted the pressure for decollectivization and it was still a time of tentativeness and experimentation.

The party secretary of Junction township, Yang Changyou, summed up his impression. He said that although things were going well there remained some serious problems. 'We still do not know whether contracting to households is a suitable way of building socialism with Chinese characteristics', he said. 'We cannot give you a definite answer on this point.' Yang expressed concern about the growing gap in living standards among the villagers: some were getting better-off; many continued living in thatched huts, farming at subsistence level to feed themselves and without much income. On the other hand, prosperous families, unable to meet their labour needs, were hiring others to work for them, a practice that leads to exploitation. 'For all these things', said Yang, 'we have to search for answers.'

Two-and-a-half years later, on my third visit to MaGaoqiao, in 1986, a subtle change appeared in the atmosphere. Priorities had shifted again. Nobody talked about the specialized 'ten thousand yuan' entrepreneurs any longer. Such households still existed but few had actually reached a high standard of wealth and many of those who tried, including the famous Mr Wu Wanwu, had apparently seen their businesses go bankrupt. Once again, but without much fanfare, the emphasis of government policy encouraged co-operatives and collective enterprises.

'This is the way to common prosperity and to help the poor', said village party secretary, Liao Wenfang. The head of the county finance department, Liu Shouli, confirmed this opinion saying that 'In the past year we have given no more loans to households and individuals; all help from the state is to co-operative and collectively-run enterprises, this is according to regulations from the Central Committee.'

In this new situation MaGaoqiao village decided to join with the state-owned Chemical Fertilizer Machinery Factory and the township's Rural Enterprise Corporation to build a small steel rolling mill on a corner of village land. This rural enterprise, apart from increasing the forces of production, was being developed, again under the guidelines of the Central Committee, as a deliberate instrument of social policy to lessen the gap between rich and poor in the village. When the mill goes into full production it is expected that 150 jobs will materialize; meanwhile thirty graduates of lower-middle school from families with the lowest incomes have found employment there. For the moment this is the party's answer to the threat of growing polarization in the countryside.

Other villagers are being encouraged to form voluntary, small-scale co-operatives. In No. 5 production team three partnerships have started up, one in the rice trade and two in small condiment shops. There is also a co-operative operating the team's grist mill/noodle factory. The metamorphosis of this eight-person operation illustrates the tentativeness of thinking about the social relations of production in the countryside.

Prior to decollectivization, poor peasant Liao Wenping and seven other team members operated the noodle factory. They received work points for their labour, equivalent to about Y500 for the year, and the team made a profit of Y6,000 which it used for reinvestment or social benefits to villagers.

In 1982, with decollectivization, Liao entered into a contract for the factory and became the boss himself. He paid the team Y2,000 rental, and hired the other seven team members as workers. They managed to reduce expenses from 30 to 25 per cent in the first year and made a surplus of Y10,000. Liao took Y2,400 for himself and distributed the other Y7,600 among the seven workers. Everyone benefited, except the collective, and Liao, with the help of the other four able-bodied members of his family, went on to become a 'ten thousand yuan' household.

Unfortunately consumers began to despise noodles 'that are the size of walking sticks'. With the improvement of living standards people wanted finer noodles which cost more to produce; they shopped elsewhere and the factory began to lose money. Faced with this business downturn a reorganization took place. After some discussion the factory became a co-operative based on the eight families. Some members of the party committee regarded this method as more in keeping with socialist ideas since there would be no more hired hands. The production team signed a three-year rental contract with the eight members and each of them invested 250 kilograms of wheat. They diversified production beyond noodle-making and distributed the income equally according to sales each month, except that Liao, elected as manager, received several yuan more per month than the others. Lacking new machinery, the noodles unfortunately remained just as thick as ever.

Although this type of organization and the thinking that set it in motion seems more in keeping with the 'four cardinal principles', it does not represent a general movement for re-collectivization of the land. Nor does there appear to be any intention to move in that direction in a hurry. The Central Committee of the party has announced that the land contracts are valid for fifty years if the contractors wish it and that children may inherit the contracts from their parents.[1] This is a lengthy time-frame. It corresponds with the period during which the government has announced that China will be 'one country with two systems', – both socialism and capitalism – until Hong Kong, Macao and Taiwan are reunited and integrated with the motherland.

Many unexpected things are bound to occur in half a century and the balance between socialism and capitalism within China and in the world will not stand still. If the events of the last fifty years are any guide great changes are in store. In the meantime, the new course in Chinese agriculture, involving one fifth of humanity, will aim to rework two problems left unresolved from the early period of socialist construction:

how to increase the productivity of farm labour so as to raise living standards appropriate to a modernized China, and secondly how to reform a style of leadership that tends to degenerate into bureaucratic commandism. These two questions have raged at the heart of political debates in China throughout the years of the Communist leadership.

To consider productivity first, Chinese farmers are noted for their industriousness. But in a densely populated place such as Sichuan province with a population of over 100 million, each person has but a tiny one-sixth of an acre of arable land; to cultivate the crops on that small plot 70 days of labour a year are sufficient. Since only half the peasants are able-bodied workers (the rest being too old, too young or disabled), this amounts to 150 days of field work for each farm worker and leaves about 200 days of free time. How can this vast reserve, the labour power of 300 million peasants, China's most abundant capital resource, be harnessed and put to work most effectively for China's modernization?

The discarded strategy of Chairman Mao stressed mass mobilizations of labour to 'transform the rivers and mountains' of China, and was based on strongly egalitarian distributive policies. The work-point system of accounting made such a strategy of labour mobilization possible. By putting politics rather than economics 'in command', people recognized the public interest first, self-interest second. It was this spirit that created the 'ten great achievements' of Junction People's Commune. By the mid-1970s, however, the most obvious and desirable transformations of nature had been accomplished, at least in places like Junction township, and then, in the absence of sufficient opportunities for employment in industry, the work-point system too often merely became a way of spreading 150 days of field work out over 350 days. It was wasteful of labour power, open to favouritism and abuse by cadres, and increasingly resented by the villagers. In Mao's declining years no new strategy emerged.

Drawing upon what they considered to be a more orthodox Marxist analysis, the new leaders of China grouped around Deng Xiaoping hold that the pursuit of self-interest must be permitted in larger measure in China's present largely pre-industrial economy in order to release the pent-up productive forces in society. Socialism, as Mao Zedong Thought taught, will be a long transition period in China during which the state-owned factories, socialist collectives and individual enterprises will continue to exist and contribute to the economy in a kind of dialectical dance. Admittedly, capitalist thinking will grow in places and the pursuit of self-interest which drives a commodity market will pose a threat to socialist values. This 'contradiction among the people' could be handled by ideological education and persuasion. The constant drumbeat of ideological exhortation in China has not diminished; people are urged to 'learn from model workers', praise selfless 'Five-Good families', 'build a cultural civilization in the village', beat back 'bourgeois liberalism' and the 'cultural contamination from the West', and 'rectify the party'. But as long as conditions of relative scarcity continue to exist, small-scale capitalist activities and markets are to be allowed, even encouraged, in order to increase wealth. This is the way to capture the 200 free days of the peasants.

The upsurge of initiative and output resulting from this new strategy is clearly evident at MaGaoqiao and elsewhere in China. Many leaders in China were mentally unprepared for this result and there is a sense of uneasiness. The feeling that things were getting out of hand, with too much individualism and 'bourgeois liberalization', led to the ousting of the general secretary of the Communist Party, Hu Yaobang, from his job in the spring of 1987. But with the economic results too valuable for hasty reactions, there is now a mood of watchful waiting and of experimentation accompanied by continuous and intense debates in party committees over future directions.

For many of the cadres I talked to, the future lay in the direction of larger farms, since small family plots of land could never lead to the transformation and modernization of agriculture. The leaders who think this way are convinced, as Engels was, that large-scale production 'will sweep over . . . antiquated small-scale production as a railway train would sweep over a push-cart'.

Already in some experimental areas in Sichuan the fields are being put together again in large blocks, with 30 per cent of the peasants contracted to do the field work; the rest are engaging in other specialized forms of rural enterprises related to processing, forestry, fishing or animal husbandry. This is the dialectical dance asserting itself. These new pioneers believe that, with the introduction of machinery on a larger scale and the discovery of suitable co-operative forms, the peasants will eventually free themselves from their physically demanding, monotonous toil and from their small-producer outlook. This vision, which is dependent on the success of the drive to limit further population growth and the transfer of a large part of the rural population to non-farm pursuits, is expected to result in a modernized, socialist agriculture.[2] As of 1986, 20 per cent of the farm labour force had shifted to industrial work in the rural areas, a development that represented a substantial change in the social structure of the country.[3]

As for the problem of bureaucratic commandism, the Chinese people and leaders see it from various points of view. Some people argue that the best way to undercut 'patriarchal behaviour, to undermine the practice of abusing power for personal interest, and to destroy a sense of hierarchy and other remnant feudal ideas'[4] is to have free commodity markets where profit-seeking individuals make their own bargains. Others do not go that far. They favour loosely knit co-operative enterprises where participants work and own a share but are free to join or leave as they choose. They argue that the possibility for dissatisfied members to withdraw their capital from the co-operative provides a material basis for bringing democratic pressure on management to change its ways.

Reforms in these directions have already given the peasants more control over the products of their labour and more room to engage in their own productive activities than at any time in the previous three decades. For some peasants this has been beneficial, for others less so, But what is certain is that the cadres are put on their mettle. Their power is diminished. There is more pressure to be responsible to those they lead as well as to those they report to at the higher level, especially since the new electoral law provides for more candidates on the ballot than there are positions to be filled. Some local cadres, finding the peasants hard to guide or control, no longer wish to continue in their positions.[5]

Many people worry that the 'cures' offered by the free market or by the free-standing co-operatives may be worse than the 'illness' of socialist collectives. They emphasize that the lack of consideration for others when one's own interest is at stake and the spontaneous money worship engendered by commodity markets both contradict socialist ethics. If a less intensive system of collective living and more individualist behaviour are accepted as means to restrict the abuse of power, then they fear the worst: the present aristocracy of power, the 'dictatorship of the proletariat', will be replaced once more by an aristocracy of wealth.

In the opinion of people who think this way, reforms in the laws and improvements in the electoral system, while helpful, are insufficient to assure the development of socialism in China. 'Socialism', according to the head of the Chinese Academy of Social Sciences, 'will not grow spontaneously.'[6] Like any other social formation it requires committed supporters. It is dependent on being able to find and train capable leadership – organizers and poets who can analyse and reflect upon experience, anticipate difficulties, make clear the choices and project the wishes of the majority. It will thrive only if such leaders have a capacity for self-criticism, a willingness to suffer criticism and honestly face up to their mistakes. It needs a people who are ideologically awakened and sensitive to the regime of a collective where certain individual rights are given up in favour of social rights and where private privilege gives way to social justice. It can grow only if it has a material base of collective organization and if every collective understands how each unit – a factory workshop, a group of teachers, a village courtyard – is related to its neighbour and to the layer upon layer of human organization and activity that is China. These things take a lot of commitment.

Returning to MaGaoqiao in early 1988 I found friends in good spirits in spite of an unusual drought that dried up the People's Canal followed by heavy rains which caused the revived waterway to overflow its banks and spill onto village lands. The flood washed away twenty-four of the older, thatched houses and put seventy families on the temporary relief rolls of the county government. During the drought, competition among the peasant households for water led to serious fighting – in a neighbouring township several people died of wounds – as farmers sought desperately to tap underground sources in time to plant their rice crop. These events brought into focus the problems attending the individual household responsibility system. Before the disasters, said team leader Wang Daoquan,

> I had to tramp about knocking on a hundred doors persuading people to come out to repair the irrigation ditches and to bank up the tractor roads. In the last five years no one felt responsible for those tasks. Things that should be done for the public welfare could not be done; everyone was busy doing his or her own business.

I learned that widow Liao died of emphysema, a loss that her family marked by an elaborate Daoist funeral followed by cremation. The verdant bamboo grove by her low thatched house provides a last resting place for her ashes. The women's leader, Chen Guofeng, wanting to defy regulations by trying again for a boy child, resigned her job in charge of family planning in favour of an older woman past the child-bearing age. 'It is easier to plan crop production than to plan human production,' said team leader Wang. By and large, though, the village is holding to the single-child policy for all new couples.

Former landlord Shi, over seventy, still tends his fields and has neighbours dropping in for odd bits of carpentry work, asking him to fix farm tools or mend manure pails. Retired village head, Zhang Jinghe, meanwhile, has given up all hope of having his grievances settled and spends his afternoons in a high-street teahouse playing games of penny ante poker. A tinge of guilt about setting this bad example for young people troubles him, but he asks defiantly, 'What else is an old man to do, except watch movies?' Perhaps as compensation for Jinghe's long and faithful service, the village has appointed his son to take charge of the bamboo products workshop, a recently begun money-making scheme that employs a dozen or more people.

After Spring Festival in February, the village reorganized as a joint co-operative divided into seven small co-operatives. In explaining this significant decision, village party secretary Liao Wenfang, his neat Mao jacket buttoned tight to the collar, referred to the party central committee's Document No. 1 for Rural Development and to similar changes throughout Shifang county. 'During the past five years,' said

Liao, 'the community became like a plate of shifting sand. Now it is time to strengthen the collective economy.'

Liao said that the new co-operatives would not be like the earlier ones:

> We will keep the household management system for a long time. I have no idea for how long. But it is going to be a two-track system, we will also have co-operative management. We have to develop this aspect. We will walk on two legs.

The co-operative rules have yet to be fully established through discussion but each year every family in the co-operative will have to renew its contract for farmland. If a contracting household does not meet its obligations, if the quotas of the state plan for grain and other key crops are not delivered, then the contract will not be renewed the following year. 'There are lots of other things a person can do,' said Liao, 'so it is voluntary. But if you take the co-operative's land you have to fulfil the responsibilities.' The co-operatives, meanwhile, will re-establish their accumulation funds for capital investment and to provide services to their members before, during and after production – better seeds, credit, technical information, machinery, sales and transportation facilities.

Team leader Wang, newly elected as head of No. 5 Co-operative, welcomed the change. No more knocking on doors. Together with his five-member committee, the same people, mainly, who led the production groups during the People's Commune, he has some real economic power to promote the public interest. 'Next year,' said the veteran village revolutionary, a smile stealing across his face, 'I think that I can retire.'

The new co-operative forms are a predictable response to the breakdown of social responsibility that followed the implementation of household management of the land. Some families, subconsciously confusing household management with private ownership, believed that they could make it on their own. The harsher realities of nature together with the anarchies of the marketplace have proved such a dream unworkable if not impossible on the densely populated Sichuan plain. In the struggle between individualism and collectivism the balance has shifted once again in favour of the more socialist-minded. Emerging is a new three-tier structure of collective ownership at the village level, co-operative leadership below that and finally household management of day-to-day production.

Out on the red earth of the Sichuan countryside it would be difficult for any outsider to know for certain what the ordinary people think about the forces set in motion during these decades of revolution. Do some regret the disappearance of the 'iron rice bowl' supplied by the collective? Do others fear that the newest reforms may be revoked? Do some dare to look forward to running water and retirement pensions? Do others dream of leaving rural life for city living?

From personal experience I would guess that different reckonings, longings, inspirations stir in those little houses among the bamboo groves. In the home of the late Zeng Xiancuan, village head in MaGaoqiao who was deposed at the time of Liberation, an ancestor shrine was re-established in the living room during the summer of 1986. It paid homage to the family forebears going back to the ancient state of Lu, and gave thanks to the Goddess of Mercy for good fortune. This family had built itself a new brick and tiled courtyard.

Next door, the neighbour, who still lived in a pounded-earth, thatched house with his family, had a different sense of the past, another vision of the future: on his wall were large portraits of the founders of Marxism-Leninism. When he noticed me looking at them he said:

> And I used to have a picture of Mao Zedong up there too, but one day when I was out doing field work some turtle's offspring came in and tore it down. What a pity! You can't get those pictures anymore.

'Humanity left to its own devices does not necessarily re-establish capitalism', Mao once remarked to the French writer, Andre Malraux, 'but it does re-establish inequality; the forces tending toward the creation of new classes are powerful.'[7] According to the course set by the reformers leading the Chinese Communist Party of having 'one country, two systems', it may be half a century before it will be known whether the collective interest prevails or a new rich peasant class becomes entrenched in China's countryside as Mao feared that it might.

METHODOLOGY AND APPENDIX

Any proposal to do social and historical research in China must pass two gates: first it must have the support of some educational or research organization; then it must gain the approval of the administrative and political cadres of the territory or unit where the researcher wishes to go. Thus after my local history project received the tentative approval of the Foreign Affairs Bureau and the party committee of Sichuan University where I was teaching, it was forwarded to the Provincial Bureau of Higher Education, who passed it up to the Ministry of Education in Beijing and to the Bureau of Foreign Experts of the State Council, who in turn sent it back to the Sichuan provincial government secretariat. China is so famous for its bureaucratic mazes that for some time I was unsure if the response to my request would ever materialize; the negotiations took four months, an illustration of the pace of many things in China.

Eventually the project was accepted and I was offered a choice of communes – two were close to Chengdu, the provincial capital, while the third was seventy kilometres to the north in Shifang county. I decided to take the distant commune. Although one of the local ones, an easy bicycle ride from the university would have been convenient, its social and economic life, being greatly influenced by proximity to the big city, might be less typical than that of the northern commune.

I began my research by asking to see the household registers of several production teams in MaGaoqiao village, also known as No. 8 Brigade of Junction People's Commune. The registers would allow me to select those villagers I wanted to interview and since they gave the age, sex, class category and educational level of everyone, I was able to choose a cross-section of poor peasants, middle, former rich peasants and landlord elements. Also as I became aware of the various occupations, special interests and affiliations of the villagers, I interviewed a selection of party members, youth leaguers, women's group, militia, school teachers, barefoot doctors, work group leaders, poor and lower-middle peasants' association members, specialized households and others. Eventually I interviewed eighty-seven commune members, of whom twenty-nine were females and fifty-eight males.

Since I wanted to study a microcosm of village life rather than do a quantitative survey, I decided to concentrate much of my interviewing in No. 5 production team. With its eighty-six households containing 356 members, it was the size of an entire village in many other, less densely populated parts of China. Located in the centre of the village at Liao Family Flats, it had the advantage of allowing me casual opportunity to observe the bustle of activity at the village headquarters, the workings of the health clinic and the school.

Other major sources of information were the statistical materials of the county, township (commune) and the village (brigade) account books. I gathered a full run of summary figures for 119 production teams, encompassing about 25,000 people, from 1949 to 1986 in Junction People's Commune, giving the population changes, labour power, farm and non-farm households, the planted area, and the ups and downs of grain yields, cash crops and animal husbandry. Another series, beginning in 1962 when the communes were consolidated into a stable three-tier form (commune, brigades and production teams), showed the income, expenses, taxation, savings and the distribution of grain to the state, the collective and the individual for the same 119 teams.

Village account books preserved at MaGaoqiao revealed the changing value of the work day in the different production teams, gave information about deficit households, subsidies to cadres, statistics comparing the levels of incomes of commune members, the use of modern technological inputs, chemical fertilizer, electrification, field reconstruction, water conservancy, construction of methane gas pits, lists of major capital assets – all valuable pieces of information for judging material progress and for assessing the social policies of the government.

The local statistical records are of two main types. There are 'work sheets' which stay in the village and deal with such matters as the grain and other quotas for each production team or work group as well as the cash and goods-in-kind distributed to each family. Then there are the accounts which are forwarded to the county Bureau of Agriculture of which a copy is also kept in the village.[1] These accounts become the basis for the aggregate figures for agriculture that are produced by the State Statistical Bureau in Beijing. The honesty of such statistics, according to Thomas B. Wiens, an American expert on the subject, can by and large be relied upon.[2]

On the other hand, there may be a tendency for villagers to under-report their income, a point that was recognized in Shifang county by various officials. By way of example, after reading the village account books I expressed surprise that the *per capita* cash distribution in 1976 was only Y16 for the whole year. Team leaders in No. 5 production team immediately expressed strong disagreement with the accuracy of that figure, saying that their *per capita* cash distribution (not including goods in kind) had never been less than Y100 and that if it had been they would have been overthrown by the team members.

County officials concurred that such a figure might be too low for a place in Junction township, but the contradiction was never resolved for me. They maintained, however, that statistical reporting was generally correct and that the pattern of trends was accurate.

I believe that a great deal of effort was made by county officials in Shifang to ensure that my time there would be a productive, positive and happy experience. Not all my requests were accepted. A visit to the county gaol was never arranged, nor was an interview with the garrison commander. But these were the exceptions. At times, particularly in the beginning, the constant attendance of extra people at interviews made it difficult to have an informal and relaxed atmosphere, especially when ordinary peasants or lower-level cadres were the subjects. Gradually, under my urgings about the need to have an atmosphere where people felt at ease if we were to succeed in 'seeking truth from facts' – a popular slogan in those days – it was agreed that interviews should take place with only the interviewee and myself and perhaps one of our research group to help with translation.

The reader may wonder, as I did, how representative Shifang county, Junction township, and MaGaoqiao village were of China's rural units. If we ask whether as socio-economic units they were subject to the same external pressures from higher authority as all other similar units, the answer must be that they were typical, average places. But every one of China's 54,000 communes and their subordinate villages obviously responded to the demands placed upon them from their own constituents and from the surrounding state in a unique way, according to their own circumstances. For a variety of reasons some struggled just to keep their heads above water, even slipping backwards at times into chronic poverty. According to Nicholas Lardy in *Agriculture in China's Modern Economic Development* (1983), from 10 to 20 per cent were in this category. Others made average progress, and still others became pace-setters.

It is true that Junction People's Commune had been favourably mentioned in newspaper accounts during the Cultural Revolution and noticed for its success in promoting rural small-scale industries, but, to judge by press accounts over the years, other communes in the county were mentioned equally and some more prominently as models in various areas of work. Junction turned out to be an average commune in an area that was somewhat above the national average, having reached 'stable and high yield' grain output in the 1970s. This situation allows us to feel confident that the conclusions drawn from this study have not been distorted by something that sets Junction and MaGaoqiao village uniquely apart from their neighbours.

TABLE 1
Results of land reform in 1951
Liao Family Flats (No. 5 production team)
MaGaoqiao village

(1)	(2)	(3)	(4)	(5)	(6)	(7)	(8)	(9)
Class of household	No.	Share of households (%)	Area owned (mu) Before/After		Share of total area owned (%) Before/After		Average area owned per household after land reform (*mu*)	Actual area tilled or used per household after land reform (*mu*)
Landlord	3	8	250	33	58	10	11	11
Rich	5	14	115	78	26	24	15.6	15.6
Small land-leaser	4	11	35	20	8	6	5	5
Middle	9	25	35	103	8	31	11.4	11.4
Poor	15	42	0	97	0	29	6.5	22
TOTAL	36		435	331			9.2	11.8

Notes: Exact population figures for 1951 are unavailable but according to the cadres the average *per capita* distribution of land at that time was 1.6 *mu*. The discrepancy between the totals of cols. 4 and 5 is accounted for in several ways: some of the land (about 11 *mu*) was distributed to neighbouring teams, some was held in reserve by the village for future population growth or for storage of water in the wintertime. It was this reserve land that was distributed for the use of the poor peasants, with the result shown in col. 9.

Source: Deng Yuanming, MaGaoqiao village clerk in 1951, and Wang Daoquan, leader of No. 5 production team since 1962.

TABLE 2

Yields of main crops 1949–58
Junction township and all-China trends compared
Output per *mu*　　　Index: 1949 = 100

Year	Grain			Oil Bearing Seeds			Tobacco (sun-cured)			
	All-China	Junction (a)	(b)	All-China	Junction (a)	(b)	All-China	Junction (a)	(b)	
1949	100	100	100	100	100	100	N/A	100	100	Individual
1952	128	109	109	121	108	108		96	96	farming
1953	128	120	120	118	142	142		115	115	
1954	128	130	130	123	140	140		105	105	
1955	138	148	148	116	146	146		88	88	
1956	137	135	155	122	150	172		89	102	Co-operative
1957	142	116	133	100	149	171		83	95	farming
1958	153	117	134	123	152	174		61	70	

Note: (a) The indices in this column derive from the information as it appears in the commune accounts. (b) In this column the post-1955 figures are adjusted to make them comparable to those in earlier years since the size of the land measure was changed in Shifang county that year. One old *mu* became equal to 1.15 new *mu*.
Sources: All-China figures in *China Agricultural Yearbook 1980*, pp. 35, 36, (Chinese edition). Junction People's Commune, *Statistics 1949–85*, pp. 7, 15, 17.

TABLE 3

Pigs in the pen at year-end 1949–58
Junction township and all-China trends compared
Index: 1949 = 100

Year	All-China	Junction	
1949	100	100	Individual
1952	155	136	farming
1955	152	170	
1956	146	193	Co-operative
1957	253	205	farming
1958	239	344	

Sources: All-China figures ibid., p. 38
(Chinese edition). Junction People's
Commune, ibid., p. 5.

TABLE 4

Analysis of population statistics in the Great Leap Forward famine
Junction People's Commune

Year	a Total Population	b %* +/−	c Peasant Registra- tion	d %* +/−	e Full Labour Power	f %* +/−	g Non- Farm Registra- tion	h %* +/−
1950	15,518	1.5	14,493	2.7	6,990	1.1	1,025	−12.6
1953	16,046	1.4	15,340	3.9	6,800	3.0	706	−35.0
1957	18,506	2.8	17,708	2.8	8,001	5.2	798	1.2
1958	17,700	−4.3	15,047	−15.0	7,500	−6.2	2,653	232.4
1959	16,465	−6.9	14,990	−0.3	7,400	−1.3	1,475	−44.4
1960	15,447	−6.2	14,917	−0.5	7,100	−4.2	530	−64.0
1961	15,811	2.3	15,381	3.1	7,700	8.4	430	−18.8
1963	16,430	5.7	15,635	5.7	8,130	5.2	795	6.0
1964	16,931	3.0	16,113	3.0	8,479	4.2	818	2.8

Source: Junction People's Commune, ibid., pp. 2–3.
* Comparison is with the previous calendar year.

TABLE 5
Rainfall in Guanghan/Shifang counties during the Great Leap Forward famine
(millimetres)

		May	June	July	August	Sept.	Total	% over/under average
	Ten-year Average 1960–70	80	125	234	203	140	782	
poor crops	1959	83	25	411	402	69	990	+26
	1960	145	56	253	367	121	942	+20
	1961	18	588	327	180	82	1,195	+53
good crops	1963	75	56	189	78	320	718	−8
	1964	59	71	365	206	163	864	+10

Source: Sichuan Provincial Weather Bureau, Chengdu.

TABLE 6
Income of commune members from all sources in 1982
No. 5 production team, MaGaoqiao village

Item	Value (yuan)	%
Total income	184,100	100
A. Collective distribution	110,500	60
of which:		
I. Distribution in kind	62,100	34
of which:	—	—
(1) Basic grain ration (141,600 *jin*)	18,700	10
(2) Grain for work days (51,200 *jin*)	6,700	4
(3) Grain for manure (34,100 *jin*)	4,500	2
(4) Grain for pigs (9,900 *jin*)	1,300	1
(5) Other agricultural products	30,800	17
II. Actual Cash Distribution	48,300	26
of which:	—	—
(1) Cash for manure	15,100	8
(2) Cash for labour payment	19,300	11
(3) Awards for overfilling targets	2,000	1
(4) Income from commune enterprises	7,900	4
(5) Subsidy for above-quota grain sales	4,000	2
B. Income from private household sidelines	73,669	40

Source: No. 8 Brigade, Junction People's Commune, *Accounts, 1982*; Table S–9, prepared by Zhao Huaisun and Zhang Changwen of the Department of Economics, Sichuan University, January 1984.

TABLE 7
Sources of collective income in MaGaoqiao village 1980 and 1982
showing increasing prosperity within the commune system
Unit: yuan

	1980	1982	1980	1982
Agriculture			415,660	510,129
Sidelines			65,481	163,932
of which:				
Farm machinery group	8,920	4,500		
Repair workshop	858	1,000		
General labour group	3,242	1,001		
Tailor shop	494	1,730		
Restaurant	16,260	14,000		
Butcher	—	9,000		
Blacksmith shop	1,159	—		
Electric supply	6,322	7,001		
Coal supply	1,097	—		
Carpentry workshop	11,390	—		
Black bean preserving	—	1,610		
Other (noodle-making, mushrooms, poultry etc.)	15,739	124,090		
Animal husbandry			12,842	5,409
Forestry			1,378	7,299
Fishery			94	604
Sub-total			495,455	687,373
Wages and profit distribution from commune industries:	17,000	83,000		
TOTAL GROSS INCOME FROM COLLECTIVE SOURCES			512,455	770,373
In *per capita* terms:			268	395

Sources: No. 8 Brigade, Junction People's Commune, *Statistics 1949–1985*, p. 30, Table D, 'Gross value of products from sideline industries of No. 8 Brigade, Junction People's Commune, 1980'. No. 8 Brigade, *Final Accounts 1980, series 2*, pp. 3, 14; *Final Accounts 1982*, pp. 25–6; *Comprehensive Statistics 1982*, p. 15.

TABLE 8

*Sources of private income MaGaoqiao village in 1982 and 1985
a comparison before/after the collective land was contracted to
individuals*

Unit: yuan

	1982	1985
Agriculture (private plots/ contracted land)	81,200	541,904
Woods, orchard, flowers, birds	19,920	12,191
Pig raising	100,000	221,695
Poultry, rabbits etc	19,480	
Five trades (masonry, carpentry, weaving etc)	19,460	218,057
Other work	19,690	
Bank interest and other income	9,870	
		Sub-total: 993,261
		Less taxes: 41,426
Total net income from private economy	269,650	951,835
Per capita income from private economy	139	491
Additional sources of per capita *income:*		
from village collective economy	— 254	nil
from commune rural enterprises	— 43	61
AVERAGE *PER CAPITA* NET INCOME	436	552

Sources: No. 8 Brigade, Junction People's Commune, *Final Accounts, 1982,* pp. 25–6, 31–3; No. 8 Brigade *Accounts 1949–1985,* pp. 30–6. *Records of the Economic Situation of Sample Rural Households* for MaGaoqiao, 1985, p. 7. Figures for 1985 are not corrected for price inflation.

TABLE 9
Families in debt to the collective
MaGaoqiao village, 1975–82

Status	Number of families in debt current year			Amount of debt incurred current year		
	1975	1980	1982	1975	1980	1982
Five Guarantee Households*	0	2	3	—	155	322
Households with difficulties	56	56	63	1,997	4,483	7,129
Dependants of state workers	23	23	22	1,270	2,143	2,666
Accidents or natural disasters	0	1	2	—	88	1,346
Able-bodied who refuse to work	0	0	0	—	—	—
Other	4	3	13	92	1,969	1,639
TOTAL INDEBTEDNESS FOR YEAR				3,359	8,838	13,102
FAMILIES IN DEBT CURRENT YEAR	83	85	103			
(Total number of families)	(414	461	492)			

Sources: No. 8 Brigade, Junction People's Commune, *Accounts, 1975*, pp. 21, 26; *Accounts, 1980*, pp. 21–2; *Accounts, 1982*, pp. 40, 42, 54. The accumulated debt by 1975 amounted to Y25,433 spread among 205 households; by 1981 the accumulated debt had reached Y74,148. *Accounts, 1981*, p. 23.

* These households, usually older people without relatives, are lacking labour power and are supported by the public welfare fund of the brigade; they are not considered 'in debt' to the collective. The five guarantees are for food, clothing, shelter, medical care and burial.

Notes: There were 492 households, (1,942 people) in the village in 1982 of which one in five had some kind of financial difficulty and relied on the brigade to help them through with loans. The average difficulty per family was 130 yuan or about half of one person's *per capita* income. The loans for 1982 amounted to about 2.5 per cent of the village income and were taken from the public welfare fund. At the end of 1982 this fund still had a comfortable surplus of 24,694 yuan which suggests that the debt situation was not unmanageable.

TABLE 10

Crop yields 1949–83: A comparison of national and local trends
(unit: *jin* per *mu*)*

		1949	1957	1965	1978	1982	1983
				collective farming			
Rice yield:	National average	252	359	392	530	650	679
	Shifang county	388	476	476	626	820	851
	Junction Commune	450	497	476	622	872	900
	MaGaoqiao village	—	—	474	617	832	868
Wheat	National average	86	114	136	246	327	374
	Shifang county	105	270	228	498	612	680
	Junction Commune	141	310	386	566	646	727
	MaGaoqiao village	—	—	409	588	675	718
Rape seed	National average	65	51	80	96	183	156
	Shifang county	75	113	171	316	327	330
	Junction Commune	89	138	222	317	338	367
	MaGaoqiao village	—	—	239	331	355	358
Tobacco	National average	—	—	—	—	—	—
(sun-	Shifang county	149	147	170	214	286	303
cured)	Junction Commune	180	150	165	177	267	320
	MaGaoqiao village	—	—	187	214	274	324

Sources: Statistical Yearbook of China 1984, compiled by the State Statistical Bureau, Beijing (Hong Kong, 1984); Shifang county, Junction Commune and MaGaoqiao village *Statistics 1949–85* gathered by author in Sichuan province.
* A *jin* = 1.1 lb; a *mu* = ⅙ acre.

TABLE 11

Output of grain and cash crops
Junction People's Commune
1963–85   Unit: tons

Item	1963	1965	1970	1975	1980	1982	1983	1985
			No. 5 Production Team					
Grain[a]	112.0	98.0	167.0	159.0	181.0	207.0	226.0	183.0[b]
Rape seed	2.5	7.8	8.9	10.3	13.0	12.6	10.8	14.5[b]
Tobacco	7.1	16.8	7.5	3.4	14.1	24.8	23.2	30.0[b]
			No. 8 Brigade (7 teams)					
Grain[a]	550.0	543.0	808.0	826.0	929.0	1,004.0	1,057.0	967.0
Rape seed	11.1	35.8	40.0	45.6	59.0	58.2	52.3	67.9
Tobacco	31.5	76.8	38.1	12.7	54.0	108.6	103.0	129.5
			Commune (119 teams)					
Grain[a]	6,410	6,455	9,325	9,685	11,130	11,585	12,860	11,318
Rape seed	129	382	451	492	650	635	640	744
Tobacco	344	786	413	162	550	1,189	1,200	1,337

[a] Grain includes rice, wheat, barley, corn and potatoes.
[b] Estimates.

Sources: No. 5 production team account sheets 1963–83, Table 1; No. 8 Brigade Accounts 1963, 1965, 1970, 1975, 1980, 1982; No. 8 Brigade Statistics 1949–85; Junction People's Commune Statistics 1949–85.

TABLE 12

Modern scientific inputs and the trend of expenses and income for
agricultural production* 1965–82
No. 5 production team
Unit: yuan

Item	1965	1970	1975	1980	1982
Seeds (hybrid)	1,284	2,594	3,400	2,927	1,580
Commodity fertilizer	3,310	2,912	4,800	9,062	8,298
(chemicals)			(4 tons)	(24 tons)	(24.5 tons)
Insecticide	46	344	380	1,187	984
Fodder (for draft animals)	50	199	267	364	200
Veterinarian services	74	115	533	234	16
Cost of tractor ploughing	—	—	600	179	—
Tobacco processing	—	—	—	157	450
Other: irrigation fees, ploughing, manure, etc.	2,040	1,812	2,653	4,750	8,187
TOTAL EXPENSES	6,804	8,853	12,633	18,865	19,715
Total Income	41,670	51,364	47,466	95,150	110,421
Expenses as % of income:	16	15	26	19	17.8

* Agriculture as used here means field crops, excluding animal husbandry, forestry, fisheries and sidelines.
Sources: No. 8 Brigade, account books for relevant years.

TABLE 13
Grain procurement prices 1955–86
Shifang county
(yuan: 50 kgms/100 *jin*)

Year	Unhusked Rice	Rice	%Rise	Wheat
1955	4.85	7.00	—	5.90
1956–9	5.10	7.30	4.3	6.10
1960	5.70	8.00	9.5	6.90
1961–4	7.70	10.80	35.0	9.60
1965	8.30	11.70	8.3	11.00
1966–78	9.50	13.80	17.9	13.00
1979–83	13.40	19.40	40.0	19.20
1984–6	15.80	23.80	22.6	20.00

Note: This chart shows what the peasants actually received as a composite price for 'quota', 'above-quota' and 'above above-quota' grain sold to the state. Rice comes in three grades and wheat in four; prices quoted here are for the middle range.
Source: Yu Dengmin, director of the Grain Department, Shifang county, document dated 27 June 1986.

TABLE 14

Cash payments to commune members from rural enterprises
Junction People's Commune 1980–2
Unit: yuan

| Year | Total Amount | Per Capita | of which: To No. B Brigade | | of which: | | |
			Total	To No. 5 Team	As payment for labour	As cash benefit	% of net income
1980	476,885	21	16,956	3,386	1,826	1,560	3
1981	611,000[a]	27	46,931	8,303	4,662	3,641	6
1982	1,100,000[a]	48	82,929	11,378	7,941[b]	3,437	7.5

[a] These two figures are approximate, arrived at by multiplying the amount given to No. 8 Brigade by 13 on the assumption that each of the 13 brigades in the commune received roughly equal shares.

[b] By 1982 No. 5 production team had 13 workers (out of 100 for the whole brigade) in the commune-level enterprises. The *per capita* cash benefit to the team was Y32 (compared to a brigade average of Y44.)

Sources: Interview with Zhu Molin, secretary for rural enterprises, Junction People's Commune, January 1981; No. 8 Brigade *Accounts, 1980* (p.29 and Attachment #2), *Accounts, 1981,* (p.20ff), *Accounts, 1982* (p.26); Article in the *Sichuan Daily,* 5 December 1980, 'Real benefits from small-scale industry'.

TABLE 15
MaGaoqiao school budgets
Unit: yuan

	1980	1984
	290 primary students 8 teachers	150 primary students 150 lower-middle school students 10 teachers
Income:		
Pupils' fees	1,160	1,410
From production teams	2,268	6,175
State subsidy	1,488	2,600
	4,916	10,185
Expenses:		
Teacher salaries	3,276	6,276
Teacher welfare fund	96	—
Pupil texts, notebooks	1,044	2,250
Sports equipment	348	350
Chalk, subscriptions, books for library	152	309
School building fund	—	1,000
	4,916	10,185

Sources: For 1980: Shi Zengfa, 1981 interview – monthly wage list, table on state subsidy, school budget, p.4; Jiang Wenguang, 1981 interview. For 1984: Shi Zengfa, 1984 inteview; Zhang Gufu, 1984 interview; Liao Wenfang, 1984 interview, 'Statistics on the Economic Burden of the Peasants in MaGaoqiao village in 1984'.

Notes: Prior to 1976 teachers received work points equal to an average able-bodied brigade member. From 1977 teachers began to be paid better. In 1980 they received 3,130 work points compared to 2,410 for the average brigade member, with the result that teachers on average received Y282 per annum from the collective distribution that year compared to Y165 *per capita* to brigade members. In addition, each teacher received Y126 per annum as a subsidy from the state for an average total salary of Y408. Like all other commune members, teachers also had their private plots.

TABLE 16

Analysis of tax burden at MaGaoqiao village – 1986

Taxes Unit: yuan		Total	Average *per capita*
State Agricultural Tax (County)		32,245	16.64
Township taxes for:			
Education	4,546		
Social assistance	2,126		
Irrigation	971		
Militia training	680		
Sub-total		8,623	4.45
Village taxes for:			
Mother & child care & family planning	5,573		
Subsidy for cadres	2,700		
Social assistance	740		
Education	607		
Irrigation	200		
House planning	250		
Sub-total		10,563	5.45
TOTAL		51,451	26.54

Source: MaGaoqiao Village Records.

Note: The tax burden per *mu* of land is 28 yuan, of which 17.60 goes to the state as agricultural tax and 10.47 is used locally.

TABLE 17

MaGaoqiao village accounts – use of funds 1965–85

No. 8 Brigade, Junction People's Commune

Unit: '000 yuan

(1) Year	(2) Gross Income	(3) Production Cost	(4) %[a]	(5) Net Income	(6) State Taxes	(7) %[a]	(8) To Public Accumulation Fund	(9) %[a]	(10) To Public Welfare Fund	(11) %[a]	(12) Revolving Fund[b]	(13) %[a]	(14) Distribution to Commune Members	(15) %[a]
1965	221	37	16.8	183	13	6.1	18	8.6	4	2	4	2	142	64.6
1975	259	68	26.4	190	17	6.7	9	3.8	5	2	5	2	153	59.4
1980	495	115	23.2	380	22	4.5	33	6.7	6	2	—	—	314	63.5
1982	687	147	21.4	539	22	3.3	23	3.4	—	—	—	—	494	71.9
1983	1,040	170	16.4	869	22	2.1	17	1.6	14	1.4	—	—	815	78.3
1985	1,377	384	27.9	993	26	1.9	—	—	14	1.1	—	—	951	69.8
At 1982 Comparable Values[c]														
1983	624			602									489	
1985	826			595									570	

Source: No. 8 Brigade, Junction People's Commune, *Accounts 1949–85*, pp.29–36.

[a] Per cent of gross income.

[b] This fund was for credit to help production teams buy fertilizer, seeds etc., at the time of spring planting.

[c] After 1982 when collective farming was replaced by household contracts, the rural accounting system was changed in China. The output from the private plots, private pig raising etc., was included in the public accounts for the first time. The accountants at MaGaoqiao said that to make post-1983 figures comparable with earlier years they should be scaled down to approximately 60 per cent. The result is indicated here, not corrected for price inflation. Statistics from the other 12 villages in the commune reveal a similar pattern of income distribution.

BIBLIOGRAPHY AND NOTES

Acknowledgements

1. Stephen Endicott, *James G. Endicott: Rebel Out of China* (University of Toronto Press, Toronto, 1980), p. 8.

Chapter 1 Back to the Beginning

A general account of the situation in China's countryside following the implementation of Deng Xiaoping's reforms in 1982 is available in Frank Leeming, *Rural China Today* (Longman, London, 1985). A collection of essays by ten American economists and political scientists in Elizabeth Perry and Christine Wong (eds), *The Political Economy of Reform in Post-Mao China* (Harvard University Press, Cambridge, Mass., 1985) offers a critical perspective on the results of the changes in agriculture.

1. Details about the former Town-God Temple and teahouses are in *Shifang shizhi xuankan* (Selected articles on Shifang history) No. 3, August 1983, compiled by the Shifang Local History Society and the Social Studies Group of the People's Political Consultative Conference of Shifang County, pp. 13-16.
2. For Deng Xiaoping's rural policy see 'CCP Central Committee Circular on Rural Work in 1984 (Document No. 1) translated in *Foreign Broadcast Information Service* (FBIS): China, 13 June 1984, K 3, and *China Quarterly* No. 101, March 1985, pp. 132-42. Grain procurement prices in Shifang county increased by 70 per cent between 1978 and 1984, see Table 13 in the Appendix.

Chapter 2 Ancestral Memories

W. T. deBary et al. (eds), *Sources of Chinese Tradition*, Vol. 1, (Columbia University Press, New York, 1960) contains a helpful summary of the main ideas of the traditional Chinese Confucian ideology. In *Morality and Power in a Chinese*

Village (University of California Press, Berkeley, 1984), Richard Madsen compares the usefulness of the Confucian moral paradigm of having regard for 'human feelings' with Mao's moral paradigm of selflessly 'serving the people', in seeking to understand the behaviour of village leaders. Background information on the geography of the red basin in Sichuan is found in T. R. Tregear, *A Geography of China* (University of London Press, London, 1965), pp. 232-9, and in Sun Chingchih (ed.), *Xinan Diqu Jingji Dili* (Beijing, 1959), translated as *Economic Geography of Southwest China* by the US Government, Joint Publications Research Service No. 15,069, (New York, 1971).

1. The six temples at Junction were the Hu Guang hui-guan (for those from Hubei and Hunan provinces), the Nanhua Gong, a Daoist-run establishment of Guangdong origin, the Confucian temple, the Lower and Upper Fire God temples and the Goddess of Mercy temple run by Buddhist priests. For a discussion of this phenomenon in Sichuan generally see Ho Ping-ti, 'The geographic distribution of *hui-kuan* (landsmannschaften) in central and upper Yangtze provinces', *Tsinghua Journal of Chinese Studies*, new series, V. December 1966, No. 2, Taipei. Accounts of Zhang Xianzhong's influence in Sichuan are in V. H. Donnithorne, 'The golden age and the dark age in Szechwan', *Journal of the West China Border Research Society*, (Chengdu) Vol. X, 1938, pp. 152-67 and George E. Hartwell, *Granary of Heaven* (The Woman's Missionary Society, the Literature Department and the Committee on Missionary Education of the United Church of Canada, Toronto, 1939), p. 72.

Chapter 3 'A Clean Snow Sweeps the Land'

The information in this chapter is mainly from interviews with the following people (those not identified are described at the front of the book in the list of 'Names of villagers who appear more than once'): Deng Yuanming, Liao Lixiu, Huang Kaiyao, Shi Shufu, Zeng Lingmo, Wang Daoquan, Deng Xicheng, Zou Jingfu – leader of village armed forces in 1951, Zhong Changqiong (female) – former landlord, Liao Shangmo – rich peasant, Huang Tianshou – middle peasant, Chang Yunshou, manager of an inn in Junction township, Ye Jichuan – deputy governor of Shifang county.

The basic documents of the Chinese land reform are in Mark Selden (ed.), *The People's Republic of China: a documentary history of revolutionary change* (Monthly Review Press, New York, 1979), 208ff. Classic accounts of the land revolution in China are William Hinton, *Fanshen* (Random House, New York, 1968) and Isabel and David Crook, *Ten Mile Inn* (Pantheon, New York, 1979). A detailed discussion of the process in Hunan province, which occurred about six months earlier than in Sichuan is in Vivienne Shue, *Peasant China in Transition: the dynamics of development toward socialism, 1949-1956* (University of California Press, Berkeley, 1980), chapters one and two.

1. An example of the existing land distribution at MaGaoqiao is given in the Appendix, Table 1, cols. 1-4.

2. The great importance of standard market towns in the Sichuan countryside is explained in William F. Skinner, 'Marketing and Social Structure in Rural China', *Journal of Asian Studies*, (Ann Arbor) November 1964, pp. 3ff.

3. The lunar New Year couplets were by Zhou Yinpo, a teacher, *Shifang Shizhi Xuankan*, (Selected articles on Shifang history) No. 3, 1983, p. 6.

4. Mao Zedong, *Selected Works* (Beijing, 1977) Vol. 5, pp. 24,29. The American scholar, Benedict Stavis, discusses various estimates of the number of people killed in China during the land reform 1949-52 in *The Politics of Agricultural Mechanization in China* (Cornell University Press, Ithaca, 1978), pp. 26-30. These estimates run from a CIA figure of 14-15 million to Premier Zhou En-lai's statement of 830,000. Stavis concludes that although it 'is impossible to know how many people were officially executed in land reform, how many were lynched by enraged peasants, how many committed suicide', nevertheless he believes that Zhou's estimate is reasonable, that is, 0.1 per cent of the rural population, or one death in every six landlord families.

5. The results of land reform in other parts of China are in Peter Schran, *The Development of Chinese Agriculture 1950-1959* (University of Illinois Press, Urbana, 1969), p. 21.

6. According to Richard Grunde, in 1937 about half the farmland in Sichuan was unregistered and its owners were able to escape provincial taxation. See 'Land tax and social change in Sichuan 1925-1935', *Modern China* (Beverly Hills), Vol. 2, No. 1 (January 1976), pp. 23-48.

7. S. Lee Travers, 'Bias in Chinese Economic Statistics', *China Quarterly*, No. 91, (September, 1982), p. 483.

Chapter 4 Taking the Co-operative Road

Interviews with: Deng Yuanming, Zhang Jinghe, Yao Shengwan, Deng Xicheng, Liao Wenping, Wang Daoquan and middle peasant Huang Tianshou during January 1984. Also interview with Zhang Shiyuan, manager, Junction township Supply and Marketing Co-operative in December 1983.

Various perspectives on the subject of this chapter may be found in *Socialist Upsurge in China's Countryside*, (Beijing, 1957); Mao Zedong, *Selected Works*, Vol. 5; Tung Ta-lin, *Agricultural Co-operation in China*, (Beijing, 1959); M. Selden and V. Lippit (eds) *The Transition to Socialism in China* (M. E. Sharpe, White Plains, New York, 1982); Benjamin Ward, 'The Chinese approach to development', in R. F. Dernberger (ed.), *China's Developmental Experience in Comparative Perspective* (Harvard University Press, Cambridge, Mass., 1980); Bill Brugger, *China: Liberation and Transformation 1942-1962* (Croom Helm, London, 1981). Two excellent novels dealing with this period are Chou Lipo, *Great Changes in a Mountain Village* (Beijing, 1957), and Hao Ran, *The Golden Road* (Beijing, 1981).

1. Interview with Deng Xicheng, January 1984.

2. Mao Zedong, *Selected Works*, Vol. 5, p. 184.

3. William Hinton, *Shenfan*, (Random House, New York, 1983), p. 166.

4. Selden and Lippit, *The Transition to Socialism*, pp. 18-19, 50, 81-6.

5. The grain crisis of 1955 is examined by Thomas Bernstein, 'Cadre and peasant behaviour under conditions of insecurity and deprivation: the grain supply crisis of the spring of 1955', in Doak Barnett (ed.), *Chinese Communist Politics in Action*, (University of Washington Press, Seattle, 1969), pp. 365-99.

6. John Gittings, *The World and China, 1922-1972* (Eyre Methuen, London, 1974), pp. 213, 225.

Chapter 5 How High the Cost of Fighting 'Paper Tigers'?

Interviews with: Huang Kaiyao and Ho Yulung, director of the Chemical Fertilizer Machinery Factory at MaGaoqiao.

Gittings, *The World and China* and Franz Schurmann, *The Logic of World Power* (Pantheon, New York, 1974) explain the crisis in foreign policy which confronted China in the late 1950s; Shigeru Ishikawa estimates the economic costs to China in 'China's Economic Growth since 1949 – an Assessment', *China Quarterly*, No. 94, June 1983.

1. Gittings, *The World and China*, p. 229.
2. Ibid., p. 221.
3. Ibid., pp. 206-07, 203.
4. Schurmann, *The Logic of World Power* pp. 257-302.
5. Ibid., p. 285.
6. Mao Zedong, *Selected Works*, Vol. 5, p. 146.
7. See Gittings *The World and China*, Chapter 12 for a general analysis of the reasons for the Sino-Soviet split. By the time unresolved boundary questions between China and the USSR erupted into armed conflict along the Ussuri River in 1969, the Soviet Central Asian and Far Eastern armies comprised 57 divisions with 8,500 tanks and a tactical air force of 1,100 planes. The United States had 60 divisions and 2,000 aircraft in the Pacific rim bordering China, about half of them in Vietnam. Ibid., p. 257.
8. Wolfgang Bartke, *China's Economic Aid* (Holmes & Meier, New York, 1975), pp. 9-26, shows that China granted US$3.6 billion, of which $1.8 billion had been taken up by 1973.
9. The case on germ warfare is in *Report of the International Scientific Commission for the Investigation of the Facts Concerning Bacterial Warfare in Korea and China* (Peking, 1952) and S. L. Endicott, 'Germ Warfare and Plausible Denial: the Korean War 1952-1953', *Modern China*, Vol. 5, No. 1, (1979) pp. 79-104.
10. According to Shigeru Ishikawa the cost of these relocations in the 'third front construction' took up half the national capital construction funds for the decade after 1964, and only 50 per cent of that expenditure could be converted into continuing fixed capital assets, 'China's Economic Growth since 1949 – an Assessment', *China Quarterly*, No. 94, (June 1983), pp. 259, 257.
11. Depending on how income calculations are made, the difference in income between the workers in the state factory and the peasants at MaGaoqiao was about 20 per cent. In 1980 the average annual income for workers in

the Chemical Fertilizer Machinery Factory was 600 yuan, while a peasant in Junction People's Commune received 173 yuan from the collective distribution and about 80 yuan from a private plot of land, an annual average of 253 yuan. When the actual family incomes are compared, however, the gap between worker and peasant families is not so wide, because the children of the peasants also had private plots assigned to them and distribution from the collective was calculated on a *per capita* basis. Thus a family of four in the factory with two people working could receive 1,200 yuan, while the same sized peasant family would have 4 x 253 or 1,012 yuan, a difference of less than 20 per cent.

Chapter 6 The Great Leap Forward

Interviews with: Deng Xicheng, Yao Shengwan, Huang Kaiyao, Yang Yongxiu, Liao Lixiu, Shi Shufu, and Wang Daoquan.

Of the many accounts of the Great Leap Forward, the most complete and balanced is Roderick MacFarquhar, *The Origins of the Cultural Revolution, Vol. 2: the Great Leap Forward* (Columbia University Press, New York, 1983). Other valuable sources or interpretations are Jerome Ch'en (ed.), *Mao Papers* (Oxford University Press, London, 1970); William A. Joseph, *The Critique of Ultra-Leftism in China 1958-1981* (Stanford University Press, Stanford, 1984); Frederick Teiwes, *Politics and Purges in China* (M. E. Sharpe, White Plains, New York, 1979); Victor Lippit, 'The Great Leap Forward Reconsidered', *Modern China*, Vol. 1, No. 1, (January 1975), pp. 92–113; B. Ashton, K. Hill, A. Piazza, R. Zeitz, 'Famine in China 1958-1961', *Population and Development Review*, Vol. 10, No. 4, (December 1984); Thomas P. Bernstein, 'Stalinism, Famine, and Chinese Peasants', *Theory and Society*, 13 (1984), pp. 339-77; Mikail Klochko, 'The Sino-Soviet split: the withdrawal of the specialists', *International Journal*, Vol. XXVI, No. 3, (Summer 1971) (Toronto), pp. 555ff.

1. MacFarquhar, *Origins*, p. 133.
2. For the first two years the village units were called management districts. MaGaoqiao village was the 8th Management District, later called the 8th Brigade of Junction People's Commune. *Sichuan Daily*, 16 February and 12 November 1960.
3. 'Resolution on some questions concerning the people's communes', 10 December 1958, *Documents of the CCP Central Committee 1956-1969*, Vol. 1, (Union Research Institute, Hong Kong, 1971), p. 124.
4. Li Dazhang, provincial governor, reported in *Sichuan Daily*, 24 June 1959; *Survey of the China Mainland Press* No. 2109, p. 19.
5. 'Mobilize the masses to discover mines', *Sichuan Daily*, 13 February 1959.
6. 'Strengthen the forces of transportation', *Sichuan Daily*, 22 July 1960 has an account of co-operation between the various counties in Wenjiang prefecture, of which Guanghan/Shifang county was a part. The Vice-Minister of Railways reported on construction of 400 indigenous-style and light modern railways in various parts of the country, *Peking Review*, No. 30, 26 July 1960.
7. 'Our Place', *People's Daily*, 25 February 1979.

8. *Resolution on CPC History 1949-1981*, (Foreign Languages Press, Beijing, 1981), p. 28.
9. Ashton et al., 'Famine'.
10. R. J. R. Kirbby, *Urbanization in China: Town and Country in a Developing Economy 1949-2000 A.D.* (Croom Helm, London, 1985), p. 35.
11. Liu Zheng (ed), *China's Population* (Beijing, 1981), pp. 4-5.
12. Ashton et al., 'Famine', pp. 614-15.
13. M. Meisener, *Mao's China*, (Free Press, New York, 1977), p. 243; MacFarquhar, *Origins*, p. 322; Y. Y. Kueh, 'A weather index for analysing grain yield instability in China, 1952-1981', *China Quarterly*, No. 97, (March 1984), p. 69. Kueh says 72 per cent of the grain loss in 1960 can be attributed to adverse weather conditions.
14. Provincial party secretary, Li Jingquan spoke of 'rather serious natural calamities' in Sichuan in 1959, but gave no details. See 'The People's Communes are the inevitable outcome of China's social development', *Peking Review*, No. 48, 1 December 1959.
15. Huang Kaiyao, retired militia leader at MaGaoqiao, November 1983. Exports of grain from China reached a record level of 2.5 per cent of total output in 1959, *Statistical Yearbook of China 1983* (Hong Kong, 1983), p. 422. Grain exports from Sichuan during those hard years remain a sensitive question and the figures have never been published. In a private interview with a member of the Board of Grain Commissioners I was told that the percentage of the crop exported from Sichuan remained constant, although it was hinted that the percentage might have been based upon the exaggerated Great Leap figures reported from the counties rather than on the actual harvest output. If this was the case, then exports could have been as much as 50 per cent more than usual. The local peasants believed this to be the case.
16. The 'four highs' were high goals, high yields, high output, high quotas for selling grain to the state, and the 'five winds' were the Communist wind of egalitarianism, commandism, blind direction of production, exaggeration, and privilege seeking by cadres. Joseph, *Critique*, pp. 95ff.
17. At that time an output of 1,000 to 1,200 *jin* would have been quite extraordinary. An extreme case of exaggeration was in the *Sichuan Daily*, 17 February 1959, where it was claimed that Pi county had an average grain yield of 3,160 *jin*; in Guanghan/Shifang county it was said that Gold Fish People's Commune had already produced 7,000 *jin* per *mu*. The paper reported the plan of Wenjiang prefecture to raise yields to 10,000 *jin* from three million *mu*!!
18. The habit of having two sets of accounts may be traced back to some unintended by-product of planning methods at the centre. According to a document issued by Mao for intra-party discussion in 1958 called 'Sixty points on working methods', there were to be three production plans: 'two are central plans – one must be fulfilled and this one is to be published and the other [with higher targets] is expected to be fulfilled but not to be published [to avoid discouragement in case results fell short]. Two are local plans – the first local plan is the second central plan, which from the point of view of a locality must be fulfilled and the other [with still higher targets] is expected to be fulfilled.' Ch'en, *Mao Papers*, p. 60. By the time this system of published and unpublished plans had filtered down through provincial, prefectural, county and commune

levels the targets were often hopelessly inflated and unrealistic, and created pressure for falsification of results. According to Ashton ('Famine', p. 626) as late as the spring of 1961 'there was no clear view from the top of what was going on in rural areas'.

19. Wang was referring to a letter written by Mao in April 1959 to brigade and team leaders in which he asked peasants to ignore unreasonable demands from upper levels. He wrote:

> You should ignore them, and pay attention only to realistic possibilities. To brag about 800, 1,000 or 1,200 or even more *jin* per *mu* is sheer bragging. Since what is bragged about cannot be done, what is the use of bragging? . . . One must not promise what cannot with effort be fulfilled . . . Honest [people] who dare to speak the truth are in the end good for the cause of the people as well as for themselves. But liars do harm to themselves and others. It must be said that some of the lies are squeezed out by a higher level which brags, oppresses its subordinates, and indulges in wishful thinking, making life difficult for those who are under it . . . We need high working morale, not lies. (Ch'en, *Mao Papers*, pp. 7-9).

(The letter is mistakenly dated November 1959 in Ch'en's collection.) Mao's letter did not leave a deep impression on Wang's mind, perhaps because Sichuan party leader, Li Jingquan, reportedly reacted against it for 'blowing a cold wind' and appended his own instructions, saying that grain output targets were not to be altered. Teiwes, *Politics*, p. 394.

20. Information, including quotations in this section, are based upon Teiwes, *Politics*, pp. 455ff.
21. Ibid., p. 480.
22. Resolutions on the rural people's communes adopted in September 1962, CCP *Documents* (1971), pp. 193-205, 695-725.
23. Nicholas Lardy, *Agriculture in China's Modern Economic Development* (Cambridge University Press, London, 1983), pp. 191-2.

Chapter 7 The People's Commune: 1962-72

Interviews with: Yang Changyou, Deng Xicheng, Jiang Wenguang, Wang Daoquan, and Wei Xiongru and Liu Shouli of the Shifang county government.

The Dazhai model for rural communes is discussed in William Hinton, 'Dazhai Revisited,' *Monthly Review* (New York) March 1988, pp. 34ff; Neville Maxwell (ed) *China's Road to Development* (Pergamon Press, New York; 2nd edition, 1979), pp. 41ff; Wang Dacheng, 'Dazhai Production Brigade', in *Beijing Review*, 23 February 1981. General Accounts of the people's communes include Chu Li and Tien Chiehyun, *Inside a People's Commune* (Beijing, 1975); Isabel and David Crook, *The First Years of Yangyi Commune* (Routledge & Kegan Paul, London, 1966); Benedict Stavis, *People's Communes and Rural Development in China* (Cornell University Press, Ithaca, 1974). Fei Xiaotung's *Chinese Village Close-up*

(Beijing, 1983) analyses the changes that have taken place in an East China village since 1936.

1. Contemporary newspaper reports about 'learning from Dazhai' in Junction People's Commune and Shifang county are in the *Sichuan Daily*, 6 November 1970 and 1 December 1974 and in *People's Daily* 11 October 1971.
2. Market days at Junction traditionally followed a, pattern of the 1st, 4th, 7th, 11th, 14th etc., day of the month. They were cut to one every five days and for a while in the 1970s down to every seventh day, on Sundays, but they were never entirely absent.
3. *CCP Documents (1971)*, Vol. 1, chapter 2, section 11, p. 700.
4. Information given to the author at the Dujiangyen irrigation exhibition, Guanxian, October 1980. A New China News Agency despatch from Chengdu of 12 October 1974 claims an even larger increase of the irrigated area in the Dujiangyen system – a jump from 130,000 hectares in 1947 to 530,000 hectares by 1974. (*Survey of People's Republic of China Press*, 1974-44, p. 137.)
5. Reports on farmland capital construction in Shifang, including the White Fish River project in Junction, appeared in *People's Daily*, 11 October 1971 and in *Sichuan Daily*, 2 February 1966, 30 January 1971, 2 June 1972, 12 January 1975.

Chapter 8 Walking on Two Legs

Interviews with: Chen Dalin, vice-director, Science and Technology Committee of Shifang county, Liu Shouli, head of the Agricultural Section, County Financial Department, Yu Yunli and Tang Zhiqin, managers of the Agricultural Bank of Shifang, Yang Wenju, director of the County Rural Enterprise Office, Zhu Molin and other members of Junction People's Commune.

Some sources giving background on the topics treated in this chapter are Yu Guangyuan, *China's Socialist Modernization* (Beijing, 1984); Jon Sigurdson, *Technology and Science in the People's Republic of China* (Pergamon Press, London, 1980); Richard P. Suttmeier, *Research and Revolution: science policy and societal change in China* (Lexington Press, Lexington, 1974); Jack Gray, 'Rural Enterprise in China, 1977-79', in Jack Gray and Gordon White (eds) *China's New Development Strategy*, (Academic Press, London, 1982), pp. 211-34; D. Perkins et al. (eds) *Rural Small-Scale Industry in the People's Republic of China* (University of California Press, Berkeley, 1977); Carl Riskin, 'Small scale industry and the Chinese model of development', *China Quarterly*, No. 46, (1979); He Kang, 'Agriculture: the Chinese way', *Beijing Review*, 12 May 1982.

1. See Appendix, Table 13.
2. For ideological reasons China's central leadership since 1978 tends to attribute shortcomings of the economy during the 1960s and 1970s to 'chaos caused by the Cultural Revolution'. A rare exception was made in 1979 during the heat of China's quarrel with Vietnam over the latter's invasion of Kampuchea. At that time an article in *Beijing Review* revealed that between 1950 and

1978 China had sent US$20 billion to aid Vietnam and help it expel the American forces. This enormous drain on China's resources helps to explain some of the constraints in the domestic economy (*Beijing Review* No. 49, 7 December 1979, p. 17).

3. Appendix, Table 12.
4. The trend of land use for cash crops in Junction People's Commune is as follows: (Unit: *mu*)

1950s	1960s	1970s	1979 and 1980	1980s
17,000	11,500	9,500	8,500	11,500

5. Alexander Hosie, *Szechuan: its products, industries and resources* (Kelly & Walsh, Shanghai, 1922), pp. 56-8.
6. *Sichuan Daily*, 24 February 1977, 'Raising tobacco seedlings vigorously in nutritious cups'.
7. Mao Zedong, *A Critique of Soviet Economics* (Monthly Review Press, New York, 1977), p. 126.
8. Article 13 of the 'Sixty Articles', in *CCP Documents (1971)*, Vol. 1, p. 101. The revised regulations are in articles 27-29 in the 'New Sixty Articles' of 1978, in *Issues and Studies* (Taibei) August 1979, pp. 109-11.
9. Interview with Liu Shouli, head of Agriculture Section, Financial Department of Shifang county, December 1983.
10. Appendix, Table 14, 'Cash Payments'.
11. *Sichuan Daily*, 5 December 1980. According to Yang Wenju, director of the Shifang County Rural Enterprise Office, from 1976 to 1982 the rural enterprises in the county provided Y11.2 million to help farm production. It was distributed as follows: Y4.5 million to buy farm machinery, Y3.5 million for support to basic farmland reconstruction, Y.5 million to support teams in difficulty with production and Y2.8 million as 'money of real benefit' distributed directly to commune members. In addition, Y45 million for labour payment in the factories went into the distribution to the peasants. Another Y4 million was spent from enterprise profits to support education, medical care and broadcasting.
12. *China Youth*, editorial, 16 January 1964, transl. in *Current Background*, No. 731, 11 May 1964, p. 4.

Chapter 9 Passing the Gate

Interviews with: work team leader, Li Shouhui, in Chengdu in October 1983, and the following members of No. 8 Brigade in Junction People's Commune in January 1981 and November 1983: Huang Kaiyao, Zhang Jinghe, Huang Kaiquan, Wang Youming, Wang Daoquan, Lan Guifeng, Yao Shengwan, Zeng Lingmo and Jiang Wenguang.

The controversies over purposes and methods to be followed in the Socialist Education Movement (Four Clean-ups) in the central leadership may be followed in Richard Baum and Frederick Teiwes, *Ssu-ch'ing: the Socialist Education Movement of 1962–1966* (University of California Press, Berkeley, 1968); Richard Baum, *Prelude to Revolution: Mao, the Party and the Peasant Question, 1962-1966* (Columbia University Press, New York, 1975); and Gordon Bennett, *Yundong: mass campaigns in Chinese communist leadership* (University of California Press, Berkeley, 1976), pp. 72, 88-91.

1. The 'Twenty-three Points' was the short title for a central committee document, 'Some current problems raised in the Socialist Education movement in the rural areas', 14 January 1965. This document, written by Chairman Mao, was given to each work team in the Four Clean-up movement. See *CCP Documents (1971)*, Vol. 1, pp. 823-35.

Chapter 10 The Cultural Revolution

Interviews with: Liao Moquan, Li Dekai, Wang Daoquan, Zhang Denglu, Yang Changyou, Deng Xicheng, Lan Guifeng, Yao Shengwan, Liao Lixiu, Jiang Wenguang of Junction People's Commune and Li Shouhui of Qionglai county.

Background on the Cultural Revolution may be found in Jean Daubier, *A History of the Chinese Cultural Revolution* (Random House, New York, 1974); Jack Chen, *Inside the Cultural Revolution*, (Macmillan, New York, 1976); William Hinton, *Turning Point in China* (Monthly Review Press, New York, 1972); *Resolution on CPC History 1949-1981* (Foreign Languages Press, Beijing, 1981). An explanation of the Dazhai work point system is in Maxwell, *China's Road to Development*, pp. 45-8. Maurice Meisner analyses the growth of the cult of personality around Mao in *Marxism, Maoism and Utopianism*, (University of Wisconsin Press, Madison, 1982), Chapter 6.

1. *Important Documents on the Great Proletarian Cultural Revolution in China* (Beijing, 1970), pp. 129-56.
2. Li Chengrui, 'Are the 1967-1976 statistics on China's economy reliable?', Foreign Broadcast Information Service, *China*, 7 March 1984, pp. K 2-15. Abbreviated version is in *Beijing Review*, No. 12, 19 March 1984, pp. 21-9.
3. 'Directive of the CCP Central Committee Concerning the Great Proletarian Cultural Revolution in the Countryside, (draft for discussion and experimentation)', *CCP Documents of the Great Proletarian Cultural Revolution 1966-1967* (Union Research Institute, Hong Kong, 1968), pp. 139-42.
4. A report of a strike in the Shifang Phospherous Chemical Fertilizer Factory appears in *Sichuan Daily*, 20 March 1967.
5. One of the major reasons that conditions continued to be unsettled in Sichuan until the end of 1968 stemmed from Mao's judgement that the February suppression of the rebels had been a mistake. The provincial rebels were released and the provincial party secretary, Li Jingquan, was removed from office. These fateful decisions led to fighting on the scale

of civil war in Ibin, Luzhou, Chongqing, Wanxian and other cities along the Yangtze River. See 'Decision of the CCP Central Committee on the Question of Sichuan, 7 May 1967', also known in Sichuan as the 'Red Ten Points', *CCP Documents of the Great Proletarian Cultural Revolution 1966-1967*, pp. 434-7.

6. *Journal of the West China Border Society*, Vol. 6, 1933-4, p. 214.
7. *People's Daily*, 11 July 1970. There are other accounts on the changes in the pig market in *Sichuan Daily*, 23 May 1964, 21 February 1966, 6 December 1970.
8. Quoted in Frederick W. Crook, 'Chinese Communist agricultural incentive systems and the labour contract to households: 1956-1965', *Asian Survey*, (May 1973), pp. 470-81.
9. The *New York Times* reports on Mao's gift of mangoes, 19 August 1968 and 2 February 1969.
10. Karl Marx, *The Eighteen Brumaire of Louis Bonaparte* as cited by Meisner *Marxism, Maoism and Utopianism*, p. 169.

Chapter 11 Family Farming Once Again

Interviews with: Yang Changyou, Jiang Wenguang, Wang Daoquan, Liao Wenfang, and Huang Kailan (female) all of Junction township; Wu Wanwu (of Yinfeng township), Jiang Yunwu (Shifang County Agricultural Office), Wang Dequn (female), head of the county Women's Association, Yu Chenggui (secretary of the county Youth League), Zhang Shicheng, (director of the Organization Department, Shifang party committee), Li Yulian, (head, Cultural Bureau of Shifang county), Xiang Qiyong (director, County Statistical Bureau), Wang Changyun, (county governor), Cheng Liangji (director of foreign affairs, Shifang county party committee), Xiao Xinhua (female) (director, Shifang county party office), Lu Feng (first secretary, Shifang county party committee).

Ma Hong, *New Strategy for China's Economy* (Beijing, 1983) and Deng Xiaoping's speeches in his *Selected Works 1975-1982* (Beijing, 1984) provide a rationale for the reform policy by Chinese leaders. Other helpful commentaries are Perry and Wong, *The Political Economy of Reform in Post-Mao China*; John Burns and Stanley Rosen (eds), *Policy Conflicts in Post-Mao China: a documentary survey with analysis* (M. E. Sharpe, Armonk, New York, 1986), pp. 252-82; Keith Griffin, *Institutional Reform and Economic Development in the Chinese Countryside*, (Macmillan Press, New York, Armonk, 1984); the introduction and chapter 7 of Tang Tsou, *The Cultural Revolution and Post-Mao Reforms: a historical perspective* (Chicago University Press, Chicago, 1986); Vivienne Shue, 'The fate of the Commune', *Modern China*, Vol. 10, No. 3 (July 1984), pp. 259-84; Graham E. Johnson, 'The production responsibility system in Chinese agriculture: some examples from Guangdong', *Pacific Affairs*, Vol. 55, No. 3, (1982); Jack Gray, 'Is China creating its own form of socialism?' *China Now* (London), No. 111 (January 1985), pp. 19-23; James F. Petras and Mark Selden, 'Social classes, the state and the world system in the transition to socialism', *Journal of Contemporary Asia*, Vol. 11, No. 2, (1981), pp. 189-207.

1. Deng Xiaoping, 'Uphold the Four Cardinal Principles', 30 March 1979, *Selected Works of Deng Xiaoping 1975-1982* (Beijing 1984), p. 188.
2. Ma Hong, *New Strategy for China's Economy* (Beijing 1983), p. 6.
3. Deng Xiaoping, *Selected Works*, p. 157.
4. Ibid., p. 172.
5. *Foreign Broadcast Information Service, China*, 30 April 1984, K 2. Also, 'Ban Yue Tan views impact of Document No. 1', *FBIS China*, 22 May 1984, K 18.
6. The average *per capita* income at MaGaoqiao that year was judged to be Y552, an increase of 26 per cent or 8.6 per cent per year since 1982 (Appendix, Table 8). Since this is somewhat higher than the rate of increase of disposable income for the village as a whole, which was 15 per cent or 5 per cent per year since 1982 as determined at comparable values from Appendix, Table 17 (col. 14), some question arises about the reality of this claim.
7. *Beijing Review*, No. 39, 30 September 1985, p. 19.
8. *Beijing Review*, Nos. 6 and 7, 10 February 1986. Supplement 'On the present economic situation and restructuring the economy', pp. vii-xv.
9. *Sichuan Daily*, 29 December 1975.
10. Quoted in Franz Schurmann, *Ideology and Organization in Communist China*, (University of California Press, Berkeley, 1968), p. 425.

Chapter 12 The Village Clinic

Interviews with: Huang Kaiyao, Wang Daoquan, Yang Changyou, Deng Xicheng; Huang Wence, head, Public Health Bureau of Shifang county; Yi Shuzhun (female), secretary, Communist Party general office, Shifang county; Tan Qijun, Zhou Zhizhu (female), Huang Kailan (female), barefoot doctors in No. 8 Brigade; Zhang Yunqing (female), barefoot doctor in No. 6 Brigade; Qing Shanfeng (female) barefoot doctor in No. 5 Brigade; Lo Chenfu, party secretary in No. 5 Brigade; Yang Zengli, director, Junction hospital; Ran Shengxiang, educated youth, director of the Chinese Medicine Factory in Junction township.

In medical circles around the world the reputation of the People's Republic of China for the advancement of health care in the countryside is an enviable one and many books have been written on how others might learn from the Chinese experience. Among these are Peter Wilenski, *The Delivery of Health Services in the People's Republic of China* (Australian National University Press, Canberra, 1977); *Primary Health Care: the Chinese Experience* (World Health Organization, Geneva, 1983); Victor and Ruth Sidel, *Serve the People: observations on medicine in the People's Republic of China* (Beacon Press, Boston, 1974); Joshua Horn, *Away with all Pests* (Monthly Review Press, New York, 1969). The *China Quarterly* has several analytical articles on the history of health care delivery in China, of which one of the most useful is David M. Lampton, 'Health policy during the Great Leap Forward', *China Quarterly*, No. 60, (December 1974), pp. 668-98. *Documents of Chinese Communist Party Central Committee, September 1956–April 1969,*

Vol. 2 (Hong Kong, 1974) has relevant documents on the question of combining medicine and politics.

1. *China Daily*, 30 October 1985.
2. See Ch'en, *Mao Papers* pp. 100-1.
3. Statistics from Public Health Bureau, Shifang county, July 1986.
4. *Sichuan Daily*, 12 January 1975.
5. *Sichuan Daily*, 26 November 1974.
6. *People's Daily*, 6 February 1973.

Chapter 13 The School

Interviews with: Zhang Shitai, head of the education bureau and Wang Dequn (female), leader of the Women's Federation of Shifang county; Shi Zengfa, Xu Fangju (female), Zeng Lingyu, and Zhang Gufu, teachers at MaGaoqiao; Huang Kaifu, graduate of MaGaoqiao primary school, the first student from Junction People's Commune to enter university (in 1975), who now teaches history in a Shifang county middle school; Wang Daofu, student in the Agricultural Technology Middle School, Junction township; Lo Jianxin, Chengdu worker who spent three years in MaGaoqiao during the Cultural Revolution as an educated youth sent down from the city; Wang Daoquan and Jiang Wenguang.

The traditions and patterns of Chinese education are presented in R. F. Price, *Education in Modern China* (Routledge, London, 1979). Other useful sources are C. P. Ridley, P. H. Godwin, D. J. Doolin, *The Making of a Model Citizen in Communist China* (Hoover Institute Press, Stanford, 1971); J. Unger, *Education Under Mao* (Columbia University Press, New York, 1982); P. J. Seybolt, *Revolutionary Education in China: documents and commentary* (M. E. Sharpe, White Plains, New York, 1973); *Documents of CCP Central Committee, 1956-1969*, Vol. 2, (Hong Kong, 1974), especially the 'Directive of the CCP Central Committee and the State Council on Educational Work', September 19, 1958, pp. 859-69; Mao Zedong, *Selected Works*, Vol. 5, pp. 404-6, 'The Question of the Intellectuals'.

1. *China Youth Daily*, as quoted by Price, *Education in Modern China*, p. 249.
2. The contents of ten Chinese primary school readers published in the 1960s are analysed by Ridley et al., *The Making of a Model Citizen*.
3. Mao Zedong, *A Critique of Soviet Economics* pp. 83-5. An attempt to defend the present policy of concentrating on material forces as being socialistic is made by Wang Zhimin in an article, 'Is there a contradiction between implementing the contract responsibility system with payment linked to output and the carrying out of communist education?', *Red Flag*, No. 3, (1 February 1983) translated in *Foreign Broadcast Information Service, China*, K 11, 21 March 1983.
4. See Appendix, Table 15 on 'MaGaoqiao School Budgets', and Table 16, 'Analysis of the tax burden at MaGaoqiao village, 1986'.

Chapter 14 Women's Emancipation

Interviews with: Wang Dequn, Zhong Tingyin, Jiang Wenguang, Chen Guofeng, Wang Daoquan, Liao Wenfang, Yang Changyou, and the following women all of No. 8 Brigade, Junction People's Commune: Zhou Zhizhu, barefoot doctor, 1969-71; Zhang Zhongqing, deputy team leader, No. 1 production team, in charge of women's group from 1966. Li Defen, treasurer, work group leader, women's group leader, No. 6 production team from 1966; Shi Zengyu, leader, Women's Association in No. 8 Brigade from 1957 to 1976, then deputy team leader of No. 6 production team; Yo Shungeng, deputy team leader in charge of side-line production in No. 2 production team since 1979, leader of women's group; Zhang Yinfeng, leader, women's group in No. 7 production team since 1966.

Valuable sources for understanding the struggle for women's emancipation in China are Elizabeth Croll, *Feminism and Socialism in China* (Shocken, London, 1978) and *Chinese Women Since Mao* (M. E. Sharpe, London, 1983) as well as her article, 'Female Solidarity Groups as a Power Base in Rural China', *Sociologia Ruralis*, Vol. xviii, No. 2/3, (1978), pp. 140-57. Another source presenting a feminist point of view is Delia Davin, *Women – Work* (Oxford University Press, London, 1976). *Women in China*, (University of Michigan Press, Ann Arbor, 1973), edited by Marilyn Young, is a collection of essays with differing interpretations of the Chinese women's movement. Radical feminist critics suggesting that socialism has strengthened the hold of rural patriarchy and that Marxist theory is inadequate for the task of guiding a family revolution are Kay Johnson, *Women, the Family and Peasant Revolution in China* (Chicago University Press, Chicago, 1983) and Judith Stacey, *Patriarchy and Socialist Revolution in China*, (University of California Press, Berkeley, 1983). For a brief comparative study of women in China and other Third World countries see *Women in rural development: critical issues* (ILO Geneva, 1980).

1. Liu Zheng, Song Jian et al., *China's Population: problems and prospects* (Beijing, 1981), p. 49.
2. Ibid., p. 159.
3. *Populi: Journal of the United Nations Fund for Population Activities*, Vol. 8, No. 3, (1981), p. 40.
4. Liu Zheng et al., *China's Population*, pp. 164-5.
5. *Sichuan Nongmin* (Sichuan Peasant), 7 June 1979, 'To dismiss people's worries about the results of bearing only one child Democracy People's Commune takes good social care of the widowed and old people'.
6. *Red Flag*, December 1973, as cited in Elizabeth Croll, *The Women's Movement in China* (Society for Anglo-Chinese Understanding, London, 1974), p. 106.
7. Luo Qiong, *Red Flag* article quoted in *China Daily*, 20 March 1985.
8. The item of Y607 in the village tax burden represents the cost of the nursery school, Appendix, Table 16.
9. *Beijing Review*, No. 36, 5 September 1983, p. 26.

Chapter 15 Festivals and Life-Cycle Celebrations

Interviews with: Wang Dequn, Lan Guifeng, Widow Liao, Huang Kailan, Cheng Guofeng, Wang Daoquan, Zhang Jinghe, Deng Xicheng, Yang Changyou; Huang Tianshou, lower middle peasant in No. 5 production team; Jiang Wenkun, leader of the Youth League at MaGaoqiao; Xin Chengyin and Gao Zhiqing, women members of the No. 1 production team in the Scientific Experimental Brigade in Junction; Wan Jingxiu, grandmother; Xu Wenqin, Daoist.

A symposium edited by Marilyn B. Young, 'Courtship, Love and Marriage in Contemporary China', in *Pacific Affairs*, Vol. 57, No. 2, (Summer 1984), pp. 209-70, amplifies some of the topics treated in this chapter. Other helpful sources are Elizabeth Croll, *Politics of Marriage in Contemporary China*, (Cambridge University Press, London, 1981), W. Parish and M.White, *Village and Family in Contemporary China* (Chicago University Press, Chicago, 1978), Maurice Freedman, *The Study of Chinese Society: Essays by Maurice Freedman*, (Stanford University Press, Stanford, 1979). An important Chinese statement on the relation of superstition and religion entitled 'Do Away With Feudal Superstitions' was prepared jointly in 1982 by a department of the CCP Central Committee, the Ministry of Public Security, the United Front Work Department, the State Bureau of Religious Affairs, the Youth League Central Committee, the All-China Women's Federation and the State Administration of Industry and Commerce of the State Council. It was broadcast over Beijing radio domestic service on 28 December 1982 and a translation appears in *Foreign Broadcast Information Service, China*, (Washington), K 17-22, 17 January 1983.

1. Adam Grainger, *Studies in Chinese Life* (Canadian Methodist Press, Chengdu, 1921),p. 57.
2. 'Do Away With Feudal Superstitions', *Ban Yue Tan* (Beijing), No. 24, 1982, transl. *Foreign Broadcast Information Service, China*, K 20, 17 January 1983.
3. Ibid., K 19.
4. Grainger, *Studies*, p. 57.
5. *Guangming Daily*, 27 February 1957, as cited in Croll, *The Politics of Marriage*, p. 1.
6. Interview with Wang Dequn, leader of the Women's Association, Shifang county, December 1983.
7. Ibid.
8. 'Gift-giving mars rural marriage', *China Daily*, 21 November 1986.
9. Zhang Weimin, 'Chinese burial customs are undergoing change', *China Daily*, 30 November 1983.

Epilogue

1. *Beijing Review*, No. 22, 1 June 1987, p. 24.
2. Parts of this discussion first appeared in my article, 'To market, to market', *This Magazine*, Vol. 18, No. 2, (June 1984).

3. *China Daily*, 'Rural Enterprises', 15 November 1986, p. 4.
4. China Historical Materialism Study Society, symposium on 'Historical materialism and reality', *Beijing Review*, No. 48, 1 December 1986, p. 15.
5. John P. Burns, 'Local cadre accommodations to the "responsibility system" in rural China', *Pacific Affairs*, Vol. 58, No. 4, (Winter 1985-6), pp. 607ff.
6. Hu Sheng, 'Why capitalism is impractical in China', *Beijing Review*, No. 134, 30 March 1987, p. 33.
7. Andre Malraux, *Anti-Memoirs*, (Holt, Rinehart and Winston, New York, 1968), p. 373.

Methodology and Appendix

1. Prior to 1982 there were two series of accounts: 'Comprehensive Annual Report of Agricultural Statistics, Bureau of Agriculture, Shifang County, for No. 8 Brigade, Junction People's Commune', (about 20 pages in length each year) which dealt with basic information on population, land and other village assets, and 'Report and Tables of Final Accounts and Distribution, No. 8 Brigade, Junction People's Commune, Shifang County', (about 40 pages). Since 1983 there is another series called 'Records of the Economic Situation of Sample Rural Households', (9 pages plus appendices).
2. Thomas B. Wiens, 'Agricultural Statistics in the People's Republic of China', in Alexander Eckstein (ed), *Quantitative Measures of China's Economic Output* (University of Michigan Press, Ann Arbor, 1980), p. 106. The Director of the State Statistical Bureau, Li Chengrui, affirms the basic reliability of statistics during the Cultural Revolution in 'Are the 1967-76 statistics on China's economy reliable?' *Beijing Review*, No. 12, 19 March 1984, pp. 21-9. (A fuller version of this article is translated in *Foreign Broadcast Information Service, China*, 7 March 1984, K 2-15.)

INDEX